Better

Also by Arianna Rebolini

Public Relations (with Katie Heaney)

Better

A Memoir

About Wanting to Die

Arianna Rebolini

HARPER

An Imprint of HarperCollinsPublishers

Portions of this book originally appeared in different form in
the following publications: "The Airlock" and "The Archive"
in *BuzzFeed News*; "The Ugly Mask" in *Catapult* magazine.

HarperCollins books may be purchased for educational, business,
or sales promotional use. For information, please email the
Special Markets Department at SPsales@harpercollins.com.

FIRST EDITION

Designed by Leah Carlson-Stanisic
Illustration by Kids/Adobe Inc.

Library of Congress Cataloging-in-
Publication Data has been applied for.

ISBN 978-0-06-329532-2

25 26 27 28 29 LBC 5 4 3 2 1

For Brendan

Come, my beloved,
consider the lilies.

—Anne Sexton, "From the Garden"

This book is not a suicide note.

—Simon Critchley, *Suicide*

Contents

Author's Note

In 2015, I published an essay on Jennifer Niven's depiction of suicide in her debut young adult novel, *All the Bright Places*, explored through the context of my own high school suicide attempt. The essay, piecemeal, traveled with me through versions of this book, whittled down to three paragraphs about the day I decided to kill myself: me at fifteen years old, walking hazily from class to class, then, later that night, standing in the bathroom holding a fistful of pills as my parents slept upstairs. I'd been reading those sentences through edits and rewrites for close to a decade, and still I could feel my body within each scene as if it had happened yesterday. Except it didn't happen. Not yesterday, not twenty-odd years ago—the day I'd been describing *never* happened, at least not as I'd remembered and then set down as fact.

I didn't discover this discrepancy until I was cleaning up the final draft of *Better*, verifying typed journal entries against the messy pages in my time-worn notebooks. I've been depressed and/or suicidal for most of my life, and there's a wealth of vague source material to bolster my false memory, but what I'd long forgotten is that I'd actually written extensively on the day I decided to kill myself—checking in every few hours, each entry revealing further psychological disintegration, until I swallowed the pills. I found these entries while looking for another. It had happened when I was twenty. I scrambled to rework the scene and panicked about the already published essay. I'd lied. I hadn't known I was lying—indeed, if I was lying to the readers, I was also lying to myself—but still what I wrote was inaccurate. Should I try to find and alert someone on staff at the site that had been through multiple rebrands and reorgs since my article ran? Should I ask them to run a correction? And what would it say? *The author tried to overdose on ibuprofen when she was twenty years old, not fifteen, as an earlier version stated. She wanted to die then, too.*

Does the difference matter? Does your answer change if I tell you that there were no external effects, that no one knew what had happened until I wrote about it, that the drama unfolded entirely in my head and hands and belly? What is truth in memory?

In her essay "On Keeping a Notebook," Joan Didion narrows down the purpose of her record-keeping—its "truth"—into the phrase *"how it felt to me."* She describes disagreeing with friends and family members over the details of her recollections, and she admits she's unbothered by their claims that her memories are flawed. She's not very skilled at, or interested in, keeping factual records. Whether something happened or "merely might have happened" doesn't matter—"for my purposes," she qualifies—because it doesn't change the felt, embodied reality of the past as it exists in the present: what it feels like and what it means now. Acknowledging the very real possibility that her memory of a snowy August night in Vermont might be wrong, Didion writes, "[M]aybe no one else felt the ground hardening and summer already dead even as we pretended to bask in it, but that was how it felt to me, and it might as well have snowed, could have snowed, did snow." It turns out I didn't spend what I thought might be my last hours saying silent goodbyes to classmates and teachers, but I might as well have, could have—if I hadn't discovered evidence of the opposite, I'd swear I did.

All of this is to say that *Better* is a book obsessed with both memory and meaning, and though I have confirmed my memories to the best of my ability, I am fundamentally more concerned with truth than fact. Most direct dialogue within these pages is pulled from electronic messages, audio recordings, or notes taken shortly after conversations. In the absence of such records, I've checked my memories against those of friends and family and altered details where appropriate. Some names and identifying information have been changed to protect others' privacy. Some timelines tangle. It serves my purposes; I hope it serves yours, too.

Better

Prologue

It's just past three in the morning and I'm lying in bed, scrolling through Google, trying to determine if I'm worth more dead than alive. I've been unemployed for a year, despite having sent out hundreds of job applications and spent dozens of hours in interviews for jobs in journalism, publishing, hospitality, office management, tutoring, anything remotely related to my mixed bag of employment history. I'm in seventeen thousand dollars' worth of debt, which was a private burden until a month ago, when I finally told my therapist, Elizabeth. This was particularly difficult since ten thousand dollars of that debt was money I'd taken from her. Elizabeth, like the majority of New York City's therapists, does not take insurance; instead, she sends her monthly bill to me, I send it to UnitedHealthcare, United-Healthcare sends me a check for a portion of the bill, and I send that money to Elizabeth. That had worked fine for the seven years I'd been seeing her—until recently, when I had started using that cash, little by little, to cover my student loan repayments, credit card bills, and rent. The reimbursement checks were unreliable and often delayed anyway, so Elizabeth was used to irregular payments. I was convinced that I'd be able to replenish the funds without her or my husband, Brendan, ever having to find out—as soon as I landed a job.

But I didn't land a job, and eventually the weight of maintaining denial became unbearable. I woke up one morning and wrote a short, disaffected email to Elizabeth, explaining that, unfortunately, the checks she had thought were delayed were never coming, because they had already come and I'd spent them and I'm sorry, but, well, it is what it is. I'll pay it back eventually, and of course I understand that she won't be able to continue as my therapist. What a bummer, but also how unsurprising, this failure, my failure. My fault.

She responded immediately and suggested we meet in a few hours, and when we did, I was determined to preempt her anger by making it clear that I was impervious to any emotion she presented, whether based in compassion, disappointment, concern, or a complicated blend of all three. I was defeated, deadened, so emotionally removed that she could chastise me for the entirety of our forty-five minutes and still nothing would stick. I'd already decided I was out. It was an act of protection, but it was also easy; in the time between my email and our meeting, I'd convinced myself that none of it mattered. I'd been failing so broadly for so long: in applying for jobs and grants and fellowships; in waking up and staying up and working on my one guaranteed source of income: writing. Brendan had become the sole earner in a job that kept him working late into the night; he was trying to manage his worsening Crohn's disease, and I could barely get myself to keep up with the laundry. Our four-year-old son, Theo's, anxiety had become a point of concern, not only to me and Brendan but also to his pediatrician and teachers, and I felt defeated by the nonstop hurdles in getting him help: the convoluted process of getting an evaluation through the school district, the scarcity of therapists who take insurance, and the sky-high rates of those who don't. I was failing, and I was watching myself fail but couldn't get myself to focus on one area and improve it. Confessing the debt was the finale, the alienation of the only person with whom I felt an uncomplicated safety. And what a relief to have finally done so, to finally be able to stop wondering when I would. But Elizabeth knows me. More specifically, she knows this about me: that I will always blow up something rather than face, let alone fix, it.

"So explain to me how this happened."

"I don't know. I messed up. When I called the insurance company the first time to ask about some reimbursement money I was still waiting on, they said two checks were in the mail."

That was true, but I'd known that their information was incorrect. I knew I'd already received and spent one of those two checks, but after the phone call I allowed myself to indulge in the delusion that maybe UnitedHealthcare had sent extra money by accident. Maybe it was a gift from the universe. Maybe I hadn't done anything wrong at all.

"The second time I called," I continued, "they said one of the checks had actually arrived, like, months ago, and I'd deposited it. But that money isn't in my account anymore. So obviously I spent it."

"You seem angry."

"I'm not angry, it's just—what do you want me to say? I spent your money. You're probably mad, and you should be mad, but there's nothing I can do about it now except pay you back. I will. I'm not going to beat myself up about it."

"Do you think that's what I want, for you to beat yourself up?"

"No."

"Look, I'll be honest. This is not a situation I ever thought I'd be in, and it will be complicated, because I'm personally affected. But I'd like to keep working together. I think it could be an exciting opportunity for you to practice managing discomfort, really get into the money stuff we've been talking about."

Better

For months, we'd been trying to address my deep-seated beliefs about money and credit that had allowed for, and even encouraged, decades of unwise spending: how none of it is real; how it's a scam; how we're all doomed, and if buying myself an overpriced candle provides a brief respite from despair or if logging on to Depop and buying a beautiful vintage coat is the only way to calm my middle-of-the-night jolts of anxiety, can't I just have that? We had spent entire sessions going through credit card statements full of transactions I couldn't recall making and working out budgets. Doing that while knowing I was keeping a monumental financial secret had required an expert level of cognitive dissonance, and now that it was out in the open, I felt a sliver of curiosity about continuing from a place of absolute transparency.

"If I'm wrong," she continued, "and I realize I can't be objective, then we'll stop—but you'll have to trust my ability to recognize that. It's your decision."

I hesitantly agreed, but the sessions proved to be tormenting. We went from one to two to three sessions a week to deal with the emotional and psychological fallout of my admitting to myself and to Elizabeth that I did care about all of it—my betrayal, my fear that I'd done irreversible damage, the debt itself—a lot, in fact. I spent most of those hours, much of those days, sleeping or crying. Twice I emailed Elizabeth after sessions to tell her that I could sense she was angry with me and it was becoming clear that the arrangement wasn't working. Both times she responded that she completely understood if I wanted to stop—she'd even give me referrals to other psychologists—but she reiterated her commitment to what she still believed was valuable work, and if we were to end our working relationship, I would have to be the one to do so. I'd never actually said as much, just dangled the reasons we should. I couldn't leave, and I couldn't get her to, either. When she helped me navigate revealing the debt to Brendan, he, too, responded chiefly with concern for my well-being. He knew something was wrong and he was relieved to find out that it was, as he said, "just money." We'd figure it out.

How much easier it would have been if it had gone the other way: if Brendan had been furious, rightfully so; if he'd acknowledged what I'd done was infidelity; if Elizabeth had reacted with icy chagrin, had formalized a repayment plan and dismissed me. Rejection would have been liberation, granting me permission to retreat into solitude, where I could manage my pain without witnesses. This, though: what mortification, how maddening, to receive compassion from people you've hurt, to have to hold it while living with the effects of that hurt. Grace burns when you're certain you don't deserve it.

I'd never been able to wrap my head around a person killing themselves because of financial trouble, having only ever been brought close to my own suicide through vague, existential despair. Now I've seen how one blurs into the other, how the reasons don't matter when they all amount to a mass of shame. So I've created a will through a free online service; I've written a letter to Theo. I've researched life insurance policies: Which plans pay out for suicide? How much do they cost? How quickly would one go into effect? I'm opening and closing tabs about survivor benefits, trying and failing to determine the precise amount of money Theo would receive through his eighteenth birthday. I write a set of instructions for Brendan in my head: Here's how to get Social Security. Here are the details of my life insurance plan. Don't pay one creditor a single cent—they'll try to convince you that you have to, but it's illegal. Don't be too proud to ask someone to set up a fundraiser for Theo; there are a lot of people who love us, and they will help.

I'm crying silently to avoid waking Brendan, mourning this thing that no longer feels like a decision, ruminating on everything that brought me here. Seven years ago, Brendan took me to a psych ward because I wanted to kill myself, and when I left I was emboldened by my recovery, steadfast in my commitment to maintaining it. I doubt I ever believed that such a thing was under my control, but I wanted to. I don't know when that optimism started to fade. Here, now, I tell myself, *Well, it was always going to end like this*.

And then, in a sharp burst of sound, Theo yells from his room, a frantic stream of mama-mama-mamas. I jump from my bed and run to his to find him sitting up, eyes shut tight as he wails. I pull him to my chest, stroke his head, tell him, "It's okay, you're okay, I'm here, I'm here." Finally, he quiets and opens his eyes, and we look at each other briefly (*Does he know, could he know?*) before he collapses back onto the bed, back asleep, just like that. I lie down and fall asleep with my arms wrapped around his body, so familiar, so small, but growing so quickly. His nightmare pulled me out of mine so that I could pull him out of his, and for now at least, our fears have quieted.

Chapter 1

Do It

Two years before Theo was born, on May 25, 2017, I decided to go to a hospital instead of killing myself. It was a Thursday, and as on every weekday, I was meant to meet Dara at her bus stop after school. I'd left my full-time job as an executive editor at BuzzFeed seven months prior, having reached a tier of management that gave me up-close insight into the company's cannibalizing ethos of employee expendability. After a round of blindsiding mass layoffs, when a manager responded to my concerns with his own concern that I'd become a toxic presence, I knew I'd reached my limit. The timing made sense, too. My first book—a rom-com cowritten with my friend Katie Heaney, loosely based on our mutual love of Harry Styles—was coming out soon, and I'd long been itching to get back to writing essays and features. I'd made connections in media and publishing; I knew who to pitch. And wasn't that the dream anyway—becoming a full-time freelancer? No boss, freedom from a strict schedule? Unfortunately, it soon become clear that I was terrible at meeting almost every requirement for that specific kind of success: the hustle, the dedication to deadlines, the will to leave the house when nobody was expecting me. I tried. It didn't work. I panicked but refused to admit defeat.

On a whim one night in November, a little over a month after leaving BuzzFeed, I searched for babysitting jobs on Craigslist. I'd helped take care of my little brothers when I was younger, and I'd been babysitting since I was thirteen. I'd always adored being with kids. I also figured it might satiate my increasing maternal urges. I applied to the first and only listing I opened, a writer couple in Queens seeking an after-school sitter to take care of eight-year-old Dara and occasionally eleven-year-old Juno, though she was mostly enjoying her burgeoning independence. I interviewed with the parents; I met the girls; I got the job and began in early December. Taking the part-time nannying position was my last grasp at making self-employment work. I told myself it was all I needed to replenish my emptied well of hope: a required daily entry into the outside world, regular human interaction, and a guaranteed, albeit small, income. The rest—the stories, the networking, the money—would follow. None of that panned out, but the upside was the girls. I adored those girls.

For three hours a day, five days a week, I was lively, smart, generous, even beloved. I spoiled Dara with attention, spending my free hours researching activities that would fill our brief time together. On walks from the bus stop to the bodega to home to dance classes and back, we invented games, told stories, imagined worlds in which we were spies being followed. When I stayed late to cover the parents' evenings out, Juno would join us for crafts or a movie, and after Dara went to bed, the two of us would hang out in her room, where she'd tell me about the music she was loving lately and her favorite recent books. After just three weeks in the job, I wrote in my journal, *Obsessed with Dara and Juno already.*

I was correct in my assumption that being around the pair would bring me joy, but I'd overestimated that joy's strength and its ability to spread into the hours when I was alone. Then it was still mostly darkness and a paralytic heaviness that my shrinking determination futilely pushed against: *Get up, get out of bed, go do something.* The gap between Ari, the sitter, and Ari, the person, expanded until one was virtually unrecognizable next to the other. By May, the osmosis I was hoping for was under way, but in reverse: my depression was seeping into the bubble of my and Dara's world. Still, I believed I could turn it around.

On May 4, the night before my birthday, I wrote in my journal, *I am immensely happy today and only wish I could always remember this. My book comes out next week, and reviews have been good. Right now Brendan is feeding the cats, tomorrow I turn 31 (!!), and the thing that makes me breathless is thinking about our future, our family. I want to start this year. Remember: today, I was very, very happy. This will be a good month.*

At the book's launch the following week, I stood with my co-author, Katie, in front of a room packed with family and friends ready to celebrate us. We'd decided to read a scene between the book's meant-to-be pair that we'd guessed, correctly, would get some laughs. Yet I felt nothing—nothing when my mother thrilled at the sight of the book (her daughter's name on the endcap!), nothing when our agent gave us individual enormous bouquets, nothing as I signed copy after copy. An acquaintance from college surprised me by showing up, and when he asked me, smiling broadly, what it was like to have accomplished such a feat, I replied—with, I hoped, the tenor of a joke—that it was just one of those things, like every big thing, where you think it's going to be this amazing, surreal life-making moment but actually feels like nothing. He didn't laugh. When we moved from the bookstore to an afterparty at a nearby bar, I was awash in guilt because the people congratulating me thought I was better than I really was, because I wasn't grateful, because all I wanted was to go home. In my journal that night I wrote, *I would very much like to be dead.*

And then, as if I'd written it into existence, death and wanting to die became all I could think about, to the extent that I couldn't access or believe in a time when I had cared about anything else. I reexamined the past few months from the perspective of this new certainty, and it all made sense. I couldn't remember the last time an editor had accepted a pitch; when was the last time I'd even sent one? I was losing patience with Dara too quickly, offering her my phone to play mindless games when I couldn't bear to engage, worried, but only distantly, that when she spoke it was as if her words were muffled, passing through static to reach my ears.

Two days before I admitted myself to the hospital, I stayed late to take the girls to Juno's piano recital, and I was surprised to discover how proud I was of her, how intimate it felt. The mother of one of the other children who'd performed tapped me on the shoulder to praise Juno's skill, as if I'd played some part in it, and I suspected that she assumed I was her mother. I was giddy over the possibility. Afterward, though, I took the girls to a pizza shop and felt my energy drain, dimming the glow of the previous hour. That night, I wrote, *Today I felt that pang I often do with the girls, of wanting this so badly for myself. And then I remember who I am and how I am.*

The following day, Katie emailed to ask if I was okay. "I just had a FEELING," she wrote, and her feeling was justified, but I assured her that I was fine. Just coming down with the flu, behind on work. My sleep schedule was a mess. Why wouldn't she believe it? Indeed, *I* wanted to believe it. I was wretched in my need to believe it. That night, while I boiled some water on the stove for boxed macaroni and cheese, I listened to the podcast *99% Invisible*. The episode is a bona fide piece of radio theater, a recording of a live performance staged at Seattle's Moore Theatre with multiple actors and original music, telling the story of Genie Chance, the young anchorwoman who had kept the city of Anchorage calm and orderly during the Great Alaskan Earthquake of 1964 by broadcasting live for fifty-nine hours straight.* Afterward, as the shell-shocked city—not yet fifty years old—began its rehabilitation, Chance's parents insisted that she send her two sons and daughter to stay with them in Texas for safety. Chance politely refused in a letter, a portion of which *99% Invisible* producer Avery Trufelman read on the air:

> *We must be together. As long as we're together, we are confident of the future. That Good Friday night, I knew we had survived miraculously. And for this reason, there must be a purpose to our lives. Apparently the children must sense this, too. For they have remained calm. They have been fully aware of the emergency, but they have not feared. We are proud that they are such dependable, responsible youngsters. I would not undermine their confidence in the future—in themselves—by sending them away for their safety. What is safety, anyway? How can you predict where or when tragedy will occur? You can only learn to live with it and make the best of it when it happens.*

And then I was crouched on the floor, water boiling over, crying so hard I felt as though I couldn't breathe.

Brendan was scared, Katie was scared, and my mother was scared,

---

* This story would be expanded into Jon Mooallem's *This Is Chance!: The Great Alaska Earthquake, Genie Chance, and the Shattered City She Held Together*, a book that helped me get through the covid pandemic and about which I've been evangelizing ever since.

and they and others asked if there was anything they could do to help, but I said no, everything was fine, because, really, what was there to do? Change medications again? Find a therapist? Join a gym? Who had the energy? Who had the money? And I heard it, felt it, thrumming stronger and louder: the command to do it, come on, come on, just *do* it. Sometimes I thought I should do it if only so that I wouldn't have to hear the command anymore, so I wouldn't have to wonder if this would be the time that I listened. Twenty years I'd spent wondering. How long can a person think about killing herself before she finally does it?

So there I was. Brendan, then my boyfriend of four years, had left for work that morning while I was still in bed, making me promise that I wouldn't sleep too late. I didn't, but I also didn't leave the bed for hours, crying, yelling in my head to just get up, until finally, suddenly, I did. I went to my desk and pulled out every bottle of the myriad psychiatric medications I'd been passively stashing for years. I poured out the Xanax, the Adderall, the Wellbutrin, the Prozac, the Lexapro—all of the pills I was currently taking, was supposed to be taking, or had been taking two or three psychiatrists ago. I didn't have a therapist—couldn't find one who took Medicaid and couldn't afford one who didn't—and lately I'd been getting my psychiatric care from a chaotic and overcrowded clinic where I never saw the same doctor twice. Visits were quick, and if I wanted to try something new, all I had to do was ask. Staring now at the fruits of those labors, I was too scared to act. So I stalled, researching lethal dosages of each medication. I read through forums and blogs where people described what an overdose on a benzo like Xanax would, or might, feel like, as opposed to that of an SSRI* like Prozac. Nothing appealed.

---

* Selective serotonin reuptake inhibitors—as of 2023, the most prescribed category of antidepressants.

I paced the apartment and saw the narrowing window of time before Dara would get off the bus three miles away. I couldn't fathom crossing that distance, literally or metaphorically. I couldn't get there, but I couldn't do nothing, and if it wasn't going to be suicide, it would have to be the psych ward. So I researched those, too, trawling hospital websites, personal blogs, Reddit forums, and even Yelp reviews, which skewed negative. What would this alternative to killing myself look like? Would I be able to keep my phone? Could I check myself out if I went in willingly? How long would I have to stay?

I picked up my phone and dialed Melissa, my best friend since we'd met on our first day at Reed College eight years prior, when we'd immediately bonded over the fact that we were both starting over at twenty-three years old. I'd always been hesitant to share my depression and suicidality with others, but it wasn't as difficult with friends who could relate—and Melissa, more than most, was one of those people. One night during our second year at Reed, while throwing a party at the house we shared with two other friends, I realized that I hadn't seen her in a while. I walked up to her attic room and found her crying on her bed, holding a bottle of whiskey and a check that would cover the next few months of her share of rent. She'd decided to go to one of the city's many bridges and jump, but she didn't want to screw us over. The conversation that followed has been lost to time, but what I do remember, so clearly, is holding the check, trying to understand how a person whose last wish was to take care of her friends couldn't see how decent—how crucial—she was; just as I remember holding her hands and saying "You are good. I promise, you are good." I needed her hands now—to stabilize me, to contain my grief—but an entire country lay between us.

"Hey!" Melissa's voice was soft—her workday in Portland, Oregon, had just begun—but also warm, calm. I already regretted calling.

"Hi, I'm sorry, are you really busy?"

"No, what's going on?"

"So I can't do it anymore. I can't keep feeling like I'm going to, you know, do something. So I think I'm going to go to the hospital?" I said, asking rather than telling, with the hope that she might tell me not to. The moment I said the words out loud, they struck me as absurd, dramatic, impossible. Surely I was overreacting, and Melissa would help me calm down, and I'd continue with my day, and no one else would have to know any of this had happened.

Instead, she said, "Okay. Good. You should."

"I don't know, is that crazy? Is that stupid?"

"Of course not."

"What's going to happen?"

"It could be simple as they give you a new medication. Or they keep you there for a bit. When I went to urgent care last month, they realized some medications were interacting dangerously, so they switched one, and it made a huge difference."

It was the first time I knew I would do it. I needed to follow through on one thing, and that thing, eventually, inevitably, had to be either the hospital or the pills. Why not the hospital? Why not this morning?

I tested the question out as a statement: "So I go to the hospital."

"You go to the hospital."

"Okay," I said. "I love you."

"I love you, too."

"I'm going to the hospital."

"You're going to the hospital. Where's Brendan?"

My plan that morning had been to keep him out of the loop until I'd arrived at the emergency room. My depression had created a world, slowly, diligently, over a period of decades, that had space in it only for me. Already, in my head, I was requesting a cab, standing at the ER desk, lying in a hospital bed. And in that projection, I was relieved—I'd done this difficult thing without having to witness its effects on anyone else.

When Brendan messaged me online as he did every day to ask how my morning was going, I typed, "I'm actually not good, and I'm going to the hospital. I was just getting my shoes on."

I shut my laptop even though I knew he was responding, as if there could be any response other than panic. Almost immediately he called me, his voice breathless, clipped, as he asked me what was happening.

"I'm just, you know, thinking about killing myself," I said, so cruel in my casualness, as though it were a lifestyle choice, as though I were considering going vegetarian or switching to a new shampoo. "So I'm going to the hospital."

"Okay, I'm on my way."

"No, it's fine, I'll just call—"

"Arianna," he said, his fear sharpened by anger. "Stop. You need to let me help you."

I relented.

While I waited, I filled a backpack with my journal, two novels,* some pens, my wallet, and a banana, and then I sat on the couch and waited. I pulled out *The Leavers* and tried, and failed, to read it. I turned on the TV and left it on the menu screen. I waited, and Brendan texted me as he got closer.

---

* *The Leavers* by Lisa Ko; *The Heart Is a Lonely Hunter* by Carson McCullers. Of the two, I'd end up reading only *The Leavers*, swapping the McCullers for Alexander McCall Smith's *The No. 1 Ladies' Detective Agency*, which I found on the bare-bones hospital library cart. (I highly recommend donating books to a local hospital if you can spare a few.)

Better

are you ok

tell me what is happening

> i'm just reading and waiting for you
>
> nothing's really changed i just like
>
> have been dealing with my brain telling me
> every day that i should kill myself
>
> and i want it to stop
>
> and literally no one in the world knows
> that so i'm sorry i didn't tell you

i'm so sorry

how long has this been happening

> i don't know like on and off for months
>
> it goes away and then i think i'm better
>
> but i was like oh god i can't babysit today
> maybe i should just kill myself
>
> which is a scary thought to have
>
> i can't rely on having you around all the time
>
> you know?

i'm so so sorry

you have to stay safe until i get there ok?

How to explain it to him? Of course I wouldn't kill myself now. Of course I was out of danger. Killing myself, in my fantasies, had most often served a singular purpose: announcing and solidifying my badness, my uselessness, my weakness against the voice—my voice, but different—telling me daily to do it. Admitting to wanting to kill myself accomplished the same goal, and I could tell because the voice was gone. I took my journal back out of my bag and wrote, *Maybe I spend a week in the hospital doing nothing but therapy and reading. Maybe I can't be reached by anyone. Maybe I put an out-of-office message up. Maybe people forgive me. Maybe their love no longer feels like a weight—like an obligation I've already abandoned.*

* * *

Brendan and I rode silently in the cab he had called, our hands clasped on the seat between us while we looked out our respective windows. The driver knew, of course, that he was taking us to a hospital, but I wondered if he knew why, if my sadness was a glaring beacon warning others against getting too close. I texted the group chat I shared with my elder sister, Danea, and our younger brothers, Jordan and Dylan; I told them I was on my way to the emergency room because I was suicidal, but I didn't want to talk about it and could they please just let Mom and Dad know? Then I handed my phone to Brendan and told him to text Dara's mother, Evelyn, and let her know that I was at the hospital and would be there for the time being. I told him to please assure her that it wasn't serious but also let her know that I wouldn't have access to my phone. I'd have to face her eventually, but I couldn't then. We walked through the sliding doors of the emergency room, and Brendan watched silently as his long-term girlfriend told the front desk and then the triage nurse and then the doctor how she wanted so much to die that she couldn't trust herself not to make it happen.

"Well, this is very real," I said while we waited for a bed. It was the first time I'd ever felt as though I didn't know how to talk to him. He nodded, reached out to rub my back. I tried to make my body tiny, folding into myself. An elderly man walked over to us, and I stood to offer him my seat; Brendan did the same for the elderly woman he was with.

"She didn't want to come," the man explained to a nurse as she wrapped a blood pressure cuff around the woman's arm. "I told her she had to come."

"Oh, it's nothing," the woman said, waving her arm in dismissal. The nurse reminded her to keep still.

"That's us," I whispered to Brendan, and he turned to me and smiled weakly. It was a recurring game we played, most often a joke. "That's you," he'd say, pointing to a woman walking a cat on a leash in Union Square; "That's you," I'd say, pointing to a man roller-skating in head-to-toe sequins. I'd hoped to inject some normalcy into this surreal afternoon, that I might remind him I was still me and we were still us. But maybe we weren't.

After six hours in the intake area, moving from one bed to the next, running out of things to talk about, and receiving a five-dollar sorry-for-the-wait gift shop voucher from an apologetic administrator, I was helped into a wheelchair by an aide, who pushed me through dimly lit hallways, past whirring industrial fans, and into and out of various service elevators. Brendan followed closely behind, carrying both of our bags. When we landed on the sixth floor of the psych wing, the aide left us at a small reception desk.

I looked around the hall. Faded drawings of homes and trees and birds and flowers hung in slanted rows along the walls. Common areas anchored the ward—to my left, a semicircle of men in hospital gowns watched a blaring television; to my right, seated patients, bodies swaying, arms waving, faced a woman who played the keyboard and sang a song I didn't know. A middle-aged white woman in a floral button-down shirt almost identical to many in my closet taunted the nurse taking her blood pressure. "You made this monster," she said through gritted teeth. "You don't want to see it bite?"

I looked at Brendan as he took in the same surroundings.

"How are you doing?" I asked.

"Pretty scared," he said, and I could see it everywhere in his face. I'd had weeks, months, years to come to terms with this decision, to research psych wards and prepare, while Brendan had had to absorb my depression, my wanting to kill myself, and the fact of this foreign, alarming environment in the span of one very long day.

I put my hands on his shoulders and promised, "It's going to be okay."

"What if you can't sign yourself out?"

"I'm sure I'll be able to. I'll ask as soon as someone comes to check me in."

"I just have no idea what to expect. What if they take your phone? Will I be able to talk to you?"

"I don't know. They might let me keep my phone. It's different for each place."

"Okay."

"It's going to be okay."

He wasn't convinced, and he remained unconvinced when a new nurse arrived to take my vitals and informed us that once I was admitted—which I currently was—it didn't matter that I'd checked myself in; by doing so, I'd given up the right to check myself out. Barring legal action, I wouldn't be released until my doctor was confident that I was no longer a threat to myself.

"But look," the nurse said, his Brooklyn accent thick and comforting in its familiarity, "I've been working on this floor for twenty-two years. I don't know you; I don't know why you're here. But this isn't a long-term residence. You're here to get better and go home. Maybe that takes a week, maybe that takes a month. But talking to you, looking at you? I think it'll be closer to a week."

A booming voice from the other side of the hall announced the end of visiting hours, and an aide took me to my room and told me it was time to say goodbye. I took my journal and books from my bag and handed the rest to Brendan.

"It'll be okay," I repeated. "Don't worry. I'll see you tomorrow?"

"Yeah. One thirty, right?"

"One thirty," the aide confirmed. "We'll take care of her. Promise."

* * *

By seven thirty that night Brendan was gone, and I was alone in a beige room, lying on a wafer-thin twin mattress that crinkled under my weight. I stared at the vent in the ceiling above me, little honeycomb holes, some black, some painted over in the same beige as the rest of the room. If I cocked my head to the side, I could make out a smiley face in the pattern. I took a quick inventory: one freestanding closet made of faded, splintering wood where I placed the travel-sized soap, shampoo, toothpaste, and toothbrush I'd been given because it was too dismal otherwise; pea green curtains covering permalocked windows; a closet-sized bathroom tucked into the corner; cinder-block walls surrounding me.

I stood, pulled the curtains back, and rested my forehead against the window, watching the sparse foot traffic on the street six floors below. Two Hasidic men, uniform in their black hats and black jackets, one following the other. Nurses walking into and out of the row of two-story brick buildings. Hospital visitors and staffers and everyone else standing cross-armed at the curb, smoking. I stepped back, wiped away the smudge of sebum my skin had left on the window.

I went back to the bed and grabbed my journal. *I'm trying not to be scared. I'm trying to remember I am not better than these people. This is exactly where I should be. And I'm . . . happy? Now that Brendan has left, my guilt is gone. I'm happy—I think maybe I'm going to get better? This is bottom, right? It has to be, right?*

The aide who'd brought me to my room popped her head in for a wellness check—"Doing okay?" Yes. "Thinking about killing yourself?" No—and let me know there were cookies and lemonade in the common room. That was also where one of the two phones was. Brendan had left only an hour ago, but he was still the only person I wanted to talk to, and I knew he would be home by now. Uneasily, I left my room and sat in the chair next to the phone hanging on the wall. When I punched in his number, though, all I got was a flat beeping tone. I hung up, tried again; no luck. On my third attempt, another patient approached with an outstretched hand, took the receiver from me, and asked for the number.

"541—" I began, but he cut me off and hung up.

"That's long distance," he said, smiling apologetically. "You've got to ask a nurse to use one of the office phones."

It felt absurd. Brendan may have had an Oregon area code, but physically he was two neighborhoods away. We'd walked similar distances on countless afternoons. But it felt worrisome, too—an indication of the facility's neglect, a harbinger of its uselessness. How many people here, themselves, had long-distance numbers? When was the last time I'd even heard the phrase?

I went back to my room, but when, a few hours later, an aide announced that phone hours would be ending soon, I walked to the nurses' office and asked for help. One of the two women dialed Brendan's number and handed me the phone. I stood, awkward in the close quarters, waiting for him to answer, and when he did, his voice sent a warm calm flowing through my limbs. I kept it short, keenly aware of my small audience, and I assured him that the place wasn't too bad. I told him about the cookies and lemonade, though I hadn't even had any, and how nice everyone seemed, though I hadn't engaged in anything that resembled a conversation.

"I miss you already," I said.

Brendan and I had moved in together two years prior, and we still delighted in each other's company. We couldn't get enough of it. We spent weekends walking the city, following extensively researched routes based on where we could find the best snacks. We spent evenings at our desks, which we'd placed facing each other and abutting the south-facing window, allowing us both to enjoy the sun; the bonus was when one of us would look up every now and then to get a second opinion on whatever he was drawing or I was writing. It was the first relationship I'd ever been in with pleasure at its core. But lately, I'd mostly slept. I'd tell him to go on walks without me, and then I'd spend the hours that he was gone crying in bed. We'd talk, but not about much, because I didn't have much to say. It was true that I missed him that night, but really I'd been missing him—I'd been missing *us*—for months.

* * *

In the middle of that first night, unable to stay asleep, I wrote down a list of my fears.

Scared again. Scared about:
—Waking up here
—Everyone thinking I'm crazy
—Not being able to leave
—The bill when I leave

—*What happens after this*

—*What tomorrow will be like*

—*That the doctors won't believe me*

—*That I won't know what to say*

—*That I'll have to get a real job*

—*That Brendan will die while I'm here for some reason and I will always have to know that the last time I saw him was here and that our last day together was full of fear*

I left my room and hovered by the aide at the front desk, a woman I'd met briefly before I went to bed, and whose name tag, I saw now, read Sylvia.

"How you doing, sweetie?" Sylvia asked.

"I was wondering if I could talk to my doctor?"

She took off her glasses, let them hang from the pink-beaded chain around her neck, and looked at me, eyebrow arched. "Why do you want to see your doctor?"

"I'm starting to feel really panicked about being here. About staying here."

"You know how to get out of here quickly? Show your doctor you're doing well. You know how to get them to keep you here for a long time? Let them see you panicked."

I took a deep breath.

"Listen. I don't know you, but I know you're here because something out there"—she waved her arm behind her—"wasn't working. Take the break."

"Okay."

"I know it's not the Four Seasons, but we've got chicken every day." She smiled, put her glasses back on. "And I hear the soup is pretty good."

Better

* * *

More than anything, it was boring. I read for hours, wrote a bit, stretched, showered, and then showered again. I'd never been so clean. On the third day, a nurse came in to get my blood pressure and suggested I check out some of the group activities.

"It looks good," she said, "participating and all that."

So I waited for the next half-hour block and ventured out. My options were bingo or music therapy. I chose the latter, which was taking place at a round table in the common area, where a counselor tapped away at an iPad. I took the last seat, joining five other patients, and the counselor gave a brief introduction. Everyone else seemed to know how it went: The counselor asked for song requests, found the songs on YouTube, and then flipped the iPad around so we could watch the videos. That morning, my fellow patients asked for the Beatles, Tom Jones, Taylor Swift. Sometimes people sang along. Sometimes the counselor asked how we felt. I felt, *This is ridiculous.* I thought, *I should have chosen bingo.*

Then someone suggested "Thinking Out Loud" by Ed Sheeran, and I remembered it playing on the radio in the car, Brendan driving, maybe a year earlier. I'd squealed and told him it reminded me of us, and then I'd started tearing up, and then I'd started laughing because I was crying, and then he was laughing, too, because it was so saccharine, so corny, but so was I, then. I requested "That's How Strong My Love Is" by Otis Redding, because it reminded me of us, too, and a thin Black man with a patchy gray beard sighed and smiled and closed his eyes. "Otis," he whispered, and when the video was finished, he asked for "These Arms of Mine."

That evening, I got a roommate, Alissa, who was a seasoned psychiatric ward returnee despite being two years younger than me. It was her first time at that location but her fourth time at an inpatient

facility, and she described amenities ranging from cold group show-
ers to outdoor meditation and yoga. "You're lucky this is your first,"
she said. "It's not that bad. But if you ever have, like, a hundred
thousand dollars, spend it on something that's actually therapeutic."

Alissa refused to spend any time in our room unless she was sleeping or showering, and she cajoled me into joining her in the common
areas. She seemed to know everyone immediately. She introduced
me to the man who'd tried to help me call Brendan that first night.
KC was younger than both of us and actively courting Alissa. The
three of us became a little clique—"The cool kids," the aides called
us when they found us playing Monopoly or cards—though I was
mostly witness to KC's overtures and Alissa's playful ambivalence.
It was KC's third time at that ward in the past two years, and he frequently complained about the fact that this forced stay was based
on a vague misunderstanding. When I told him I was there because
I was suicidal, he shook his head, let out a low whistle, and said,
"Man, they're never going to let you out." His favorite gag was
trying to convince everyone else I was Ariana Grande; sometimes
it worked.

Nicole, the woman who'd been shouting about turning into a
monster, warmed to me after I told her I liked her shirt. I was jealous
because I hadn't been given civilian clothing privileges yet and was
still stuck in the standard-issue hospital gown that left me perpetually
freezing. A few times a day, Nicole would try to tell me she knew
me from somewhere outside. At first I said no, I don't think so, but
eventually I just started to shrug. Maybe!

"They're so mean to me here," she told me one morning while we
waited in line for our medication. I put my hand on her shoulder and
then quickly removed it; no touching allowed.

"I'm sorry," I said, hapless and awkward with the guilt of knowing
I was benefiting from factors of circumstance and, worse, enjoying

it. I'd been treated kindly, patiently, with a sort of winking acknowledgment that I didn't really belong there, and I knew it was because I was young or attractive or white or because, through an opaque process of genetics and environment, I'd been assigned depression—the most palatable of mental illnesses. Most likely it was all the above.

"Let me ask you," Nicole continued quietly, conspiratorially. "They giving you pain meds?"

There was Joey, who was loud and gregarious, regularly stealing extra snacks even though the nurses always confiscated them, even though the other patients yelled, "Joey, man—you're a fucking diabetic."

Every time Brendan came by, Joey asked him to bring a six-pack of Corona at his next visit and then mimed smoking a blunt, yelling "Party time!" His smile was crooked and ever present, which made it hard to square him with the man in the story he told me about how he had ended up at the hospital; hard to see him as the man whose front door had been forced open by cops, the man who had stood in his living room pressing a blade against his neck because—he told me plainly—everything hurt too much.

I liked Rafat the most, though it wasn't until my fourth night there that I heard him speak. Up until then, I'd only seen him pace from one end of the hall to the other, wearing a fleece blanket around his shoulders like a cape. One night, we were alone at the common room table when he held a piece of paper out to me and asked, "Do you know words for these other words?"

In a shaky scrawl, he'd listed "apocalyptic, opponent, pretended, emancipate." He was writing a poem, he explained, and he needed alternatives that would give him more opportunities for rhymes.

"Apocalyptic is hard," I said.

He nodded.

"Maybe you could use a phrase . . . something about the end of the world? 'World' could have some good rhymes."

"Yes!" His voice lowered as he ran through some options: girl, curled, unfurled.

I told him I'd think more on it—maybe we could even brainstorm rhymes for the words he'd already picked—and that I'd love to hear or read some of his poems. "I'm a writer, too," I said, and he beamed. He jumped up and went into his room, returning with another sheet of paper, this one wrinkled from multiple foldings. He sat back down and flattened it on the table in front of us—stanzas written in every direction, a palimpsest of lines atop others only partially erased. I couldn't make out his handwriting, and he refused to read it aloud before it was finished, but he explained it was about him and his dog, whom he missed desperately. "Animals are the most beautiful thing," he said.

Once he started talking about animals, he didn't stop. He recalled being a young boy in Bangladesh and finding a nest in a tree on his family's property. His mother had warned him not to blow on the eggs because if he did, the mother bird would destroy them. He had been paralyzed by the fear of unwittingly ending their lives before they even began.

He told me how, just a few years later, while walking through the fields behind his home, he had happened upon recently hatched parrots trapped in a hole in the ground. He had loved them immediately, and he'd wanted them. He didn't care if they weren't his; he had found them, and he would save them. But he was far from home, and he'd have to cross a pond to get there. So he took off his lungi* and wrapped the baby parrots in it one by one, each nipping

---

* "Like a skirt, but for boys."

at his fingers with its tiny beak as he made the transfer. The lungi made a good wrap, but now he was naked. He used the pond as cover and held the bundle of birds high in the air, wading farther and farther into the center until he couldn't take another step without being completely submerged.

"I shouted for my mom," he said, and then mimicked her shock and anger. "I cared for the birds every day, for a long time. One day I gave them little chickpeas and then some water, and then!" He clapped his hands. "It turns thick into sludge in their bellies. All dead."

I was silent, shocked, watching for his reaction. But he laughed, so then I laughed, for the first time since arriving. What had happened to this man to bring him here?

*   *   *

Brendan visited daily at first, bringing snacks for me, and then, too, for a few patients who never had visitors of their own. I told him about the people I'd met, how happy the nurses were that I was socializing, how my doctor said she was seeing a real improvement.

"What does it feel like, getting better?" he asked. "How does it feel different?"

"It feels like—" I stopped; I couldn't explain. I motioned as if I were wiping a window clean. It was a lightness, a newness. It was a wind blowing away the dust. It was seeing everything I'd do from there on out as if along a path freshly cleared.

Brendan updated me on the outside world, everyone who was asking how I was doing. I was overcome with love, something heavy and felt, but almost immediately the heaviness became guilt. How vexing to love, to hold another's fear as your own. How dreadful to be loved, to have the power to cause such fear.

On his fourth visit, I told Brendan not to come by anymore. I knew if I told him he didn't have to come, he'd still insist on it, so I told him instead that his visits were no longer helping me. That, rather, they were reminding me of the effects of my hospitalization on the people I loved. It was almost the truth. More accurately, his visits were no longer helpful enough for me to justify the pain they caused him. The foreignness of that ward had worn off for me—I knew the best seats for lunch, the best sessions to attend, which aides would let me get away with using a pen, which patients would be down to play cards. The fluorescent lights had warmed, the couches looked less disheveled, the strangers were familiar. It was only when I saw it through Brendan's eyes that I became frightened again, ashamed.

This was why, too, I told my family not to come and told Brendan to relay the same message to anyone else who asked: No visitors. My mother talked with Brendan daily. If he hadn't been part of the family before, this cemented his place in it, and my mother texted him the way she texted us: tacking on unnecessary information about the house, the siblings—"I'm so happy she's getting help. Jordan is home. He and Carlo are opening the pool."—just for the connection, just because it was something to say. I felt for her, but not enough to welcome her. The ward became a stand-in for my depression, something I'd become accustomed to—in which I'd even come to find comfort, despite its asperity—but also something I'd unilaterally decided no one else could handle.

*   *   *

Contrary to KC's prediction, I was discharged after just six days. I was eager to leave, and I knew I could—I was restless, I was better, I wanted my restart—but I was scared, too. What if the only reason I felt okay was because I was separated from the real world and its tremendous pressures? What if I could be okay only in here? Alissa promised that I would be fine, and we exchanged phone numbers and email addresses. She told me about all the artists she knew, all the raucous, elite parties she could get me into, all the rich men she dated. "There's nothing like the friends you make in inpatient," she said. "Just good to have someone out there who can really understand."

I imagined myself transitioning into a life that was completely new. How, after all, could I go back to the one I'd been living? How could anyone from my past fit into my life now that I was part of this club? Wouldn't recovery be more dramatic, undeniable, if it aligned with a ritualistic shedding of everything I had been before? But the fantasy was brief and swift. I was planning on a rebirth, but if that involved forsaking any version of myself, it would be the one in the hospital gown, scared to leave her room. If I had to decide who to leave in the past, it would be everyone who'd known her.

Just good to have someone out there who can really understand. But I wanted leaving the hospital to mean that I no longer needed someone who could understand. I wouldn't need to commiserate with someone who knew what it was like to be a person who ends up in a psych ward, because the whole point of this was that I would no longer be that person. I wanted a clean break, and I was obstinate about the necessity of the divide. I was still far from realizing that recovery, at its best, is more expansion than transformation.

I couldn't sleep that last night, unable to ignore the blood I could feel and hear pulsing behind my ears. Every bit of me was overheating with kinetic, anxious energy. I kicked off the thin, starchy top sheet and tried my old tricks: going through the alphabet and thinking of places that start with each letter, counting to see how high I could go. When those failed me, I abandoned the effort and sneaked out of my room, quietly so I wouldn't wake Alissa, and I asked the pharmacist for a sleeping pill.

"I'm going home tomorrow morning," I told him, and he smiled as he handed me the pill in a tiny cup and some water.

"You'll do fine," he said, and I returned to bed.

It didn't work. I gave up again and moved to the dimly lit common area. I grabbed a forgettable thriller from the sparsely populated library cart but couldn't focus. My last option was writing, but I didn't want to go back to the room and disturb Alissa while looking for my journal in the dark. Sylvia was at the desk, so I wasn't nervous about asking for paper and any sort of writing tool.

"You going to write me some poems?" she asked.

"Trust me, you wouldn't want them," I said, and she laughed. She pulled some printer paper from a drawer along with a golf pencil and handed both to me. "Any chance you have a marker or anything? It's just, my hand kind of cramps with the little pencil."

The security guard sitting next to Sylvia looked up from his phone. He was an overnight shifter; I knew him only by his voice, which was usually holding forth too early in the morning about billionaires in DC and political corruption. "We can't give you a pen."

"No, I know, I just figured if you had some arts and crafts stuff."

"Someone stole the carton," Sylvia said. She opened another drawer and dug up a colored pencil, lime green, dull. "You've got to give this back, you hear me? Someone else gets it—" She flipped it in her palm and gripped it tight like a knife.

I understood, and I promised I would return it, and then I took the pencil, thanked her, and walked back to the couch. "So cute," she said to the guard when I looked to be far enough away to be out of earshot.

Most of the women who worked there referred to me with pet

Better

names—little miss, sweetheart, pretty girl—and it made me feel safe, cared for. It also made me feel young and pitiful, and I thought I must have looked it even when I'd been able to change back into my own clothes. I still wasn't allowed to wear my bra—they couldn't risk my hanging myself with it—and I was still shuffling around in the infamous psych ward grippy socks. I still couldn't close my door, couldn't make a phone call without a chaperone. The first time I'd met Sylvia, I'd asked her for a bar of soap, and though she'd sighed as though the request was bothersome, she'd packed me up a brown paper sack with extra socks, soap, shampoo, lotion, toothpaste, a toothbrush, and tissues and given it to me with a smile. I was at so many people's mercy. While that was originally part of the allure of the ward—there is a paradoxical liberation in ceding control of your life, in releasing yourself from the terror of obligation and decision making—such abdication is attractive only when it's done willingly, when you control the parameters. By now I'd become resentful of it. Thankfully, it was time to leave.

Chapter 2

Better

My parents picked me up at nine the following morning. I'd called my mother the night before to tell her I was being discharged, and she'd asked what time she and my father should arrive. I'd paused.

"Is it going to stress you out if we come?" she'd asked.

"Maybe."

"We don't have to talk about anything."

"So we'll just sit in silence?"

"You know what I mean. We'll get bagels."

I'd dreaded the idea of transitioning directly from the distance the hospital accorded to the hyperintimacy my mother's love required. Could we ignore the past six days completely, make small talk about the current events I'd missed? Should I joke about it, ease their minds? Would she cry? What I was feeling was less a stress than it was a hardening, an aversion to sentiment made manifest. I was more inclined to take the hour-long walk home alone, to indulge in the symbolic labor of putting physical distance between my current self and the self I had dispatched at the hospital. But there was the inconvenient fact that I'd left my phone, wallet, and headphones with Brendan. I had no podcasts or music to keep me company, no way of calling a cab if the symbolism started to seem less important with each passing moment in the sweltering humidity of New York in June. I had no money for food or water, and I was starving already. My mother and father wanted to be there for me, they wanted to care for me, so I let them.

"Yeah, okay. Come pick me up."

And now here she was, walking briskly from the elevator to the reception desk. I sidled up behind her while she spoke with the aide at the front desk.

"There you are!" She spun around and pulled me into a hug. She eyed the brown paper bag I held, containing the few things I'd arrived with, along with mementos from art group and those travel-sized toiletries I can't help but hoard. "That's all you have?"

"I left all my stuff with Brendan."

"So that's it? You're ready to go?"

I signed some discharge papers and made two follow-up appointments, and then, yes, I was. I said goodbye to the staff and a few of the other patients who were lingering by the desk.

"Be good," a nurse said. "I don't want to see you back here."

"I will," I said. My mother took the bag from me, rested her hand on my back, and led me to the elevators.

"They seem so nice!" she said as the elevator doors closed.

"They are."

"And it wasn't bad at all! Do you know the places I've seen? You made it sound like it was terrible."

"Did I?"

"Well, that man came up to me when I got out of the elevator—he was so nice, what's his name?"

"I don't know, Ma. There were a lot of men there."

"Bald? Big smile."

"Ah. Joey."

"So sweet. He insisted he knew me! Probably knew I was your mom."

"Yeah, maybe."

"And those nurses? So nice, everyone."

We stepped outside, and suddenly, for the first time since I'd walked through the front doors a week ago, there was the sun. High and hot, its warmth radiating through my face, my chest, my arms—my whole body hungry for it.

"Your father's parked around the corner, but he's swinging around. I told him he didn't have to come, but he insisted. He's been so worried about you."

My father pulled the familiar black sedan to the curb, and I slid into the back seat, where a bouquet of assorted flowers lay. "Are these for me?"

"Of course they're for you, silly," my father said, his voice light and playful as he glanced at me through the rearview mirror.

"Ari, I'm so sorry," my mother said. "I wanted to get you really nice flowers, at a real florist, but traffic was so bad, and we didn't pass any, and I had to just grab some from outside a deli."

"Mom. These are fine. They're beautiful."

She twisted around from the passenger seat and grabbed my knee. "Okay. Fine. But I want you to know I really meant to get good ones."

"I know you did."

Already we were back to normal, and I was comforted by the

quick return to the status quo. My mother's anxiety expands to fill whatever space we're in, and in that moment, I was relieved for the excuse to shrink. We're a family replete with mental illness: my mother's anxiety and ADHD, my father's depression, their children's depression, bipolar disorder, obsessive-compulsive disorder, eating disorders, and anxiety—so my hospitalization hadn't been earth-shattering news. It had been my first inpatient psychiatric stay, but twelve years prior, I'd called my mother during the middle of my first semester at Fordham University and asked her to help me pack up my dorm room and take me to an intensive outpatient facility for my bulimia.* During high school, my mother had seen the scars on my stomach from my brief dalliance with cutting. We'd been through family counseling and shouting matches. The details varied, but we'd done this before.

My father found a parking spot right in front of my apartment building's entrance—"Rock star spot!" he said, as always—and I led them to the second floor. I'd insisted to Brendan that he go to work that day, promising that I'd probably just take a shower and a nap anyway, but before he left, he'd taped a sign to the front door: "So happy to have you home" in looping red cursive letters, a beaming smiley face next to it. On the kitchen table sat a crystal vase full of pink and white peonies.

My mother groaned, gesturing at the bouquet. "His are so much nicer than ours! That's what I wanted to get—that's what I *meant* to get."

"Mom. Stop."

My father looked at me and sighed. "Lin, it's fine."

---

* That was my first failed attempt at getting an undergraduate education. It would take three schools and eight years for me to get my degree.

I dropped my bag and nuzzled up against our cats, Marceline and Mila. My father brought out the bagels and I made some coffee, and then, while we ate, I broke the silence as if we were already in the middle of a conversation.

"So yeah, it really wasn't that bad."

"That's good!" my mother said.

"You think it helped?" my father asked.

"Definitely."

"You know, I knew you weren't doing well," my mother said. "When we were upstate for Dylan's graduation? I knew it." She turned to my father. "Didn't I say that? 'She's not doing well.'"

She'd been right. Two weeks before the hospital, Brendan and I had made the overnight trip to Syracuse with the rest of the family to watch my youngest brother, Dylan, graduate from college, and I was in the throes of it—unable to maintain a single conversation, holing up in the bed-and-breakfast instead of celebrating. Still, I bristled at her claim on my sadness and the implication that I hadn't been nearly as good at hiding it as I'd thought. I refused to let her have what I perceived as her desired satisfaction.

"Oh, really? I was feeling great that weekend. I just had a cold."

"Well, anyway." She waved her hand as if brushing the thought aside. "You feel okay now?"

"I do. My therapist today, for our last session, said sometimes you just need to make it impossible to kill yourself for long enough that your brain stops thinking about doing it. Or wanting to do it, I guess."

"Yeah? That's good." She paused. "We just want you to be healthy, you know. We don't care about anything else."

"I know. I am."

We finished our bagels and I nudged them out the door, telling them I wanted to catch up on some sleep. We hugged and kissed, and then I was alone. I lay on the floor and the cats walked to me, Mila climbing onto my stomach, Marceline gently butting her head against mine. The silence was conspicuous. I was grateful for it. I went for a run and saw the faces and heard the voices of everyone who was still on the ward. I felt the vividness, the immediacy, of my time there slipping away. It was bittersweet.

Afterward, I went to work announcing my return to the world on social media, which, for most of those who saw it, served as an announcement that I'd been gone at all. I sent emails and apologies to people I'd ghosted: a reiki practitioner I'd been seeing for weeks until I'd bailed on an appointment and then ignored her calls; a publicist friend who'd been brainstorming with me about a potential author feature I could pitch to the few extant outlets that hadn't yet abandoned literary coverage. I posted a photo of the cats on Instagram with a short, contextless caption saying I was back from the hospital and doing well.

I saved my most daunting email—to Dara and Juno's mother, Evelyn—for last. She was the person to whom I owed the most, practically speaking, and whose family's lives would be most directly affected by the ways I needed to change mine. It didn't matter that nothing I'd learned about Evelyn in the past five months would make a heartless response remotely realistic, that she'd never been anything but compassionate; I was still holding enough underlying shame to gird myself for reproach. I apologized for having left them in the lurch and, on top of that, having to leave the position after the school year's end. I explained that though it broke my heart— and truly, it did—I needed the structure of a nine-to-five. I needed a so-called *real* job.

Of course, Evelyn's response was understanding, revealing not even a hint of blame. She gave me the last bit of absolution I was looking for and, through that, the freedom of unfettered hope. I published a breathless blog post about the hospital, what had led me there, and where I hoped to go now, and I was invigorated by the congratulatory and appreciative responses that flooded in. My mind tunneled toward a specific future, and at its core was *better*. It wasn't a relative state; it was an absolute. Not *better* as in improved, but *better* as in finished, as in done with all of that.* Not a fluid recovery but a static peak: an achieved ideal of life and self, an inherent better*ness*. It was a shining, weighted thing, and every joy and accomplishment that I could see so vividly in my future—my marriage, my child, my professional success—orbited around it, thriving in its anticipatory glow. Believing in that future provided a high that came with an almost manic sense of invincibility, mighty enough to overpower the quiet fears that my resolute optimism wouldn't last.

Immediately, the high transformed into work, specifically writing. In the first few months, I couldn't stop writing—mostly in journals but also for my modest newsletter subscriber base. I wrote about life before and after hitting rock bottom. I wrote so that I'd have a record of not only my suicidal self but also my leaving her behind, a portrayal against which I could hold myself accountable. I wrote so that others could witness my transformation, so they could forgive all my failures preceding it, and so their celebration of my recovery might function as another safeguard against depression's return. I wrote because writing about all the ways I was better—how I was running again, seeing friends, getting on the train, and finding wonder

---

* Yiyun Li begins her 2017 memoir about suicidal depression, *Dear Friend, from My Life I Write to You in Your Life*, with a brief commentary on the very American obsession with "before and after," noting the appeal of such a neat and "definitive" phrase as well as the unlikeliness of its promise: "[F]or each unfortunate and inconvenient situation, there is a solution to make it no longer be." What is *better* in mainstream usage if not another unlikely promise of *after*?

in the everyday—amplified my enjoyment of it and my gratitude for it. I wrote because it also felt good to hear from people who'd been where I was, to feel like my laying bare my experience could help someone else.

I also read. It struck me that I could best guarantee a permanent banishment of suicide by studying the work of writers who had killed themselves and try to suss out what had gone wrong with them. The stacks of books on my desk grew with journals, novels, essays, and poetry by Sylvia Plath, Virginia Woolf, David Foster Wallace, Anne Sexton, Osamu Dazai, more avenues for research opening with each book I read. This self-directed education became an integral part of my recovery—not only for what I might learn for the future but also for the work it required of me in the present. I needed my recovery to be a project because I didn't know how to understand emotional and psychological well-being absent productivity. My desire to die has always been inseparable from my fear of being unable to function. Functioning means working—as in laboring, as in making money, as in gaining external and material success—and working means proving my worth. Better put: my desire to die has always been directly related to my fear of failed ambition.

Though I'd have been loath to admit it out loud, my feverish reading and writing brought a particular and familiar excitement: here, finally, was the thing that would break me through. I'd spent the past year trying and mostly failing to monetize my writing, to make a name for myself. I was adjacent to the world I wanted in on, envying the editors I pitched and the writers I made a living writing about. It was easier to decide that my depression was the reason for that failure rather than the result. I wanted to learn how to be and stay better, but I couldn't abandon the suspicion I'd always held: that the answer was achieving professional success. The solidity of my recovery would be ensured less by my analyses of suicide and depression and more by the success of its output.

That belief held firm despite the countless pieces of evidence I'd gathered that proved the opposite: I'd spent the past decade ticking off achievements that, before achieving them, I'd believed would banish a depression I was so certain was caused by professional failure. I'd graduated from college, settled into a healthy relationship, gotten a full-time job at a media outlet during the height of its popularity, earned a salary I'd previously thought unimaginable. I'd published a book. These were supposed to have been the milestones that would turn my life real—not an amalgam of hypothetical futures but rather a solid foundation of achievements on which to stand. None of it had worked. I still wanted to die. Rather than concluding that the metrics were flawed, I decided they weren't enough.

So now I did more. I was grasping. I tried teaching myself to play guitar. I read about naturopathy. I cooked. I meditated. I floated in a sensory deprivation tank. I woke up early to write and practice yoga and pull a daily tarot card. I color-coordinated my journal with washi tape, gel pens, and highlighters. I brainstormed how to turn these habits into an essay series, a column, perhaps, for a popular but respected online women's publication. On June 11, fewer than two weeks after leaving the hospital, I wrote, *I'm doing A LOT and I can't help wondering if I'm trying to stave off depression. All the ways I'm getting better. Still working toward it. What will be the goal? The "climax"? My book? Getting a job? Getting pregnant?*

The goals varied, but without question each required performance. My recovery relied upon a coherent narrative and an audience to follow it. It could never be entirely for myself, because it needed to be not only validated but celebrated. It would be worthless otherwise.

Better

I don't blame myself for guessing at the magical missing piece of recovery. I do still think one or maybe a few exist, but none was where I was looking.

* * *

Amid my new project, I was applying for full-time jobs, albeit ambivalently. The applications, the cover letters, the rounds of interviews: it all carried dread, weakening my optimism. It brought me down to reality, and I was slowly remembering that I hated this reality. Three weeks into the process, I felt inklings of wanting to die. *Today is the first day I thought of suicide again, no doubt because I've put myself out there,* I wrote. *I think about my future and I can't breathe. What is important? [It creeps back in, don't let it, don't let it.]*

Then a miracle, or so I thought: The job I'd initially applied for at BuzzFeed four years earlier—books editor—was open again, but within a different division. I'd essentially spent my first tenure training under the original books editor, who was leaving now. It was perfect, serendipitous even. I was back in the office by July and ecstatic, but again, of course, not for long. Soon my exhaustion and general overwhelm would insist upon my attention, and it would become more and more difficult to wake up early enough not to have to rush to work, and then to wake up, full stop. I was in constant negotiation with what I'd always assumed was laziness, a moral failing, and my remedy was an obsession with systems. I needed discipline, routines; those would be key if I wanted to deserve this dream job, if I didn't want to squander the opportunity. I cycled through the most extreme versions of hope and disappointment, hinging entirely—as silly as it seems now—on a single daily decision: Will I leave the apartment today?

On November 8, 2017, four months into a job I was genuinely enjoying, I woke up and decided: *no*. As was usually the case with *no* mornings, it followed a banner day. The previous morning, I'd put on a nice outfit, then chatted with a colleague on the train. I'd schmoozed at a work lunch, knocked out two posts, wasn't ignored once in the team chat. It was no wonder I was so beat today; certainly, I deserved a break. I knew what was waiting for me in the retreat, but I told myself it didn't have to be that way. My coworkers worked from home all the time. My doing so didn't need to precipitate a meltdown. I could be normal.

It didn't work. *I stayed home today,* I wrote in my journal. *I need to stop. Makes me weepy. Everything is making me tired. Everything is too much. I'm angry. Yesterday was so good. I don't know.*

It was easy to blame the retreat, the bed, the sleeping, the staying home. That was where I felt worst, so those were the circumstances that warranted close inspection. That was the space in which to locate the fix. My home was an extension of myself, and as long as the problem was confined within its walls, it was familiar, domestic, manageable. If that could be the case, if I could *convince* myself that that was the case, the problem wouldn't be this idea of a better life in which I'd invested so much faith and labor; it would be me. And this time it would be different. This time, I could fix me.

On December 2:

> *I'm doing the thing → feeling bad & explaining it away → my behavior is the cause. My decisions → because I stayed home, because I let work build up, because my sleep schedule is all fucked. I want this to be the case because if it's the other option— that I'm not "better"—then I'm as far away from recovery as I ever was. No progress.*

Better

On December 6:

I promised Brendan I'd no longer work from home. I made it two days and felt the pull today. Got dressed, waited for him to leave. Conspiratorial. Two selves. "No one understands." I got back in bed fully clothed, considered sleeping. I got back up. I'm on the train. Sort of a victory. Thought about having to lie by omission all day, building layers of lies (or secrets) to quarantine me. But I'm on the train! So. Yesterday was very good. There is a correlation between the best days and the pull.

But then, December 7:

Didn't go to work again. So sick of myself. Stomach tense. All I can think about is all the things I haven't done, all the balls I've dropped, all the ways I'm sinking.

As we moved into the new year, the pattern continued, the ups and downs, and my faith in my systems waned. In January, I wrote,

I have one good, productive day and it wears me down, perhaps because of the futility of it. Perhaps because I'm certain routine & organization is the key to steadiness & ease & then I do it & the result is a sort of emptiness. What am I missing? (Trust the process.)

In February, I started probing the flaws in this rigid, unforgiving *better*:

What is it that pulls me back to bed/sleep/giving up after just one good & productive day? I think it's the never-endingness of it.

The way "good" can just stretch out, unstructured, in a terrifying
way. Yesterday at around noon I was overwhelmed by dread and
fear—a sort of, okay, if this is what I'm working toward, if this is
what's left after working away all the dysfunction & self-sabotage,
what . . . is it?

I was approaching the problem but landing just aslant. I was right
to feel disillusioned, even betrayed, by those outward-facing achievements, but I was wrong to conclude that the hollowness of life on the
other side was an effect of my limitations. Rereading those entries
now, it's impossible not to see the glaring, repeated juxtaposition of
"good" and "productive." Each required the other. To be good was
to produce; to have a good day was to go to bed with fewer items
on my to-do list than there had been when I awoke. But good how?
Good as in positive, enjoyable? Clearly not; those "good" days left
me distraught. More likely, it was the moral good, the worthy good,
which I was conflating with measurable output. In April, I began a
new, short-lived daily practice of opening my journal every morning and naming three things that would *MAKE TODAY GREAT!*
Without fail, I listed variations on the same few never-ending tasks:
respond to X emails, brainstorm X new posts, spend X hours on the
book proposal. Who would possibly be surprised to hear that the
great days never came?

On May 30, having long since abandoned the lists, the schedules,
and the daily gratitude, I wrote:

I woke up this morning, sat disappointed in myself for five or so
minutes, thought about killing myself, and then literally thought,
okay, I should pick one thing and do it every day for a month,
meaning one of my stupid, tiny "habits" that I keep trying to
track, which I (and the world) seem to think will be the key to

*mental health—or stillness, at least a foundation. And then
I thought, am I really going to open up my journal and write
ANYTHING that begins "Starting tomorrow . . ." HAVE I
LEARNED NOTHING?*

*But okay. Despite no evidence of previous success—a success
rate of zero—I will try to commit, again, to waking up early,
journaling, stretching, ET CETERA. I will keep creating
systems, new metrics by which to fail.*

The trap of the clearly defined, externally verifiable *better* is, iron-ically, that it often keeps us from pursuing and exploring potential joy. We want to be certain we're better before we move forward be-cause we want to feel safe in the knowledge that not only will we succeed but we'll deserve to. We'll appreciate our achievements, because we'll have finally, fully, rid ourselves of the sickness that contaminated all the other successes that came before. But if we're committed to the linear narrative of recovery—and why wouldn't we be, when the alternative is the ever messy and unsatisfying cycle?—we have no way of determining if any postlow wellness is in fact the climax. If there's always the possibility of a *better* better, we'll never know if it has arrived. And if our dream for the future hinges on reaching that unknowable destination, how can we possi-bly expect to meet it?

* * *

I've always known I wanted to be a mother, but the desire became urgent and overwhelming in the year leading up to my hospitaliza-tion. Pregnancy announcements were popping up among friends and friends of friends, and Brendan and I were at least planning to get married. He was hesitant about the baby timeline, always the more cautious of the two of us, but I was determined to prove that it was something we could handle—financially, logistically, and emotionally. I used my outward overenthusiasm to mask my own ambivalence. I was still falling into and out of extended periods during which I wouldn't get out of bed, avoided socializing or even leaving the house, became distracted by the fears and self-beratements crowding my head. I wanted this thing—this baby, this family, this life—so desperately, but I couldn't rid myself of the suspicion that I hadn't earned it, couldn't handle it, and each time I remembered this, I collapsed into the depressive state that had inspired the suspicion to begin with. Any past hope mutated into pitiful delusion.

In March 2017, two months before the hospital, Brendan and I took a weeklong trip to New Mexico. On our second day there, we visited the Santuario de Chimayo, a nineteenth-century Roman Catholic shrine that sits atop dirt believed to have healing powers. The modest adobe and weathered-wood church draws roughly 300,000 pilgrims a year,* but that day the crowd was sparse as we walked through the garden and chapels. Finding a line outside the chamber containing the pocito—the small well of blessed dirt— we decided to take a detour down the street, toward a handful of cafés and shops.

We entered a stand-alone shop, the words VIGIL STORE painted in

---

* The native Pueblo people, having lived in the area since the twelfth century, believed in and sought the dirt's healing powers centuries before the Spanish conquest, but the modern pilgrimage is rooted in the Catholicism the Spanish brought. The details vary across retellings, but the predominant legend says a local member of the Penitentes brotherhood, searching for the source of a mysterious light on a nearby hill, found a crucifix planted in a patch of glowing dirt. After three failed attempts to bring the crucifix to a local church—the crucifix kept ending up back in the dirt—the man petitioned to build a sanctuary at the site.

large letters above a sun-faded corrugated metal porch cover. Bundles of dried chilis hung below the sloping roof, and a sign advertised santos, wood carvings, and ice pops. Inside was bright and lively, walls lined with shelves holding statues, candles, and stacks of dried spices in sandwich bags. I lingered by a display case holding rows of small silver charms in the shape of body parts—isolated limbs, bellies, hands, lungs, the whole lot labeled "milagros." A salesman approached from behind the counter and asked if I needed any help. I tapped on the glass above a woman's torso, silver breasts falling on a rounded belly.

"What are they . . . for?" I asked.

"Well, let's say I broke my leg," he said. "I would buy the leg charm and maybe I'd bring it to the chapel, right? And I'd pray for recovery. And maybe I'd hang it up on the chapel wall, as a thank-you, after it healed. Or maybe I'd hold on to it so I could give it to a friend when he broke his leg. Why did you point to that one?"

"Oh, I don't know." Brendan was standing next to me now, and I couldn't admit I knew exactly what it depicted and why I wanted it. "I just love it."

The man pulled it out of the display case and placed it on the counter between us. "Well, what does it look like to you?"

"A pregnant belly."

"So let's play a game. Why would a person buy that one?"

"To get pregnant?" I was embarrassed; I felt like a child.

"Sure, or maybe to ensure a safe pregnancy."

He walked away abruptly to help another patron. The conversation was finished. Brendan left, too. I picked up the milagro and turned it in my palm. I wanted to need it, but I didn't, and I wouldn't, not anytime soon. It felt disingenuous—or worse, bad luck—to buy it in preparation for a vague future. It seemed to me, superstitious to a fault, to be the type of thing that needed to be energized from the start: pursued, chosen, and purchased awash in honest intention and necessity. Another employee walked past me, and I called for his attention, pointing to a different charm. This one was an open hand, fingers curved up to form a slight cup—brushed silver, blackened in the creases between the fingers and the wrist where the clasp was attached. It was tiny, delicate, no longer than half an inch. He threaded it onto a black satin cord, and I took it to the cash register, where the man who'd explained the pregnancy charm was waiting.

"Now, why'd you pick that one?"

"I'm a writer. A lot of stress on the hands." I laughed awkwardly, curling and extending my fingers as if to illustrate the claim.

"That's great." He pointed to Brendan, who was again at my side. "Why would he pick the hand?"

"Well, he's an artist, so—"

"Good guess! Why else would someone pick the hand?"

I wasn't trying to be dense; I didn't know. I felt foolish and out of place. I shrugged and handed him my credit card. He swiped it and then popped open the cash drawer. "Open your hand," he said, and I did. He dropped a quarter into my palm. "Prosperity."

"Ah." I smiled and handed the quarter back to him, but he waved it away.

"Prosperity doesn't only mean money, of course. There's a reason it's called a helping hand."

I unwrapped the necklace in front of the shop and wore it back to the sanctuary, where we made our way back to the pocito. We stood outside the open door, waiting for our turn while a middle-aged woman sat on the ground and rubbed dirt onto the stomach of a man kneeling before her. It was a moment of such vulnerability, such intimacy, and I felt guilty to have seen it. But wasn't that intimacy the point; wasn't each of us sharing in it? We were all ostensibly there in supplication, pleading for myriad rescues. It was a place for humility, but humility didn't require shame.

When it was our turn, we ducked through the low doorway and found the room to be somehow smaller than it appeared from outside. It was a solemn and sobering niche with nothing but a window and, in the center of the stone floor, a small hole revealing the underlying dirt. This, the holy dirt, was soft and cool to the touch, a brighter rust red than the surrounding ground. A bright yellow-and-orange plastic shovel—a beach toy in another life—stood upright in the mound. Brendan and I scooped out just enough dirt to fill the ziplock bags we had been told to bring and then quickly rubbed some on the sites we thought could most use some healing. I dusted my forehead ("for my sick old brain," I said) and Brendan did the same for his stomach. I knew that he, a skeptic and atheist, was humoring me, and I loved him for it. We walked silently back to the car. That night, I dragged a small handful of dirt over my womb, sanctifying it in preparation for the baby I prayed would be there soon.

Initially during the planning of this trip, I'd told Brendan that we should elope in Santa Fe. I had dangled the possibility in front of him like a joke to see if he would grab it. He hadn't, but he also hadn't explicitly rejected it, so I'd spent hours privately researching the logistics while knowing that the chances of its actually happening were minuscule. Still, I'd told Dara and Juno that I'd be getting married soon, and they were thrilled, immediately helping me Google hairstyles and dresses. It wasn't the truth, but it wasn't exactly a lie, either: Brendan and I had decided to get married in a small civil ceremony in the vaguely near future. But I didn't want vague, I wanted definite, I wanted immediate, so I pretended I had it in spaces where it didn't matter what the other person believed. It didn't matter if the girls assumed I was getting married sooner than I really was. My relationship was only adjacent to their lives.

It also didn't matter one unremarkable afternoon, when Katie and I visited an occult shop on a whim, and I lingered by the premade spell kits. The saleswoman, garbed in crushed velvet and a mess of silver chain necklaces, approached and told me that she offered custom charm bags for customers who needed something specific. What was I looking for?

I told her—so quickly it took me by surprise—that I wanted something to help with fertility. She clapped her hands and smiled, then dashed around the store gathering stones and herbs and powders. She placed them in a velvet purple satchel, cupped it in her hands, closed her eyes, murmured words I couldn't hear, and blew softly into the puckered opening before tying it shut. She handed me the pouch and explained that I would need to charge it with my own energy before placing it under my mattress. Katie was as surprised as I was, saying she hadn't realized that Brendan and I had decided we were ready. I was embarrassed and backtracked, saying it wasn't official or anything. I took the spell home but never used it. What if it worked?

In all of those moments, I wanted to know what it would feel like to have the type of life—to be the type of person—for whom rites of passage were not only possible but imminent. I wanted to embody that potential, and I wanted people to witness it, if only briefly. I imagine that if I hadn't believed so vehemently in my depression's ability to disqualify me from those milestones—that I carried a defect that fundamentally separated me from those peers who were achieving them—I wouldn't have felt such urgency. If I didn't see the baby, the marriage, the type of professional success that could be screenshotted and posted on social media as confirmation that I was finally, fully better, maybe I wouldn't have been rushing so frantically toward them. In my mind, though, those broadly acknowledged landmarks of adulthood could be both proof and guarantee of my final, permanent recovery.

Better

Watching Dara and Juno didn't satiate my desire for children; it stoked it. I spent a third of my life in a home, with a family, that looked so much like the one I wanted for myself: successful, creative parents with vibrant lives of their own; kind, curious children; an environment of palpable love and respect. I knew, of course, that I wasn't part of their family, but I felt lucky to be in its orbit. As my depression worsened, though, my role as a caretaker, and my proximity to family and motherhood, no longer made me optimistic. Instead, it taunted me with its impossibility, humiliated me for ever thinking I deserved it.

Two weeks before the hospital, late on a night when I'd once again told Brendan to go see our friends without me, I wrote:

Sometimes all of it seems so close—the baby, the family,
the career, the life—and then I'm here again and I see its
impossibility. Lately depression is physical, unrelenting. Every
bit of my body at its edges—the jaw tensed, stomach tight,
nauseated, head heavy, crowded. I think about boring a hole into
my skull. A little drill. I want to smack it out. Could I really say
goodbye?

  But, also:
—Could I ever love Brendan well enough?
—Could I ever be a mother?
—Like this?

On my first morning at the hospital, I met with a group described as my support team—a psychiatrist, counselor, social worker, and nurse—only one of whom I'd see again over the course of the next six days. They asked me all the questions I'd answered the day before. I worried that my lack of emotion, namely my lack of tears, might seem suspicious or suggest I was faking my despair, so I explained I wasn't really feeling sad; I was feeling nothing. I'd just published my first book, I was in a great relationship—still, nothing.

"Can you tell me something in your life you're excited about?" the psychiatrist asked.

My instinct was no, but I took a second to sit with it, which was when the sting of tears finally hit. I knew what I wanted, but I didn't believe I could have it. If I could believe it, maybe I could feel excited.

"I want to have a family," I said. "But I don't want to have a family like this."

When I started seeing Elizabeth two months later, I sat on the couch at our first session having honed this inkling of an idea into a clearly defined mission.

"I want to have a baby," I said, "but I need to know I won't be a mother who kills herself."

* * *

It's no coincidence that I started my project of solving suicide with Sylvia Plath. I'd never gone through a Plath phase, hadn't ever even read *The Bell Jar*, but it was impossible to travel in the sad-girl amateur poet circles of my teens without gathering intel on their patron saint. I knew she'd been a mother. I knew she'd put her head into an oven. I knew she'd been young when she had done it. I wasn't intimately familiar with Plath when I left the hospital, but I would be. The details I discovered in those first few months were devastating: how her one- and two-year olds were asleep in their bedroom when it happened; how, hours before she died, she'd placed bread and milk on their bedside tables, opened their window, and plugged the kitchen door frame with towels; how the note she left had read, simply, "Phone Dr. Horder"; how her death happened close enough to her nurse's arrival to thrust her suicide into some public skepticism. Did she mean to be found? To be saved? Would death by ambivalent suicide make it any more or less tragic—are there hierarchies of tragedy?

For my purposes, those distinctions were pivotal. My logic was inexplicable, but somehow, I felt as if her suicide's being accidental would count as a win on the side of my survival. If it had been a mistake—if she simply hadn't been careful enough—well, I could be careful. Otherwise, I was left hunting for signs of our emotional and psychological separation. If Sylvia* *had* meant to leave her babies, I needed her despair to be exceptional. I needed to find in her writing evidence of pain, anxieties, anger, and hopelessness that so obviously surpassed anything I'd ever experienced. Mostly, though, I saw echoes of myself.

Sylvia had wanted a baby for years before she had her first, and she, too, inflated the shift into motherhood with meaning. The meaning was inconsistent. Sometimes, having a baby would be the thing that would heal her; other times, it would be the culmination of having been healed. This was a catch-22 that permeated all of her plans: motherhood, marriage, popularity, publication, or, most important, critical acclaim, would make her better, but also, she would need to be better already in order to achieve them. In a bout of "paralysis"—as she frequently describes her lows in her journals— she laments in her journal the disappearance of the "clearly defined immediate and long-range objectives" she'd once carried with gusto. She supposes she'd like to write and admits to "fearfully, dimly"

---

* At the risk of sacrificing propriety, I've decided against changing first-name references to Sylvia Plath throughout the editing process. Sometimes, while writing, I thought of her as Sylvia and others as Plath, and the distinction was instinctual but also, I think, telling.

wanting to have a child. Giving birth, she explains, would set her on "a bloodily breached twenty-year plan of purpose." That purpose is key. Plath is continually distressed by her difficulty in defining what she believes *must* be her firm, unambiguous role in the world. At just twenty-five years old, she bemoans having been "rejected by an adult world, part of nothing"—a conclusion she's drawn through brutal self-assessments in comparison with her peers.

Throughout years of extensive journaling, Plath describes an adulthood spent hungry for different identities, but she's stymied in an obsession with determining which next step would be best—as if there were a single right answer and as if she had only one chance to choose. Her angst isn't unwarranted. Certainly, most women in the first half of the twentieth century didn't have an abundance of time or resources to weigh their limited options for their futures, but Plath's ambition and proven talent exacerbated that urgency, turning every decision into a small agony. She can't face one opportunity without imagining all those she might sacrifice by taking it, and the result is stagnation and self-deprecation. She yearns for an external validation of who she is so that she might be relieved of the pressure of figuring it out herself—and, ideally, the impossible standards she has set as stipulations. Motherhood might—she imagines, she hopes—do just that.

But just as Plath has specific and severe requirements for qualifying as a writer, she must first "*deserve** to conquer childbirth." What would suffice? Namely, as she notes in the very same sentence, she'd first have to "conquer [her] writing and experience." But that contingency doesn't offer much guidance, either. Even that repeated verb—*conquer*—evokes the unrealistic expectation of life as a series

---

* Emphasis mine.

of culminating, definitive victories. Certainly, in her mind, bouts of depression are proof that she hasn't won. She hates the process, has no patience for it, and is disgusted with herself for not getting to the end more quickly. She suspects she doesn't want to write so much as she wants "to have written." She ping-pongs between blind faith—not only in a better future but more significantly in her ability to single-handedly manifest it—and a complete dissolution of the self when she either fails to achieve her goals or does achieve them but decides that something must be wrong with her for not feeling completely fulfilled by them. She measures her value as a person by her output and professional success, so her work can't be just work; it is fraught with consequences. Her professional success, her critical acclaim, is the prerequisite of the future she wants but also inseparable from her self-actualization: "I live for my own work, without which I am nothing."

When I started seeing Elizabeth, I think I imagined therapy as a kind of certification course: I'd do the work, the work would be approved, and I'd get to have a baby. In the outside world I was pretending that pregnancy, and therefore stability and success, was imminent, but in therapy, at least in the beginning, I believed I really *was* working toward it and that soon it wouldn't have to be an act. Inevitably, though, as months and years passed, as friends got pregnant, I'd downplay my periods of depression, anger, frustration, and fear. I was never successful in hiding them, and when Elizabeth asked about my hesitation to be honest, I explained that I couldn't tell her everything because if she knew everything, then surely she'd realize, and be obligated to tell me, that my becoming a mother—a mother lost in a dysfunctional cycle, unable to part from suicidality—would be immoral, irresponsible. I was desperate to preserve my initial optimism, and so I was willing to sacrifice all of the progress my previous honesty had created.

"Why on earth would I tell you that you shouldn't have a baby?" she asked.

"Because I can't just fall apart when I have a kid," I said. "And obviously I can't stop falling apart."

"What happens when you fall apart?"

"I don't know. I stop working. I stop leaving the house. I sleep too much. I fall behind on everything until I push myself into a full panic."

"And what does that look like with a child in the picture?"

"I don't know. It can't be good! The tasks aren't just 'answer emails' and 'make breakfast'; they're literally 'keep this human alive.'"

"True. What would happen if you became a mother and for a bit you couldn't handle caring for your child—for any reason, not just depression?"

I knew what she wanted, and I knew I didn't believe it, but I said it anyway: "I could ask for help."

"You could ask for help."

Suicide is inherently a solitary process and act, so I wanted conquering it to be the same. Asking for help is such an unsatisfying answer, so easy to dismiss. The problem with asking for help is that I have to do it. I got pregnant with Theo a little over a year later, faster than either Brendan or I had expected, but now that he's here, all that time spent trying to figure out if I had deserved it—earned it—feels silly, or maybe just beside the point. I am a mother, and that is a fact; a mother is a mother whether or not she wants to die.

I read about Sylvia's marriage and look for signs that she wasn't *really* happy, wasn't really in love. I look for something I can use as evidence of a lack that made it easier for her to leave, so I can point at it and convince myself that my love is deeper, fuller, stronger than hers, that it will succeed in keeping me alive where hers failed. I pore over the photos: Sylvia standing next to Ted, gazing down at the newborn daughter in his arms. Is her smile tight, her body a bit rigid? But then there's a photo where it's as if she and Ted can't get close enough to each other. His arm is around her waist, and she grasps his hand with both of hers—see her fingers, curled around his, holding tight; her head is lifted skyward; her smile is wide, spreading high into her cheeks and eyes. It's 1956, and she looks to be in absolute bliss. She'll be dead in seven years. Was her suicide present even then, a seed rooting within her?

I've spent years trying to figure out how happy *Sylvia's* happy was, but her journals reveal her indefatigable attempts to do the same. She writes about her joy as diligently as she does her sadness, often as a measure of preserving that joy, though I've found no evidence such work ever provided a respite. Either Sylvia is panicked about losing her joy, telling herself to hold on to it, or she is interrogating it. She knows her happiness and suicidality exist in a disorienting cycle, but she's certain she can break it with enough discipline and diligence. Part of that diligence is an intense scrutiny of the moments in which she's felt better:

February 10, 1958: "How clear and cleansed and happy I feel. Why?"

September 18, 1958: "Much happier today—why?"

December 16, 1958: "Is it dangerous to be happy?"

One week after her twentieth birthday—in an entry she opens by declaring, "God, if ever I have come close to wanting to commit suicide, it is now . . ."—Plath frets over the knowledge that she *should* be happy, given what she's achieved. She's a student at Smith College; both *Seventeen* and the now-defunct *Mademoiselle* have published her short stories and poems; she lives in the "free, spoiled, pampered country of America" with "a few lovely clothes, and one intelligent, handsome boy." She suspects others would be happy in her place. She wonders if others who *were* in her place—other women writers, that is—were similarly disillusioned. "Why did Virginia Woolf commit suicide?" she writes, and now the question resides in a chapter, a book, asking the same question of her. "If only I knew," she continues, suggesting the answer could keep her from following Woolf's lead, but in the next sentence the object of her desired knowledge shifts to something narrower. "If only I knew how high I could set my goals, my requirements for my life!" Was Virginia happy or unhappy? Did she suffer from a misalignment of goals and their expected effects? What difference does it make?

Perhaps Sylvia read Woolf's journals, just as I do now, alongside hers. Perhaps she, too, noticed Woolf's unease within happiness, her lack of faith in its strength. At thirty-eight years old, with two novels and a wealth of literary criticism under her belt, Woolf wonders why "life [is] so tragic," laments her tendency to "think too much of whys and wherefores," and grieves the fact that, globally, "[u]nhappiness is everywhere." But she notes all of this at a remove. She's still "happy with it all"—or would be, "if it weren't for my feeling that it's a strip of pavement over an abyss." The "strip of pavement" might be life, or it might be happiness; either way, it's precarious.

Whether we're analyzing our happiness or despair, the result is a distrust and dissection of emotion in general. To realize happiness, like its opposite, is necessarily ephemeral and arbitrary, impossible to pin down—is that the moment fear enters?

On June 6, 2011, I wrote: *I'm so happy it is beginning to frighten me.*

On January 2, 2018: *I'm trying not to be scared of emotional stability and/or happiness.*

On March 18, 2022: *Happiness is dangerous because it's always entrée to disappointment.*

Better

Though I was no longer nannying for Evelyn and Richard, I'd happily continued watching Dara and Juno a few nights a month. I'd also started sending Evelyn bits of writing, paragraphs that would become essays that would become this book.

"You know what really struck me?" she asked one night as we stood in her kitchen discussing this very section, while the girls were upstairs, long asleep. "That word—*joy*—when you're talking about the moments people try to remember or hold on to. I mean, how many times do you think you've experienced real joy? You know? What kind of life are we expecting?"

It was impossible then not to see the evidence everywhere, not only in my reading and writing but also in my thinking: our requirements of wellness, the standards that condemn us to failure, the implied *enough*. Not "Am I happy?" but "Am I happy enough?" Am I successful, alive, engaged enough? Am I good enough, am I recovered enough? Do I love Theo enough? Am I—have I ever been, will I ever be—enough?

We can call this an analysis of recovery, but it would be disingenuous to ignore that it is also a suspicion of it. To examine happiness is to prod it, doubt it, seek out its inconsistencies lest it turn out to be fraudulent. This skepticism is justifiable in a society obsessed with happiness, optimized wellness, and toxic positivity—are we living our best lives?—but it's dangerous to create a hierarchy of happiness, and then use that hierarchy as a gauge for your wellness and safety. Put contentment through the wringer long enough and often enough, and disillusionment will inevitably squeeze out. Is this the happiest I could be? Is there a Platonic ideal of *better* I haven't accessed? Am I left vulnerable, at risk, until I do? As I searched desperately for the cracks in

Sylvia's happiness, for the clues she missed, I ignored the fact that doing so required probing my own happiness. As long as I was relying on comparison, I would be playing defense, always looking for absolution. It was never going to work.

"Tell me more about this book you're working on," Elizabeth said after we'd been meeting for a few months, during a session to which I'd arrived already feeling defeated.

"Basically, it's about the fact that I want to start my real life but I also still kind of believe that eventually I'm going to kill myself. So I'm looking at people who've committed suicide to see if I can figure out what they did wrong, so I can avoid it."

"What have you found?"

"Nothing."

Chapter 3

The Airlock

I wake up in Theo's bed the morning after planning my suicide, ashamed of the previous night's conviction and relieved that it's been wiped out. I'm embarrassed by the evidence that remains, the tabs still open on my phone's web browser, the letter to Theo, which I stuff under a stack of legal pads in my desk drawer. I return to the plan I've developed with Elizabeth and Brendan: consistent and clear-eyed budgeting, following through on personal therapy and couples counseling, going to bed at a reasonable time, the usuals.

For most of my life, indulging in the fantasy of killing myself—getting as close as possible to it before rejecting it—has become the only way I know to move past suicidality. It has been with me, part of me, almost as far back as my memory reaches, the source of a counterintuitive safety because I know the possibility is always there. With it comes a short-term relief granted by the idea of a permanent one: relief at the idea of relief. And so my death is a near-constant presence in my life, traveling back and forth on a spectrum between comfort and despair. It is, like Sylvia wrote in her journal, "as if I had to plunge to the bottom of nonexistence, of absolute fear, before I can rise again." Now that Theo's here, though, my suicidal fantasies are stuck in the pole of despair. I can't use them to calm myself down, but I also haven't figured out an effective alternative.

The day we brought Theo home, I was overwhelmed with love and relief and pain when I wrote in my journal, *How could I ever possibly leave you?* I think I had known this before getting pregnant—that having a child would root me in this world—but I couldn't anticipate the day-to-day repercussions. I didn't realize that having to stay wouldn't necessarily translate into wanting to. I can't leave him—I don't *want* to leave him—but the impulse toward suicide lingers. I haven't unlearned it. I imagine it painfully, but it remains my knee-jerk response to even the most benign conflicts.* Indulging in the fantasy of oblivion has served a purpose, but it comes at a cost, both then and now. In *History of Suicide*, the French historian Georges Minois looks at the Stoic philosopher Seneca, who analyzed the pain of those who "lose their taste for life and the universe" before killing himself in AD 65 at about sixty-eight years old. Seneca described a "sickness" that both comes from and results in constant inaction—unless, of course, it leads to the ultimate act of suicide. Among first-century Romans, though, this type of suicide would

---

* A TikTok video by an unnamed user, captured and shared across social media platforms, describes this phenomenon so casually that I'm taken aback and delighted when a screenshot of it pops up on my Instagram feed. A young white woman stands outside on a sunny day sipping an iced coffee, a text overlay above her head reading "it's so over for everyone the second I learn to stop shifting to suic*dal ideations the second something doesn't go my way." At the time of screenshotting, it had 3,844 likes.

have been rare. More likely, Minois states, those who lived with "this spiritual malaise" never left the contemplation stage of suicide. "Its most typical manifestation," he writes, "was floating in a perpetual state of indecision between life and death." I'm floating, now. I'm stuck in the in-between.

* * *

The writer and therapist hannah baer* gives this stuckness form and physicality in *trans girl suicide museum*,† her slim but revolutionary treatise covering suicide, gender, capitalism, drugs, and the internet, accurately described by the publisher as "one part ketamine spiral, one part confessional travelogue from the edge of gender." Imagining suicidality in the form of the museum transforms it: suicidality isn't so much a personal characteristic or psychological symptom as it is a space where baer resides or travels through. It encompasses not only

---

* baer does not capitalize her name; her book title is also stylized in lower case.

† While baer's ideation of the suicide museum is broadly illuminating and valuable, it would be disingenuous and harmful to engage with her theories without acknowledging that first and foremost they are intended for trans readers, which I am not. In baer's own words, she wrote *trans girl suicide museum* specifically so "no other trans girls (and no trans guys, and no non binary people, agender people, or anyone else who has deviant gender and does suicide) to feel that they have to die in order to get through it." The distinction is vital and must be made explicit because research shows trans and nonbinary populations—especially trans women—are disproportionately represented among adults who've had suicidal ideation; trans youth are more than two times as likely to attempt suicide as their cis peers; suicidality in the trans population as a whole is inextricable from external factors like discrimination and harassment, violence, lack of access to gender-affirming health care, and societal rejection of gender identity; and trans people are at significantly higher risk for factors that increase suicidality universally, such as abuse, poverty, estrangement, and incarceration. (More on this in chapter 9.)

rumination on suicide but also indulgence in habits that amplify the fantasy: "[a]s much spending the hours between 3 and 5am scrolling-through-old-pictures-on-your-external-hard-drive-looking-at-your-bone-structure-from-when-you-were-a-kid-and-teenager as it is suicidal ideation."

What's remarkable about the museum is that it is also the site of defense against suicide, if only because—until the moment of killing oneself, should the moment arrive—the process of suicide necessarily includes surviving it. In one wing of the museum sits "the most normal white sterile high-ceilinged art gallery room you can picture," except instead of art on the walls it houses a "yellow metal seesaw." The suicidal person sits on the low end; above the high end gapes a "mechanical cisgendered vagina ready to dump transphobia" until that person is "flung into space, sucked up into the trash chute, and gone." It's a brutal, overwhelming, and unfair fight, but it is a fight nonetheless—and though the museum is primarily a place of loneliness, it has space for others who have similar reasons for visiting. baer envisions the gallery when a friend calls and says they're "thinking about ending it":

> I imagined us together squatting on the low end of the seesaw, feet in leather stirrups fastened to the floor with big metal bolts, making sure we stayed down. I was behind her with my arms around her waist like a motorcycle passenger, while hundreds of things fell on the upper side of the seesaw, pouring down, trying to tip it: their parents, their dead ancestors, the surgeon that performed gender affirming surgery on them, hundreds of pounds of trash, especially bad trash, like dirty diapers, hypodermic needles for hormones, hypodermic needles for dope, dog shit bags that ripped open . . . raining down trying to tip the seesaw.

The museum makes sense because it contains space for all of the outside components that shift the desire to die from the body to its environment. Through the trash chute, baer explicitly names and alludes to specific risk factors—the transphobia, the drugs, the poverty—that are problems with societal solutions, issues we'd prefer to ignore lest we be compelled to acknowledge that sometimes the desire to die isn't strictly irrational. At the same time, extending the boundaries of suicidality from the body to the museum walls emphasizes the distance between the suicidal person and the nonsuicidal person—even, too, the distance between two people whose suicidality is born of vastly different lived experiences. (There is a reason that this is specifically the *trans girl* suicide museum.)

Describing her complicated relationship with her mother, baer writes, "Part of the museum is not being able to see very far and so it makes it harder for me to comprehend her experience or do the heavy lift of teaching her about mine." Museums are sturdy, insulated, built to last; she can't see beyond the museum's impenetrable walls, meaning that she can't see beyond herself and her suicidality. More specifically, the museum blocks meaningful connection with those who don't visit it, or won't.

There is a tipping point of suicide, but the museum has surprising safeguards against reaching it. That friend sitting on the seesaw with baer lived, as does baer. The two hunkered down, and the vagina chute failed to overwhelm them. This is the hidden hope within the transfer of suicide from the body to the environment in which it resides: it isn't the self we must escape but rather our surroundings. Or, as baer writes, "It might seem like your body is the problem . . . but it's actually the museum." There's an exit somewhere; it's just a matter of finding it. It's easier said than done.

Victory inside the museum is possible, but only temporarily, conditionally, if we continue to come back. baer worries about being trapped in the museum. During those periods in which she isn't visiting daily, she still returns to "pay [her] respects, periodically, with little offerings." Here suicide isn't only a museum, but also an "altar"—one that has been impossible to leave completely. If suicide is a cavernous museum, if it is a sacred apse, if it is a process that includes rumination and ambivalence, how easy might it be to spend an entire life within its limits? When do we start to get too comfortable, to even resist escape? "I feel this pain now," baer writes, "the ambiguity of the museum, not just not knowing if I'll ever escape, but if I did, where I would even be, would I even want that life . . ." She knows that even at her best—when she's able to see a future she's excited about—she's never shed her "readiness" for death, even in absence of the "wish"—and she worries whether she ever will.

baer recounts sitting on an airplane and calmly considering the possibility of its crashing; she writes, "I guess that's the question I'm asking—will I always feel OK about leaving." It's one of many questions punctuated as a statement in the book—she's seeking answers, presumably, but does she really believe there's an answer she doesn't already know? These questions and their variations—*Will I always be ready to go, no matter how well my life is going? Will there be anything that removes my ambivalence toward death, that would make me actively fight for my survival?*—are key to the liminality of the suicidal space. I've lived the entirety of my adult life with the presumption that only when I've definitively rejected suicide—when I've confidently, unequivocally decided I'm committed to life—will I be able to allow myself to stop worrying about it. But maybe that's never going to happen. Is the disposal of that ambivalence a requirement of recovery?

Almost thirty years before he would leap into the East River, the playwright Spalding Gray, while "lost and desperate" trying to pin down his identity, wrote a list of possible future roles in his journal. In just nine items he covers a large swath of human (and superhuman) experience:

1. *a world traveler*
2. *a Zen monk*
3. *a lover*
4. *a movie star*
5. *a dancer*
6. *a maker of a group to carry out my vision*
7. *a suicide victim*
8. *god*
9. *a family man just in love with Liz*

Clearly, these aren't all mutually exclusive, and in fact Gray would manifest a few of them: he'd travel the world, act, "carry out his vision" through ambitious theater groups, and have a family.* He would also kill himself. That "a suicide victim" is on this list—a rigid rhetorical format whose entire function is to break down ideas into discrete items—suggests the belief that an eventual suicide would define him, that it would negate any of the other identities he might have embodied before. More clearly, it reveals his ongoing,

---

* Like Plath, Gray elevated his career to a state of urgent, critical importance; also, he was distraught by its inability to fulfill him. In February 1980 he wrote, "I hope I can get down to some writing. It would be the only thing that could save me." Just three months later, feeling "out of it and ragged," he'd reached the disillusionment part of the cycle: "I'm not at all sure that the work can sustain me anymore. Feel at the END." His work didn't save him, but he couldn't imagine anything else might, either.

active consideration of suicide's possibility. Maybe we don't have to categorically disavow suicide to survive, but at least we can try removing it from the options we're weighing.

* * *

I've begun a group chat with the five women who've known the extent of my suicidality for about as long as they've known me. They know it so well because they've also been there, or at least close to it. The five of us, Melissa among them, happened to land on the same dorm floor fifteen years ago when we started at Reed College, and we continued to live together in various groupings for the following decade. Now we're spread across the country—Melissa, Rose, and Natasha remain in Portland; Juliet has settled in Pittsburgh; Annelyse hops around the world—and I ache for them daily. No boundaries exist among us—or, I should say, no shame exists in revealing the depths of our depression or anxiety, and no explanations are needed when one of us must drop out of the chat because, for whatever reason, it's not something she can handle at that moment. They are brilliant women in every stage of life; they are accomplished and self-actualized, but still, at various times and to varying degrees, they're not so keen on living, and so we talk often about the reconciliation of these states and realities, debating whether or not that reconciliation is possible or even necessary.

The chat is one of a handful we share—others reserved for memes and shitposts, general life updates, pictures of Theo—but this one is called The Airlock. An air lock—the small chamber attached to rocket ships and submersibles in which pressure is equalized before an astronaut or diver enters outer space or the deep, dark sea—is itself a metonym for liminality. The name comes from Annelyse's mother,* her shorthand for suicide in the sense that, if used incorrectly, an air lock could be quite an efficient and irreversible escape hatch. Its only purpose is transition; its entire existence is a state of in-between, and its isolated opportunity suggests a sort of quantum suicide.

This specific group chat, similarly, is reserved for those times when we're neither here nor there. My relationship with it mimics my relationship with my suicide, and so our use of it brings to mind similar concerns: What are the repercussions of frequent, ongoing examination? What are the costs and benefits of dwelling in a space that both affirms and confirms the validity of suicidal thinking? At best, one of us helps the other out of whatever hole she's fallen into;† at worst, we all wallow in our yearning for oblivion. *We all feel it, nothing to be ashamed of* so easily turns into *We all feel it, maybe it's healthier to accept this instead of even attempting to get better.* In an essay about Sylvia Plath following her suicide, Anne Sexton wrote of her friend, "We talked death with burned-up intensity . . . as if death made each of us a little more real at the moment. . . . We talked death and this was life for us." Sexton would kill herself nine years later. We try not to make death our life, but sometimes we struggle.

Putting aside our shared depression, anxiety, suicidality, we are also joined by having witnessed too many deaths in our twenties and thirties. Two friends died during our second year at Reed, one from cancer and another from a seizure. Three more have died in the twelve years since our graduation, one from a chronic illness and two from suicide. During the spring semester of our first year, on the

---

* (We come by it naturally.)

† Indeed, our most used reaction emoji in The Airlock is ⬬.

night before spring break, a freshman named Jessica killed herself in the room below mine. Melissa, Natasha, and I didn't find out until we were already in the car on our way to Natasha's family's home in Ashland, Oregon. I hadn't known Jessica well; the only memory I could conjure up—and I was desperately trying—was her stopping at my open door while I sat on the floor, building a shoe rack. She'd told me that she, too, loved Regina Spektor.

Jessica's suicide plagued me, obsessed me, especially because it had happened as I was considering my own suicide. I dreaded returning to campus but couldn't justify that reaction. I was no one to her; she was barely anyone to me. The night before we would return to Portland, I sat awake in the guest room and wrote:

> *I was awake above her until four in the morning, crying about a boy. When did she do it? And how? And when did they find her? And who found her? They found her in her room. How did they know to look? Did she leave a note? Did she leave the door unlocked? Who found her? Who found her? Where was the commotion? Shouldn't there have been some kind of commotion? When did she think about it? When did she decide? Sometimes I think I'll kill myself for almost any reason, but she did it. And it's awful. Why didn't I know? But how would I have known? She must have been so incredibly sad. And scared—I wonder if she was scared.*

The following year, Melissa, Natasha, Rose, and I moved into a nearby house that we named the Birdhouse—we were the birds, wide-eyed and hopeful. The house came with a cat and a backyard with a compost heap. We painted the front door robin's-egg blue. We filled the cabinets with groceries and covered the walls with art. We got cable (we were the only college students we knew of who had a DVR) and hosted *True Blood* viewing parties that often devolved into kitchen raves. The sadness was inconstant.

Nearing the end of the school year, for reasons so banal I can't even isolate them—I missed too many classes? I couldn't keep up with the work? I was insecure and off Prozac and unable to maintain my eating disorder?—I stayed up late one night looking up ways to kill myself that wouldn't scare me too much. I had no access to drugs. I couldn't fathom jumping from some great height, was too daunted by the fact that it would require leaving the house. I landed on bleach. My meager research said it would hurt—badly—but would get the job done, so I grabbed a jug from the basement and sat next to it on the floor of my bedroom. I opened it and closed it. I wrote individual goodbye notes to everyone in my family and in the house, sobbing all the while.

Eventually I'd written myself out of my conviction; I'd successfully diverted my attention from myself to everyone I loved. I was lucky to love so many. I tore up the notes and threw them into the garbage, covering them with rotting food scraps for good measure. I put the bleach under the sink.

The experience echoed one from three years earlier, when I had been twenty years old and on the brink of dropping out of college for the second time. My bulimia was back with a vengeance. I was two months off Prozac, which I'd stopped cold turkey without letting anyone know. Any hope I'd had for that second attempt at continuing my education was rapidly diminishing. I was living in a house on Long Island with my sister and two of our best friends, trying to hide the breakdown I knew was coming, but it was emerging rapidly and loudly. Two days after Christmas, I spent the day drinking alone and tracking my disintegration:

Better

2:10 p.m.:

Things are good. Things are ok. I'm stepping out and moving on and doing all of the things I do to fake progress. I must keep moving.

4:19 p.m.:

My heart hurts. Either my heart or my stomach, I can't tell. There is such clarity in these moments of chaos. My life will be only what I make from it. There is nothing else. It terrifies me to think that me, my core, can change and I won't even know it.

5:08 p.m., in letters big enough to fill the page, each line traced over itself so many times that the pen strokes push patterns into the paper:

I want to SCREAM

5:30 p.m.:

I'm not scared. I am scared of nothing. (I am scared of everything.) I have such high hopes for my life. Travel, writing, music, education. I just don't know how to get off the couch, you know? I want to be able to exist in my body without clawing, writhing. I want to be still, but not stagnant. Calm.

6:01 p.m.:

The funny thing is Christmas was so perfect. The most grown-up Christmas I've ever had. I cried while praying before bed,

*thanking God for such a perfect life. I have more love in my life
than I know what to do with. I want to get better. I really, really
do. Please just let me get better.*

I don't know how many minutes or hours elapsed between that
last entry and the next, which has no timestamp but is titled *MES-
SAGE TO READERS: If I die tonight, or tomorrow night, etc.* I think
I imagined it as a noncommittal suicide note, a letter someone could
find if they had reason to look, but if not, and if nothing happened,
could just exist as one melodramatic journal entry among many. I
hadn't quite committed to killing myself, but I was toying around
with the idea. I told the reader what song to play at my funeral[*] and
asked, if possible, to give me a green burial. It's maudlin and cringe
inducing, and, reading it now, I know I was motivated in no small
part by the desire to create art, not only to make something beautiful
but, more important, to leave it behind. But I know I meant it, too,
when I wrote: *I love you. Thank you. I tried to do as much with my little
life as I could.*

I went to the medicine cabinet and pulled out a bottle of ibuprofen. I read the label. Recommended dosage: two pills. I usually took
four. I poured out a handful, rolled them around in my fist. I put a
few back into the bottle; I read the label again. I swallowed thirteen.
That moment standing over the bathroom sink was layered: at the
base was sadness, but above it, closer to the surface, was frightful
certainty that the sadness was unassailable and that it would never
end while I was still alive. My sadness needed to build up to fear,
to panic. Sadness is a dulling agent; it's the fear that activates the
body. It was fear that energized me enough to make the decision and

---

[*] Jolie Holland, "Mexican Blue."

follow through—to get off the couch in the empty, dark living room, but not with an aim toward getting better. After I swallowed the pills, I returned to the couch and waited to find out if this thing—if anything—would happen. It didn't. Eventually I went upstairs to my bedroom and fell asleep.

When I woke up the next morning, the only thing that had changed was that I didn't want to die anymore. I was embarrassed at the emotion I had indulged in and grateful that no one in the house knew anything about it. Mostly I was relieved and, surprisingly, re-vitalized. The two pages following my *MESSAGE TO READERS* are torn out, just two thin columns of jagged paper in their place, sentences reduced to letter fragments. Whatever I'd written, I didn't want to take it with me into this bright future, in which I reveled two days later: *Too much to say. My heart is full!!!!* I'm surprised I let any pages from that day remain.

Checking into the hospital in 2017 was drastic, but the fact is that that night—twenty years old and daring myself to take an above-the-recommended-dosage of a nonprescription pill—remains my only attempt. It feels silly to designate it as such, and I hesitate to do so here,* but while it was tame, it wasn't half-hearted. I swallowed a bunch of pills and spent a few hours scared that it might work, pretty sure that it wouldn't. I needed to know: What would it feel like, the second, the minutes, the hours after setting your suicide into mo-tion? And I got my answer, albeit in a tiny dose. What I discovered is that the best way for me to realize I want to live is to inch myself right up to the edge of death. I didn't have to think about suicide for months, because I knew, ultimately, that I would regret the decision. My conviction didn't last, but the revelation—that getting as close as

---

* Not even suicidality is immune to impostor syndrome.

possible to suicide without enacting it could make me want to live—remained. It turned into a strategy: pushing suicide back by walking toward it. It could never have been a long-term solution, but for a while it worked.

Donald Antrim describes a similar practice in his memoir *One Friday in April: A Story of Suicide and Survival*, in scenopoetic and often discomfiting detail. His respite comes from enactment, as if running through his suicide's dress rehearsal. He writes countless suicide notes. He lies down on his kitchen floor, arms crossed over his chest, and he imagines himself as a corpse waiting to be found. He drags a knife along his wrist, guessing at the pressure he would need to apply to break the skin. He practices; he pretends. And for a while, these rituals silence the voice inside telling him to do it for real. "[W]e pick up the pistol, the one in the cabinet," he writes, speaking for all who've been suicidal, as he does frequently throughout. "[We] hold it for a moment, and that helps—the bullet will be there when we need it—and we can then place the gun back in the drawer."

The habit brings to mind the psychologist Thomas Joiner's theory that the ability to kill oneself is acquired through acts of self-harm—that we must train our bodies, inure ourselves to self-inflicted abuse, if we want to thwart our firmly planted survival instinct. Each wound—each cut, burn, bruise imposed on oneself—works toward the wounded's "develop[ing] the ability to beat back [the] pressing urge toward self-preservation." This on its own isn't enough to push a person to suicide or make them high risk. The self-harm must co-occur with that person's feeling "real disconnection from others" and "that they [are] ineffective to the point of seeing themselves as a burden on others." But fear of death—specifically fear of the method and moment of dying—is a significant hurdle to suicide, if not the last one standing before the act. When my brother Jordan spent years cycling through various levels of suicidality, he told us that the only reason he hadn't killed himself yet was his fear of dying. For how much longer could that fear hold him back?

Joiner's theory addresses physical harm specifically, but we can extend the notion to consider psychological or existential harm, too. When I got pregnant, Elizabeth referred me to a reproductive psychiatrist* to take over my Lamictal and Effexor prescriptions. Dr. Lambert explained the benefits and risks of staying on the medications and helped me manage them as they interacted with pregnancy and, later, postpartum anxiety and OCD. During one of the many sessions we had in which I recapped every slight disappointment I'd reacted to by reminding myself that I could always just kill myself, she said, "I wonder about the damage done by constantly imagining your suicide."

"Right," I replied, "like I'm cutting off any possibility of healthy responses to stress."

"Well, yes, but more so the psychic damage. That fixating on your own nonexistence can actually chip away at your sense of self or reality."

In other words, it's a tenuous border between fantasizing about oblivion and begetting it. I have spent most of my life in a protracted negotiation between living and dying, striving for an impossible objectivity that would make the answer clear. When I'm down, I'm

---

* The first psychiatry fellowship in women's mental health was launched in 2002, but reproductive psychiatry specifically was described as an "emerging field" as recently as 2023. I didn't know it existed until Elizabeth made the recommendation. I extend to you the same caveats she gave me: reproductive psychiatrists are pricey and uncommon, but if you can get your insurance to cover it and if you live in a progressive city like, say, New York, it's worth pursuing. As the subspecialty grows, hopefully its accessibility will, too.

adding to the list of evidence that suicide would be a reasonable action. When I'm up, I'm probing: Is this happiness real? How long until it's gone? Fundamentally, this kind of existence is a wavering between the suspicion that I'm doomed and the hope that I'm not. I'm never fully separated from my nonexistence.

*　　*　　*

In the trenches of our multigenerational familial mental illnesses, I have long recognized that my father and I are on the same side of the unspoken divide within our family: those with depression and those without. Though I'd never confirmed this link with my brother Jordan explicitly, I counted him among us, too. This connection, like an undersea river, mostly ran below the surface of small moments of compassion and camaraderie. In 2008, when I'd spent most of a postbreakup weeks-long low in bed, Jordan left his *World of Warcraft* discs on my dresser with a note saying that they had given him something to care about when nothing else had mattered. In 2017, when I texted the sibling group chat on the way to the hospital, Jordan responded directly, off thread: "I love you. Don't let it win."

A month after I left the hospital, Brendan and I got married in an intimate service at New York City's marriage bureau—just us, a city clerk, and one of the handful of photographer-slash-witnesses who advertise their services on the sidewalk outside the entryway. We celebrated the wedding shortly after with a pool party in my parents' backyard, in the middle of which my sister, Danea, called me to the edge of the pool. Jordan had made a brief appearance before disappearing into his room, and Danea let me know he was going through some kind of breakdown. She and my parents were trying to calm him down, but they thought I might be better equipped to help. I'd been drifting on a diamond ring float and was too drunk to handle the situation gracefully, but I knew it didn't matter. I followed Danea inside and into Jordan's bedroom, where I found him curled in bed, crying, my father sitting at his feet. I asked if I could talk to him alone, and when everyone left, I climbed into bed behind him, wrapping him in my arms.

"What does it feel like?" I asked.

"I just feel scared of everything," he said. "Like I can't see a way out."

I tried to use his own words back to him. I promised him that people got through this—I had, and he would, too.

"If I don't get to kill myself," I said, "you don't get to, either."

Nine months later he was admitted to an intensive inpatient facility. Throughout the intervening months, he'd pleaded with us daily. He wanted to kill himself; the need plagued him constantly; he was furious that we wouldn't just give him our blessing—or at the very least admit he was right to want to die. In the days before his hospitalization, his alarming texts became urgent, growing into multiple-paragraph miniessays and then into emails. He had nothing to live for; was he even living? One night I woke up from a dream of pulling an endless, ever-replenished flow of razors out of his hand, and I worried that it was a psychic message that he'd done it.

"Please don't go yet, okay?" I texted him. "Just wait a little longer at least."

He responded, "I'm already gone. This is just my body."

His life felt empty, made unreal, so he let flourish the idea that it wasn't even a life. Consciously or not, he was nurturing an environment in which it would be easiest to leave: What's suicide to a person who's already dead?

David Foster Wallace's "This Is Water"—the commencement speech Wallace delivered at Kenyon College in 2005, three years before he'd hang himself and four years before it would be published and packaged for the gift aisle—has become a shorthand for mindfulness, but it, too, touches upon the fear of a living death. The speech begins with a parable:

> *There are these two young fish swimming along, and they happen to meet an older fish swimming the other way, who nods at them and says "Morning, boys. How's the water?" And the two young fish swim on for a bit, and then eventually one of them looks over at the other and goes "What the hell is water?"*

What follows is a message of compassion, patience, and awareness. Wallace describes the drudgery of adulthood, how quickly one can default to self-centeredness, and how easy it is to get stuck there without realizing it. He worries that the message might be written off as "just a banal platitude," but, he warns, "in the day to day trenches of adult existence, banal platitudes [in this case, that "the most obvious, important realities are often the ones that are hardest to see"] can have a life or death importance."

Wallace's worry is unnecessary. The speech references suicide too often and too casually to fit neatly into "banal platitude" territory. It lends a direness, an urgency, to the otherwise benign advice: Fail to exercise this awareness, and you risk your life. But survival isn't enough for Wallace; he's less concerned with physical death than he is with an empty, sort of zombie existence. In one of three references to people "shoot[ing] themselves in the head," Wallace clarifies, "[T]he truth is that most of these suicides* are actually

---

* Here Wallace uses a less familiar form of "suicide," the noun referring to the person who does it.

dead long before they pull the trigger." What pressure to lay upon oneself—to be ever watchful, a sentry against a subtle, creeping death. It isn't enough to live. One must live right. And there is a right way to live; Wallace is sure of it. He is sharing, after all, the "capital-T Truth" about life. The problem with believing in and living by a "capital-T Truth" is that it tends to be unforgiving. It demands absolutism in a world of nuance. It recasts so many valid experiences as failure.

In this case, the "capital-T Truth" is about "simple awareness . . . of what is so real and essential, so hidden in plain sight all around us, that we have to keep reminding ourselves over and over: 'This is water. This is water.'" But is it fair to call this kind of awareness "simple"? Wallace describes a living death, but his is a cause, not an effect, of suicidality. It is a failure to live properly, not considering the possibility that years spent interrogating the validity of one's life might actually create the stasis one fears. Does Wallace's suicide mean that he failed to maintain such an active awareness? Or could it mean that such an active awareness was pointless?

We can't effectively examine the living death without establishing what qualifies as life. To do so, we can look at the word itself and its extension into etymologically connected words and their definitions. See *vitality*, from the Latin *vita* (life), as in power, force; the psychologist Ben Dean further defined it as "a sense that one's actions have meaning and purpose." See *inspire*, from the Latin *spīrāre* (to breathe), as in to influence, infuse, or communicate. See *animate*, from the Latin *anima* (to rouse, quicken), as in to make motion. These are fundamentally social, energetic ideals, requiring engagement with our community and environment. They suppose an opportunity to effect change, to wield power—at the very least, in terms of our autonomy. Just as we can't will ourselves out of depression, we can't will ourselves into active, purposeful life when stuck in a world that inundates us with, and requires our participation in, systems that distract, exhaust, separate, and dehumanize us. When Plath defines her "chief" fear as "life without having lived," what exactly does the life she fears look like? Years spent tethered to suicide? Perhaps. But that isn't the entirety of the living death—it might not even be its definitive element.

* * *

Back at the Birdhouse in 2010, the morning after the bleach and the notes, just like the morning after the ibuprofen, I woke up full of optimism. I'd survived the night; I'd made it out alive, again. It was a Saturday, and I was alone in the house. I found a video of Wallace delivering his speech and watched it no fewer than three times. I showered, got dressed, took the bus to a tattoo parlor, and got "this is water" tattooed on my wrist. The tattoo hasn't aged well, for a number of reasons. The letters have bled. ("Like water!" I joke when people ask about it.) Wallace was brilliant, but his legacy is polarizing, complicated by claims of his misogyny. Most significantly, though, the meaning of the phrase has shifted over the twelve years I've worn it. That morning, and for a while, the sentence was a reminder to myself to recognize the mundane miracles of life. *This is water; this is good.* Later, it came to be a wake-up call, urging me to investigate the state of my reality, which I'm often so mired in that it becomes imperceptible. *This is water; is this good?* Now I don't know. Now, sometimes, it embarrasses me. Exhausts me. Must I be in an everlasting state of vigilance against an encroaching "partial death"? What are we asking of ourselves?

If the tattoo links me to anything good, it's the version of me who

Better

wanted so badly to live, and to keep choosing to live, that she decided to inscribe her arm with a message that would reach all future selves, outlasting the fading ink and the morphing letters. Probably the words haven't saved me, but maybe she did, or I did—that day, at least.

Chapter 4

The Archive

In the months before Jordan checked himself into an inpatient program, I sat next to him through information sessions and emergency room visits at psychiatric facilities and hospitals, each of which I'd scrupulously researched online, as if a "what to expect" section on an institution's website could be an accurate indicator of its living conditions and therapeutic offerings, as if a review from a patient who'd been treated three years ago had any bearing on what Jordan's experience would be. There was nothing I could do beyond show up, ask him to live, and hope he would listen, but playing at control can be a powerful tool for maintaining sanity while trying to help a loved one who wants to die.

During one of those meetings, this time at an intensive outpatient program at a Long Island facility Elizabeth had recommended, a well-meaning social worker ran through the now familiar list of questions meant to determine Jordan's psychological and emotional fitness, his risk level, and his access to support.

"Are you able to recognize that this feeling will go away?" she asked. He shook his head no; she nodded. "It's hard to see that now, but one of the skills you would learn here is the ability to correct your thoughts. To understand that all feelings are fleeting. Just like happiness comes and goes, so does sadness—you know?"

She invited someone called a peer specialist into the office, a man named Rob who looked to be in his forties and had perfected a smile that balanced support and concern. He leaned against the social worker's desk, wearing beaded bracelets that clicked as he waved his hands.

"Two years ago, I was where you are," he said. "And I mean exactly, man—sitting in that exact chair. I know you can't see that it'll get better. I couldn't. But it doesn't matter if you believe in any of this, you just have to do it. Go to the sessions, take the meds. Shit, make some corny art, who cares?"

Jordan put his head in his hands, folded his body in half, and I rested my hand on his back.

"Even if you can't do it for yourself, do it for someone who loves you," Rob said. "And I know you have someone who loves you because she's sitting right next to you, and that's something beautiful."

We left with some pamphlets and a promise to check in with Jordan's insurance about what they would cover. I knew we wouldn't be back. We got in the car and Jordan connected his phone to the Bluetooth. A ringing chord gradually loudened, and I recognized the sweet soprano of Adrienne Lenker, his favorite. I remembered the CDs he'd brought to Portland when I texted him in the summer of 2012. It was a month after graduation and I'd hit a breaking point after weeks of mania, subsisting on coffee, cocaine, and leftovers from the restaurant where I was waitressing. I asked him to fly across the country and then drive me back home to New York. He did. We spent a week on the road. I couldn't tell you one thing we talked about, but I know it felt safe. Two years later, he sent me a drunk text from a party—"NEVER FORGET ARI AND JORDAN ROAD TRIP 2012!!! THE GUN HAS NO TRIGGER!!!!"—referencing the Dirty Projectors song and album we'd listened to on repeat, and it made me laugh on an otherwise sad night. Now he rested his head against the passenger window as I drove, singing along in a whisper I could barely catch: "And I know that someday soon I'll see you, but now you're out of sight."

A month earlier, Jordan had bailed on plans to hang out with some visiting friends, and I'd called my mom, shouting, outside of a Williamsburg flower shop. She wasn't taking this seriously enough. He was going to die. We were going to lose him. When he finally agreed to hospitalization, the first weeks passed with little improvement. My mother asked me and my siblings to take him some photos. Recent ones, she said, maybe some with his friends. She wanted us to present him with proof that he'd enjoyed life—even recently.

"He's convinced himself he's never really been happy," she said.

"Is that possible?" I asked Elizabeth in a session shortly after. "That we only thought he was happy?"

She shook her head. "He's been happy."

"But what if he's never happy again? Is that possible?"

She hesitated.

"Am I allowed to ask that?"

"You're allowed to ask anything," she said with a smile that faded quickly. "But yes, it is possible. It's incredibly rare, and it's way too early to worry about that."

So I gathered mementos: a custom photo book I'd designed for our grandmother but then made copies of for my three siblings, with page after page of photos from hikes, bars, holidays, and beach trips, a paean to our unlikely bond; the trail guide we carried while backpacking the west coast of Ireland with so little money that we'd had to sleep on strangers' couches; a rose quartz crystal Jordan had teased me about the previous Christmas. But the trail guide was wire spiral bound, meaning sharp, so it wasn't allowed. And when I asked about the crystal, the nurse considered her answer, clearly torn, mouth twisted, but ultimately landed on no, for fear he'd try to choke himself with it. ("I'm sure he wouldn't," she assured me, apologetically. "But we can't take risks.") And when I handed him the photo book, he added it to a pile of other books I'd brought him—essay collections, meditation guides, fantastical zines—and I imagined it staying there, gathering dust.

Since I couldn't bring him to—or force him to look at—tangible memories, I tried tricking him into remembering by pretending I couldn't, asking him questions that I hoped would force him to revisit his happiness, to believe in his joy. What was the name of the guy we'd sat next to at the bar in Ireland the night we didn't have a place to stay? Oh, right, Jack, yes. And, okay, was he the one who had taken us to a weird beach with his friends? Like middle of the night, totally empty? Yes, yes, of course—it was so impossibly cold. The morning after that beach trip, we'd woken on the floor of Jack's living room and Jordan had said it was one of the top five experiences of his entire life. Now he confirmed the details without emotion.

* * *

We rely on memory to tether us to the good. We curate the happiest moments of our lives and ourselves in photo albums, on social media, in the pages of scrapbooks; they are the ropes we toss into the abyss of depression so that if—or, as is so often the case, when—we're there again, we might climb back out. Many of the moments

Sylvia Plath records in her journals are celebrations. She rejoices in her stories and poems being published, in her talents earning both praise and professional opportunities. She shores up her resilience by writing of suicidal lows that had passed, of her confidence in her ability to prevent another from returning. She's curious about art and research and those around her; her analyses of the works of her contemporaries vibrate with life. She has the capacity for joy—and she knows this, loves this, about herself—but she is terrified of losing it. She sees the moments in which she can't access that joy as evidence of her forgetting it and believes that, if forgotten, such joy might as well never have existed at all. In even the briefest experience of doubt or despair, she sees the threat of joy's permanent retreat, and she fights that outcome by tying joy to the page, refusing to lose happy memories to time lest she come to doubt that they had ever happened at all. "[S]ometimes, in a panic, mind goes blank," she writes. "[The] world whooshes away in void. . . . [a]nd I forget the moments of radiance. I must get them down in print."

Plath describes herself in multiple accounts as "clinging" to her past, a word that evokes the desperation of a person who is certain that her survival depends upon it. It's easy to understand why. If a person lives in perpetual fear that the self she is in one moment will be lost to and forgotten by the self she becomes in the next, wouldn't she want to leave that future self reminders of who she's been—of who she really is? Plath writes memory like an incantation, hoping that by capturing remembered feelings and experiences in writing, she might conjure them back: "How all this life would vanish, evaporate, if I didn't clutch at it, cling to it, while I still remember some twinge of glory."

Plath doesn't record only the good, though; she is equally, if not more, determined to set down the details of her life and mind when she's at her worst. Just weeks after an entry considering suicide—

and despite Plath's having "vow[ed] to go to bed early"——she stays up deep into the night "because it is more important to capture moments like this, keen shifts in mood . . . than to lose it in slumber." Virginia Woolf reveals a similar motivation in her journals, writing, in a bout of career-related depression, "I must hurriedly note more symptoms of the disease, so that I can turn back here and medicine myself next time." The journal becomes a medical record, the writer both patient and doctor.

Whether we look to memory to bring us out of depression or prevent its return, whether ours is a record of joy or despair, whether the past is an escape or a specter, the truth remains: an obsession with the past induces stasis. Plath records, revisits, and reworks even the most mundane moments of her life, and the result is a constantly looping cycle of steps forward and then backward. We see this, too, in the work of the turn-of-the-century French writer Édouard Levé. Ten days before hanging himself in 2007, Levé handed his editor the manuscript of *Suicide*, a novel framed as a young man's communications to a friend who, with little warning, had shot himself in the head. Levé was forty-two years old. Despite using the friend as narrator, the book can be, and often is, read as Levé's own protracted suicide letter, its context forcing a blurring of the boundary between fact and fiction. The narrator says to his friend, "This was perhaps what you feared: to become inert in a body that still breathes, drinks, and feeds itself. To commit suicide in slow motion," and it's easy to imagine it is, in some way, Levé talking to himself.

Like Plath, Levé's deceased quasi protagonist had a palpable anxiety about forgetting. The narrator describes how he held on to and revisited his day planners, how he was so distressed by the entries that contained details he couldn't recall despite having written them. Even worse was his understanding that countless more moments——

more than he could grasp—had gone both unrecorded and forgotten. "Where had they gone?" the narrator recalls him wondering. And then: What did they mean? He experienced these losses as existential devastation, creating a profound, debilitating panic over the possibility that his understanding of himself was incomplete. What of himself might he have lost over the years? Could he have been more? The narrator recalls his friend's three-day visit to Bordeaux and his discomfort on the return trip upon finding that landmarks he would have seen just days earlier were now unfamiliar. Maybe he had been looking at the other side of the road on the way there, the narrator recalls his deceased friend considering. Maybe he'd been lost in thought when he'd first seen them. "You looked for explanations rather than believe in the shortcomings of your memory," the narrator writes. Within his lifelong fear of forgetting, the friend had come to believe that whatever he remembered was a result of his *decision* to remember, paired with the will and strength to do so. Remembering, that is to say, must be active.

Memory and its losses consume not only the deceased man in *Suicide* but also, apparently, Levé himself. Before he wrote *Suicide*, he published *Autoportrait*, a slim autobiography of just over one hundred pages. It is a narrative-less series of facts about himself—declarative, often banal, statements about his habits ("I do not keep track of how much money is in my bank account"), his likes ("I do not like the big toe"), and his memories ("I had a female hamster called Pirouette"). They are presented without analysis, commentary, or discernible chronology. Their significance, if any, is determined by the reader. The significance for Levé seems to be the whole—the neat, exhaustive presentation of a complete life—rather than its disparate parts. It is the act of creating the list, the verb, which Levé collapses into two load-bearing words at the bottom of the first page: "I archive."

Better

This obsession is inseparable from a dream or fear of the future. How religiously a person records the past and how tightly they clutch that record is directly related to their distrust of the present—or, perhaps more accurately, their distrust of their present self. We can write the past with the goal of using it as data for optimizing our future, but no amount of historiography can lead us to a concrete answer to the question of what the best future would be. An integral part of archiving is imagining the unknowable self who will eventually read it, a self who—if we can just get onto the right path—will have banished their badness. This future self will luxuriate in her success, having finally mastered some great truth of existence. How quickly this daunting, perfect, impossible self becomes a hurdle in moving toward the very goals we imagine she's achieved. Plath sees each moment's choice as a narrowing of the expanse of options before her, and she is distraught over her inability to see all possible ends laid out for comparison before choosing the best one: "Life is so only-once," she writes, "so single-chancish!"

Virginia Woolf, however, revels in her future self as she writes in her journal, fixating specifically on Virginia aged fifty. She writes about and to this self, relishing the eventual rereading of her entries more than the present writing of them. "How I envy her the task I am preparing for her!" she writes a week before turning thirty-seven. "There is none I should like better." This future self will know her better than she knows herself, now; she will be able to look back at what Woolf envisioned as she wrote and "will be able to say how close to the truth [she] came." The following year, Woolf's preoccupation with Virginia-aged-fifty remains. She relays minor dissatisfaction with the contents and "style" of her current diary and then dismisses it swiftly for the sake of this future self: "Never mind; I fancy old Virginia, putting on her spectacles to read of March 1920 will decidedly wish me to continue. Greetings! my dear ghost . . ."

She romanticizes the past and idealizes the future. Where she resides, in the present, can only disappoint. But what happens when that dream of a future is suddenly the present and it hasn't brought with it all of the clarity and success we imagined? I don't know if Woolf was disillusioned when she became her fifty-year-old self, but I do know she killed herself nine years later.

* * *

If a person can't experience a moment in the present without imagining the way they will eventually remember it—the future it will lead them to—decision making can be terrifying to the point of paralysis. But this inertia induces even more panic over the time they've lost to idleness. "This second is life," Plath writes. "And when it is gone, it is dead. . . . The high moment, the burning flash come and are gone, continuous quicksand. And I don't want to die."

What high stakes to place on any given moment, that each one forgotten becomes a tiny death among a ceaseless stream. Plath's requirement for staying alive is keeping the past active in the present. "Life piles up so fast," Woolf writes, "that I have no time to write out the equally fast rising mound of reflections." But if the past is quicksand, sinking, or if it is an ever-increasing heap, then living in it will either pull us down or crush us. Either way, we're stuck.

There can be deceptive comfort here, in in-between places both literal and figurative. It's part of what drew me to the psych ward and what inspires fantasies, when I'm feeling most overwhelmed, of admitting myself again. Throughout six weeks of Jordan's hospitalization, I lived in a limbo of my own making by checking into one hotel after another, setting up temporary homes in rooms ranging from mold ridden to near luxurious, depending on how self-indulgent I was feeling when I booked them. I could tell myself and everyone around me that I was doing it because Jordan's hospital was a ninety-minute trip from my Brooklyn home, and so temporarily moving closer to him made it easier to be there during daily visiting hours. I could say that, and it would be true but incomplete. I knew I didn't have to do as much as I was. I didn't have to fall deeper into credit card debt in order to support Jordan. I didn't have to scramble for Wi-Fi so I could call in to work meetings, didn't have to take sick days and then vacation days when I realized I couldn't keep up. I didn't have to drive from hotel to hospital to home and back again, over and over and over. "You know he'd understand if you have to take a break," my mother told me, and I knew she was right.

Mostly I did it for myself. My life was paused because I couldn't emotionally separate myself from Jordan, sitting in that common room eighteen miles away. During the one week that I tried to handle everything from home—when I tried going back to the office, waking up early, doing my stretches, trusting my family to visit him on the days I couldn't get onto the train—it took just two days for me to end up crying on my living room floor. I called Danea from down there, my phone resting on the hardwood panel next to my head, my body splayed like a starfish.

"You know those videos of dogs who freak out when you put those snow booties on them? And they just look too terrified to even take a step?" She did. "That's what I feel like. I'm a little dog stuck in booties."

She understood, and it helped, for a bit. Saying it out loud made me feel better about my inability to keep up with or even care about work. Her commiseration was validating and reminded me that it was perfectly acceptable to function at half capacity instead of abandoning all efforts entirely. I could go through the motions without feeling quite present, get up and get dressed and go to the office and answer emails because that was what the company was paying me to do. It didn't have to be all or nothing. But the next morning I got out of bed and stood paralyzed in front of my closet. The reality of reentering my other world was too daunting. So I messaged my team to say I'd be working from home, and I went back to bed, and I woke up three hours later to messages from my boss, and I thought, for the first time since I had left the psych ward, *Well, I should probably just kill myself.* I booked another four nights at a hotel instead, this one the fanciest, most expensive yet. I wasn't home for more than two nights a week until Jordan was discharged.

My life was paused because I wasn't able to move forward, at least not in the way I'd come to define forward progression, and I needed my environment to match my emotional and functional suspension—to in fact necessitate it. There is only so much you can do from a hotel room in an unfamiliar town, and the bulk of it is ordering room service, going shopping, taking baths, watching movies, reading books. It was an acceptable, which is to say forgivable, break, an approximation of a functioning person in a functioning life, a way of shutting down while pretending that I wasn't doing so. Still, the societal mandate of productivity is so ingrained that even with outside permission, there's no escaping the internal guilt of our inaction.

Plath longs for relief but she can't grant it to herself without a good reason. She wants to have a baby ("that most fearsome first woman's ordeal") at least in part because doing so will let her "elude [her] demanding demons and have a constant excuse for lack of production in writing." The archiving, the tracking and recording: all of it is work, and so, in the moment of laboring, it can scratch the itch of productivity. But that also means it can, and often does, become another set of tasks that overwhelms us. And for what? We can spin the rigorous documenting of our lives, the plotting of our futures, and the analyzing of our past into necessary exploits, but to do so is dually harmful: it never allows true rest, and it stalls true progress. *Why is it so hard to write in here every day?* I wrote in my journal at one of those many hotels. *There are so many things I'd like to track, the absence of which makes me feel chaotic, ungrounded. An unnecessary source of anxiety of my creation.*

* * *

So what do we do with the past if it isn't powerful enough to pull us out of suicidality, but might be powerful enough to arrest us in the present? Do we memory-hole it, leave it to lie untouched and all but forgotten? As with any tool for survival, its efficacy is determined by the person trying to use it. The moment when I am most certain that my history of suicidality is a justification for killing myself is also the moment when the idea is most dangerous: when I want to die and I'm looking for a reason to. If the past is precedent, well, which span? Those times I survived suicidality or those times when it returned? In Yiyun Li's *Dear Friend, from My Life I Write to You in Your Life,* her 2017 memoir about suicide, literature, and human (mis)connection, Li argues that "our memories tell more about now than then," and this, of course, is the rub. We read of and remember a past self, but we can't help manipulating her in the process: like with all memories, as Yi writes, "we choose and discard from an abundance of evidence what suits us at the moment." We write to a future self, but we don't know her and we can't meet. Our dream for her is really our dream for now. There is no escaping the *now*; it absorbs everything it touches. For Yi, who confesses having a "troublesome relationship with time," the present offers little respite:

> *The present—what is the present but a constant test: in this mud-dled in-between one struggles to understand what about oneself*

has to be changed, what accepted, what preserved. Unless the right actions are taken, one seems never to pass the test to reach the after.

A battle won, a test passed. After, finished, better. Within these frameworks, working toward these goals, the present—that is, life—is always sacrificed.

"Nothing is real except the present," Plath writes, but the meaning shifts with her moods. Most often she engages the idea in bad faith, dissolving the future, ignoring the fact that the future is just a present she hasn't experienced yet. She invokes the notion only in moments when her present is an intolerable pain, when it's most clear that all her years of faithful archiving have failed to offer an escape. She talks herself in circles: "[N]othing is real, past or future, when you are alone in your room with the clock ticking loudly into the false cheerful brilliance of the electric light. And if you have no past or future, which, after all, is all that the present is made of, why then you may as well dispose of the empty shell of present and commit suicide."

But there is so much more possibility in the statement. If we choose to believe that the present is all that matters—if we invest in believing this—we admit that fleeting moments of happiness aren't enough to shore up our future resilience, but we also free ourselves of the paralyzing fear of failure yet to come. It's a worthy goal. We might work toward experiencing the past and future gently and briefly: delighting in a triggered memory, sharing an old joke with a friend, naming a goal to work toward, scheduling a future event for something to look forward to. We might give both less weight, relieve ourselves of the burden of carrying not only our history but every imagined future—every hypothetical life. We could welcome, instead, a lightness, even deliverance. For all of Levé's protagonist's obsession with remembering, he ultimately resents it. He is its captive. In *Suicide*'s epilogue, comprising a collection of found verse written by the deceased friend, a single line speaks volumes: "To forget frees me."

* * *

Another day, another hospital visit. I walked into the familiar lobby, said hi to the familiar nurses, had my bag checked, and put on my wristband. I found Jordan at a table with my mother, and she looked up at me and smiled in the way that meant it wasn't a good day. We talked about group therapy. We talked about his upcoming birthday—twenty-eight!—and what type of cake we should bring. I talked about work, and he surprised me by asking if I'd ever lost interest in writing when I was where he was.

My first thought was no, and I didn't know if that was a good or bad sign—if it was evidence that I'd come so far out of my low as to have forgotten its details or if it meant that Jordan's low was at a depth I'd never reached, never survived. But then, at my worst, I *wasn't* writing outside of some short and dismal journal entries. That was a fact. Maybe I wanted to, or maybe I felt as though I had to, but I couldn't fathom doing it. I'd lost interest in living, which means I'd lost interest in the things that made up my life, that made my life feel like something worth continuing.

So I said, "Yeah, of course. But honestly, the way you feel now—doubting you ever felt happy because you can't remember feeling it—that's how I feel, but about how depressed I was last year. If it makes you feel better."

He nodded.

I squeezed his shoulder and said, "Make a list of all the things you thought you enjoyed, even if now you can't remember what it felt like." I didn't believe he'd feel the happiness he felt then by re-membering it—I wasn't even sure he'd believe he felt that happiness then—yet I couldn't help but ask him to look to the past. Maybe he could at least believe in the possibility of happiness, whether past or future. Maybe our mother was right and memory can help us, but more as a buoy than a rescue boat—not enough to bring us to safety, but enough to keep us afloat while we wait for whatever can. But there is so much pain in the waiting, the fear in not knowing how long the pain will last this time.

Jordan's hand rested on a piece of paper, white with a large brown oval with jagged edges painted just off center. I pulled it gently from him.

"What's this?" I asked.

"He had art therapy this morning," my mother said.

"Oh, cool, did you like it?" He shook his head. "I loved art ther-apy. One time, one of the guys, older, really shy, painted these blue and purple figures—they kind of looked like trees? And when the counselor asked what he was working on, he said, really quietly, that they were friends and the purple part was their love. I swear it's the only thing I heard him say the whole time."

"I love that!" my mother said, squeezing Jordan's hand. "Isn't that sweet?"

He started to cry, and I tried not to. I looked at the painting. The brushstrokes were short, doubling back on themselves; it was a vio-lent cover-up of his first attempt, now visible only as a bright specter behind a rust-colored veil.

"Can I take this?" I asked, and he nodded. And I took it home and stored it in my desk drawer under a pile of unused and abandoned notebooks and planners. And I thought, *I'll show you this when you're past this. You'll look at it, but it won't mean anything. You won't even remember what it felt like to make it.*

Chapter 5

The Ugly Mask

Years before either of us had been hospitalized, Jordan and I sparked a rhetorical sibling divide by sharing our reluctance to pass down our genes. It was July 2014, when Danea was living in Los Angeles and Jordan, Dylan, and I were spending a week at her place. We sat around a patio table in the apartment complex courtyard of a friend of a friend of a friend, drunk and about to get drunker. I had my first salaried job writing at BuzzFeed, the closest I'd ever gotten to work that I both enjoyed and believed to be valuable; I was in a new relationship that was going so well it made my skin crawl in anticipation of its inevitable end. I was restless and itching for conflict. When I brought up the fact that I didn't think it would be responsible for me to have a child, given our family history of severe mental illness, I knew Jordan would be on my side and the others would be aghast.

"What is wrong with you?" Danea asked.

"Our genes are great!" Dylan insisted.

Better

Jordan handed me a sweating bottle of rosé and started unravel-
ing a roll of duct tape. We were unyielding in our argument: Yes,
sure, we're smart, we can have a good time—it's not like we *hate*
ourselves—but we also have this tendency to feel sadness so impenetrable that months can elapse without any other emotion breaking through; to feel meaninglessness so calcifying we can't fathom
getting out of bed. And it didn't come from nowhere. Look at our
mother, whose anxiety has translated into a house so crowded with
stacks of unopened boxes, bags of clothes, and decades-old para-
phernalia that we can barely find paths through rooms. Look at our
father, his depression at times so profound that as young adults we'd
staged an intervention to make sure he wouldn't kill himself. Look at
his mother, whose lifelong depression had begun in 1940s Italy, when
the cure was being sent into the country to "calm her nerves." We
couldn't, in good conscience, bring someone into this life when we
had so often felt, almost irreversibly, the desire to leave it.

"I'm not trying to be dramatic," I said. "I'd just rather not risk
passing it on." I was lying, at least about the drama. I love being
dramatic; I love being contrarian. I'd gone into the conversation to
test out a concern as a conviction. It was safe, noncommittal. My
hypothetical child's potential inheritance did worry me, but at the
same time I was well aware I'd abandon all methods of birth control
that instant if Brendan wanted to. Maybe I wanted Danea and Dylan
to persuade me out of my lingering doubts.

"You honestly don't think it would be a net positive," Danea said,
more dare than question.

"I honestly don't."

She rolled her eyes. Jordan shrugged. He wrapped the duct tape
around my hand and the bottle and then took my phone to get a
photo: Edward Rosé-hands.

"You're idiots," Danea said.

"We know," Jordan agreed.

Jordan hasn't changed his mind about having kids. Clearly, my stance wasn't so solid. That day in LA, Jordan and I were arguing with a narrow, individualistic focus: We didn't want to transfer the suffering we'd experienced onto someone who had never asked to be born. Maybe I eventually decided that the gamble was worth it; maybe I just really wanted to be a mom. Maybe it was selfish. I worry sometimes that it was. Would I have chosen to live had I known what living would be? At my worst I've resented my parents for bringing me here, but I've also been overwhelmed with gratitude and awed by the sheer luck of existence. It's a mindfuck of an exercise: we can't imagine nothingness without the lens of our consciousness perceiving it. When I've been suicidal, my emotional state wasn't dominated by a desire to die so much as by a wish to never have been. I sought a corrective to the mistake of my existence. A month before my hospitalization, I wrote, *I want to go to sleep and never wake up. Or just to never have been woken. I didn't ask for this. I didn't ask for this.* How dramatic it feels, typing it out now. But it *is* dramatic amid suicidality, only then the drama is dire, rather than—as it seems in retrospect—maudlin, histrionic.

Underlying our argument, whether we were conscious of it or not, was something more sinister but which offers more insight into the experience of the chronic desire to die. Individually, our horror at the possibility of passing down our depression is built on premature guilt for causing another person's suffering, and premature fear of that despair whirling in the person we're meant to protect and love above all. But zooming out, it reveals a rejection of the proliferation of depression across humanity. It smacks of eugenics; acceptable—barely so—only because we were discussing it in the context of an intimate and deeply personal decision. Just as much as it is about the fear of passing down an excruciating desire to die to someone who never asked to exist, it is also, inherently, a reinforcement of the idea that a depressed life is not worth living. My choosing to have Theo doesn't mean I've come around to believe the opposite. I hope a depressed life is worth living; quite often I'm sure it is. Still, I'm desperate for evidence that Theo has evaded it. Still, I watch in trepidation for signs. Has he been infected?

*   *   *

Brendan and I decided it was time to start trying for a pregnancy in 2018, about a year after we got married. I had a seemingly stable job leading books content at BuzzFeed that came with a salary that eased some of our financial stress. I had access to eighteen fully paid weeks of maternity leave, a substantial package in the US. Elizabeth had proved to be the only therapist I'd ever felt at home with, and she—along with medications whose side effects were manageable and that showed no signs of failing—was helping me steady my moods. Jordan was out of the hospital, and though he wasn't miraculously exuberant, his depression hadn't yet returned with a vengeance, which meant that my and my family's lives weren't dominated by fear.

Brendan and I settled on the decision under the assumption, based on my long history of ovarian cysts and inconsistent periods, that it would take some time for me to get pregnant. A month later, I was holding a positive test. Immediately, I pushed aside my current, incomplete journal to start a new one meant to represent this momentous transformation. Throughout the entries during pregnancy, I alternated between writing about Theo—unnamed until two days after his birth*—and to him. I liked the romance, the intimacy, of

---

* It was down to Theo or Calvin, after *Calvin and Hobbes*, and though Theo is absolutely a Calvin, we have no doubt that we made the right choice. Theo agrees.

leaving behind a document made specifically for this unknown and unknowable child. Though I tried my best to reject it, part of the appeal was the somber but poignant possibility of the journal becoming a tool for accessing a mother whose death had obliterated any chance of establishing a vital, reciprocal bond.

This was mostly a passive result of habit. I was no longer actively preoccupied with my death, but it was as if its absence required a substitute. And so I swapped in Theo's, and that fixation flowed along a spectrum between preparation and prevention. I was obsessed with tracking milestones, staying up late into the night trawling forums and firsthand accounts of stillbirths, SIDS, and other various pre- and perinatal tragedies. It was indulgent and voyeuristic, a source of shame that I shared only with Elizabeth, and, even then, the confession was censored. Whatever I was trying to achieve—catharsis, relief in finding people who have survived my greatest fears, comfort in remembering that as yet I didn't have to—my unseemly craving wasn't sated until I was in tears. That fear extended, as to be expected, far into his future. I'd spent so much time scared that I'd kill myself, but now that this baby inside me was real and alive, that my body was creating and protecting his, I dwelled on the possibility of *his* suicide. *Who will you be?* I wrote halfway through the second trimester, but beneath that question lay another, unwritten: How will you hurt?

As soon as Theo arrived, bits of his personality were apparent. Other parents had told me this would happen, that I'd be shocked at how clearly defined his quirks and sensibilities would be. Here's what we found: a baby who came out raring to go, as if trying to bypass all of the required stages so that he could participate in the world. His legs never stopped kicking. His pediatrician, witnessing his nonstop motion and then, at two months, his attempt to push himself up, let out a low whistle and wished us luck. As a newborn and then infant, Theo would abruptly pause in the middle of playing or babbling and gaze at nothing I could pinpoint, quiet, as if lost in contemplation. When he was just six days old, I recorded a video that I often revisit. I'm holding Theo with one arm and filming with the other; his face fills most of the screen. His lips are pursed, a small dribble of milk from the corner, and his eyes scan slowly back and forth, up and down, in an expression that mimics deep consideration. It lasts fifteen seconds. At the time, I sent it to my family group chat saying, "Sometimes Theo likes to pause in the middle of breakfast to think about things."

Then it was a joke, but if I'm being honest, part of me believes it. I catch those breaks still, constantly. When it happens, I ask him what he's thinking about, trying to sound playful and curious, trying to mask the underlying dread that this is the beginning of a lifetime of isolating interiority. He never shares, and I never push. I tell him it's all good; he's allowed to keep some things to himself. It is his right. Still, his hypersensitivity and attunement to my moods are undeniable, intensifying with each passing year. He has always been attached to me, literally and metaphorically, and at four years old that manifested in constantly checking on my well-being. It became claustrophobic. Wasn't I allowed to be stressed in my own house, wasn't it unreasonable and unrealistic to expect me to mask any sign of frustration? As the check-ins became more frequent, I assured him that he didn't have to worry about me, that he should never ever feel as though it was his job to change my feelings.

"Yes, it is," he said. "I feel everything you feel."

The theme continued, becoming a source of overpowering distress. Theo would register any shift in my tone, more often than not a result of annoyance that had nothing to do with him, and ask, "Are you angry, Mama? You're talking angry." At bedtime—it was always more urgent at bedtime—he told me to be happy, and I reminded him that it was okay to be sad, that everybody got sad sometimes and it was nothing to be afraid of.

"Why do you feel like I have to be happy?" I asked.

"Because that's how I love you," he said. "That's how I don't get so sad."

A few months into pre-K, I took him to get cheeseburgers after pickup, just the two of us. I asked him if he'd had a good day, and he said no, he'd cried a lot. I told him I was so sorry that he felt so sad and asked if something had happened. He shrugged, unbothered, and said, "Every day at school I'm scared that you're not okay. Only when I'm with you I know you're being safe."

This development was a source of tension between me and Brendan—not angry but still disruptive—as I insisted it was pathological and required medical intervention and he admitted that he wasn't convinced it was that serious. The reality likely lies in the middle. I'll catch Theo holding back tears, self-censoring no matter how many times I tell him it's okay to be sad, and within seconds I'm ten, twenty years in the future, trying to stop him from killing himself. It's an unproductive, even detrimental, preoccupation. It helps no one. Finally, we've reached an accord, agreeing that, diagnosis or not, he—and we—would benefit from seeing a child psychologist. But I haven't mastered dismissing the intrusive thoughts.

One recent night, as I lay with Theo in his bed, trying to cajole him into sleep, I told him it would be easier if he closed his eyes. He told me he hated to do that, that it was too scary. This wasn't news; the year prior, he'd cried after day care, saying he hated nap time because the teachers made him shut his eyes. That night, I asked why it was scary.

"When I close my eyes, I close everything," he said, and hearing it was like taking a bullet. I apologized in a tone of communicating sympathy, of hating that he was struggling with this fear, but, really,

Better

I was apologizing for what I can't help but perceive as my role in his fear, my passing along such a recognizable burden to him.

* * *

So has Theo been infected, or am I overreacting, projecting? Might this be run-of-the-mill toddler preoccupation—nothing more than an expected, 100 percent normal stage of his psychological and emotional development? And if he *is* anxious or depressed, well, what of it? To what extent? Will he be powerless against it, condemned because of it? Will he resent it? For as long as I've known I've had depression, I've wondered if, given the option, I'd choose to be rid of it. If I could isolate this thing in my brain or body and pluck it out, would I? If I could recreate my reality, would I opt to have never had it at all? How much of myself is intertwined with whatever modern science has hypothesized depression is: Chemical imbalance? Missed signals in the brain? Genetic inheritance? And who would I be without it? Is it someone I'd want to be?

Kay Redfield Jamison describes her ambivalence regarding her bipolar disorder,* having come to understand it as "a distillation both of what is finest in our natures, and of what is most dangerous." Her initial reluctance to seek treatment stemmed in part from her determination that her "changeable moods, energies, enthusiasms" weren't indicative of illness but rather "an extension of [her]self"— and though she has since attributed her survival to psychiatric medication, she also acknowledges that many of these medications do

---

* Throughout *An Unquiet Mind*, Jamison refers to her diagnosis as "manic-depressive illness," the accepted terminology when the book came out in 1995, but I've substituted this for the current diagnosis name here.

alter our sense of self, sometimes dulling the qualities we hold most dear.

My first brush with psychotropic medication was at eighteen years old, when I was prescribed Prozac during an eating disorder treatment program. I resented the idea that I had to depend on medication, and I'd go on to spend years in a self-directed cycle of starts and stops. My resistance came both from fear that the pills would eradicate some essential part of myself and a hard-headed rebellion against what I considered a great injustice. It was the principle of the matter: I shouldn't have to take medication to live. This was an arbitrarily established rule, disregarding the millions of people who, for thousands of myriad reasons, require medication to live, and I suffered because of it. Today, I'm grateful to have found the medication cocktail that keeps my depression mostly manageable, with side effects that are mostly not terrible. Many others haven't found theirs, and still more, understandably, are too scared to try.

It's a bum deal, but it's one of few solutions at our disposal, at least while we wait for better clarity on where depression lives and how its treatments work. Medications ease symptoms—not always and to varying degrees—but scientists are skeptical of the theory they're built on: that depression is the result of a chemical imbalance in the brain. Though SSRIs target serotonin, their success might in fact be due to a "generalised emotion-numbing effect." Studies have revealed "barely distinguishable" results comparing antidepressants with placebo pills. On Reddit's r/antidepressants forum, user u/GullibleThug offered an analogy in response to a post asking why SSRIs work despite the theory that they're built on "be[ing] . . . disproven:"*

---

* This is an oversimplification. Though the once dominant hypothesis has come under scrutiny, it hasn't been categorically debunked.

Better

Picture a bucket of water that is leaking water through a hole in the bottom. As long as one fills more water continuously [sic], the bucket still has water, but it is hard to say that the water that is added continuously [sic] fixes the problem.

It's an illuminating, layperson-friendly illustration of SSRIs' imprecise mechanism, albeit a bit imprecise itself. (SSRIs don't pour serotonin into our brain; they just make it more available.) Regardless, the takeaway is clear: these medications might work, but they aren't ideal. I imagine mine now as a stopgap, holding me steady until a better option comes along. If we gather that these pills function through broad "emotion numbing," then I wonder: Are the emotions that I feel more strongly when I'm in a low—alongside the more obviously detrimental effects such as lethargy, weepiness, and fear—symptoms of my depression or not? Would a more precise cure still affect them? Where does my depression end and I begin?

* * *

"Don't let it win," Jordan texted me the morning I chose to live, and years later I'm stuck on the *it*. If *it* is depression, it's an independent and opposing entity—if *it* wins, I lose. I've identified less with this version of the depressive and suicidal experience as I've gotten older. Partially this is because I'm exhausted by the notion that depression is a war comprising daily battles for survival. But on a more basic level, I've become resistant to the idea that depression isn't part of who I am.

By the time Jordan was hospitalized, I was deep in Plath's journals and letters, looking for evidence of what had gone wrong. Now I searched with new urgency. Naively, perhaps willingly so, I believed these documents held secrets that would save Jordan if only I could identify them and translate them into action. Mostly what I found was a young woman desperate to write her way out of fear and continuously coming up short. And so I wonder when I read Plath's insistence on separating her depression from herself—by giving it a body, agency, the ability to exert pressure upon her—what such transference accomplishes.

In Plath's poetry and prose, depression is a monster, vividly drawn—"A great muscular owl . . . sitting on [her] chest, its talons clenching and constricting [her] heart"—or a "demon" that "feeds" on her attempts to share her fears with others. Surely these avatars are a means of better describing, and therefore better understanding, an otherwise inscrutable thing, and the comparisons are apt. Depression can feel like a being that acts at once upon and through me, and when it leaves, it absconds with all traces of its motivations. When I am happy, it isn't enough to say that I've forgotten my depression or vice versa; I can scarcely believe in it. Outside of a depressive episode, I can know I wanted to kill myself, but I can't feel it. In its grips, the opposite: I feel that any happiness I've ever known was merely misapprehension. We want to explain what depression feels like, so we describe it as an animal, a demon, a malevolent force, and then that is how it exists—corporal, apart from us, dangerous. Attempts to communicate depression and suicidal thinking—to others but also, perhaps more significantly, to ourselves—are paradoxically both powerful and insufficient.

My mother doesn't rely on metaphor, but her conversations with and about Jordan have always held steadfastly to the assertion that his depression isn't him. It is something that is being done to him; it is a parasite, a possession.

"I told him to write a list of reasons to live," she said during one of our many drives between the Long Island hospital and whichever hotel I was in at the time. "The next day I asked to see it, and you know what he did?"

"What."

"He comes out with two lists, and he says, 'Okay, here it is, but I also wrote a list of reasons to die.' And you know what I did?"

"What."

"I took the pen and wrote in big letters at the top, 'Jordan's Depression's List.'" I nodded, but she was looking at the road. "That's not Jordan talking," she said.

I think of Danea on the phone with me during one of his worst weeks, when there was no getting through his unwavering insistence that he would never get better. "I look at him," she said, "and I want to say, 'Jordan, are you in there?'"

It's Jordan's depression, but couldn't it also be him? Couldn't it also be me? Shouldn't we be the ones to decide? We resist the idea that a person's suicidality might be rooted in truth, might be, at least partially, valid. But that aversion is always based in fear, biased toward living at all costs, rejecting the possibility that a person might, simply and honestly, want to die. The stakes are too high to say anything other than a version of "No, you don't" to a person who wants to kill himself, because we think—we need to believe—that if the suicidal person can be convinced that his suicidality is an illusion, he won't follow through. I understand why we hold this assurance with a death grip: *This is not you. This is a symptom.* But what if it's both?

Let's say a symptom manifesting as desire is still desire. Let's say a person can assess his life, recognize his decision to end it as irrational, and still want to do it anyway. Let's say that telling a suicidal person he doesn't want the thing he wants turns that person paranoid, makes him doubt every emotion he feels, shifts his understanding of himself into something slippery, precarious. Let's say this disorientation makes him doubt not just his mind but then, too, the world around him, which he now knows he understands through a broken brain. Let's say the desire goes away, and he thinks, *Oh, they were right*, but that doesn't make the desire's return any less scary, because it's still desire and he's still being told it's not. And let's say that, trapped in this cycle, he decides that the only thing he knows for sure is that a large portion of his life is spent in a state of unreality and he's exhausted trying to parse the true from the false. Let's say he doesn't know if he's killing the true self or the false self when he does it, but he does it anyway. Couldn't we also say, then, that "This isn't you, this is just a symptom" is not enough?

And if it isn't enough to call the desire to die a symptom—if "symptom" doesn't do enough to capture the desire's totality—what are the implications? If the desire isn't foreign—if it is part of and made of the suicidal person—what does that say about that person, their quality of life? What does it mean for their future? Plath distances herself from her depression not only through metaphor; she also imagines separate selves. On January 10, 1953, she pastes an image of herself into her journal. The photograph, a simple, unremarkable headshot, is from two months prior, during a depressive episode so low she had described herself then as being "beyond help" and intent on killing herself. Plath refers to her face in the photo as an "ugly dead mask," describing "[t]he pouting, disconsolate mouth, the flat, bored, numb, expressionless eyes . . ." A mask suggests something shallow, surface level, something that can be removed to reveal a true face beneath, but Plath goes on to describe an intrinsic existential split. The photo—the mask—isn't simply a disguise, it is a doppelgänger. The woman in the photo harbors a "foul decay within," not "the cheerful, gay, friendly person that [Plath is] really inside."

Plath cleaves herself this way, and over the course of the twelve years that her journals span, we see a waning confidence in her ability to determine her real self versus the fraud—the former vibrant and successful; the latter, a shameful failure. At her most depressed, she shifts fluidly from first to second person, trying to ground herself through the act of writing as distinct from the other self she's writing to: "You have forgotten the secret you knew, once . . . of being joyous, of laughing, of opening doors." More often, she berates that separate self, coursing through a litany of flaws. In 1953, during the summer before her first, near-fatal suicide attempt, Plath's writing is a mess of *you*s and *I*s, a muddle of desperation and contempt. She begins an undated entry "Letter to an Over-grown, Over-protected, Scared, Spoiled Baby," and it reads like one side of a bitter lovers' quarrel. Writing in the first person, she tries in vain to prove her goodness, promising many carefully chosen accomplishments—a list of intentions, but also a desperate attempt at ingratiating herself to her depression, as if she knows she's possessed and making a case to be exorcised: "I will learn about shopping and cooking. . . . I will write for three or four hours Each Day. . . . I Will Not Lie Fallow or Be Lazy." Her affirmations become directives, less optimistic and more frantic. Her fear is tangible when she writes, "You just better learn to know yourself . . . before it is too late."

Surely such a separation can be essential for the suicidal person as well—if not as a source of comfort, at least as a way of talking oneself out of the act. I'm sure that many people, whether depressed or suicidal or not—myself included—have relied on missives to themselves: spoken affirmations, motivational phrases on Post-its, a good old-fashioned journal. These methods can affirm and encourage our ability to change, develop good habits, improve our lives in whatever ways we've decided to, regardless of however we've failed to do so in the past. One needs a way to remember—as banners that hung on the walls of both Jordan's and my psych wards announced—that we are not our thoughts, and that those thoughts, that fearful voice so hell-bent on delegitimizing any evidence of talent or goodness, can be disregarded and discharged. But splitting ourselves into good and bad actors becomes an issue of literal deadly consequences when it's a suicidal person doing so; it all but demands the model of warfare. Within this framework, even the most trivial or brief failure, however you define it—sleeping in or staying up too late, eating more than you'd like or restricting your food intake, blowing past a budget—signals an enemy advance. It requires an aggressive response, brooking no room for patience or gentleness; compassion can't exist on the battlefield. We celebrate the emergence into *better* as if it were a military victory: Plath glues the photo of the ugly mask to the page as though it's an enemy's head on a stick, as if it might scare away the next onslaught of depression.

Alternate terms for suicide such as "self-murder" and "self-homicide," though less common, slot perfectly into this theme of violence. Their reflexiveness aligns with the current guidelines for covering suicide in the media, most notably Reporting on Suicide, an extensive resource developed by the American Foundation for Suicide Prevention and other experts in the field. Reporting on Suicide, along with the National Institute of Mental Health and the World Health Organization (WHO), unequivocally denounces the phrase "commit suicide," suggesting "die by suicide," "take one's life," and "kill oneself" as safe alternatives. The reasoning is rooted in perceived negative connotations—"Commit," WHO explains, "implies criminality"—but I can't help side-eyeing the memo, regardless of the good intentions and research driving it.

Reporting on Suicide provides its credentials up front, assuring the reader that its recommendations were determined in collaboration with "international suicide prevention and public health organizations, schools of journalism, media organizations and key journalists as well as Internet safety experts." Whether those groups comprise people actively living with suicidality is anyone's guess. I'm reminded of linguistic debates within the broader disability community: How long did similar medical institutions insist that we use "person-first language" when referencing disabled people—the clunky "person with autism" as opposed to "autistic person"—before taking into account the opinions of the communities they were discussing? How loudly did those people have to shout—those who resented being separated from what they considered part of their identity, who explained that it was actually *more* insulting to imply that their disabilities removed their dignity—before those in power listened?

Ironically, when the word *suicide* first appeared in the mid–seventeenth century, it connoted the exact opposite and was viewed as a neutral alternative to the more common phrases used in discourse dominated by censure. Familiar "self-" forms filled the pages of Christian tracts condemning suicide and damning those who dared to so much as consider it. *Felo de se*, derived from the Latin *felonia de se* (felony of the self), was born in medieval England at a time when suicide was a gruesomely punishable crime,[*] and while its parameters loosened over time, its legal context was ingrained.[†] The arrival of the word *suicide* coincided with a wave of (mostly poorly received) philosophical and humanistic defenses of the act. As the term gained popularity, a consistent divide formed: writers who

---

[*] Given the fact that the felons in these cases were dead, the punishment was primarily a means of warning others against doing the same, and the families of the deceased bore the brunt. Nevertheless, they were brutal, including everything from forfeiting the deceased's estate to the king, to staking his body at a crossroads.

[†] The last recorded felo de se verdict occurred in the United Kingdom in 1938, though suicide remained a crime there until 1961.

supported a person's freedom to die adopted "suicide," while those against it stuck to "self-murder," "self-homicide," and "self-killing."

The distinction isn't incidental; it has consequences. The "self-" forms might have been used to emphasize criminality, but I find a more subtle argument against them and their modern equivalents. These phrasings—to "kill oneself" or, worse, the vague and prim "take one's life"—establish a separation of the person from the act, the actor from the acted upon. "Death by suicide" doesn't divide the person who's died, but it does remove their agency. This terrible, terrifying, unthinkable thing is no longer a matter of self-determination but rather something done to them. To say that a person commits suicide, to place them firmly and solely in subjectivity, is to acknowledge their humanity even in their death.

These separations are tempting as ways to preserve and privilege one aspect of the self, to isolate the one who wants to live as rational and the one who wants to die as irrational. As if one could isolate a healthy existence, a sane existence, a happy existence—what is the opposite of suicidal, anyway? I can't help but read a willful, even optimistic, delusion into the term. What does it matter who is killing whom when both victim and murderer inhabit the same body? Whom does the distinction serve? I found the battle against suicidality compelling when I saw it as a clean narrative—low, then lower, then rock bottom, then fight, fight, fight, and then, finally, victory. I never thought to consider it any other way. Linguistic nods toward war are everywhere in articles meant as self-help for the depressed: "Eight Ways to Actively Fight Depression." "To combat depression" we must "tak[e] on this internal enemy." Exercise, and maybe we'll "defeat" it. At nineteen years old, in the depths of a suicidal low spurred by taking myself off Prozac, it wasn't depression I was fighting. *I hate this Ari*, I wrote. *I don't know why she's back. I need her gone.* How better to push her out?

Better

I suspect we spin survival into combat, into heroism, so that we won't be punished for living with it. I suspect, even more so, that the idea proliferates because it defangs suicidality. It makes suicidality more palatable, less terrifying, to those who don't live with it, those who don't want to consider the possibility of a person—not an interloper, not a monster, not a disease—wanting to die. I think of the pleas of heartbroken survivors: "She wasn't herself." "It was the depression that killed him." The need to absolve the deceased of censure is surely an act of love, so it is understandable, but it's also misguided. In execution, it unwittingly but loudly confirms a fear that plagues so many people who are suicidal, namely, that a person can't be remembered with love—indeed, doesn't deserve love—unless their mental illness is excised from their true being.

What I know for sure is that every journal entry I've ever written while freshly out of a depressive episode, high on the belief that this time it's for good, has been followed, eventually, by an entry written from the familiar pit. On February 17, 2017, three months before my hospitalization, I opened my journal just past midnight and wrote, *Maybe one state isn't more real than the other—when I'm happy, this feels fake, and vice versa.* By April, I was as obsessed with the distinction between fiction and reality as I was with suicide—a word so heavy with intent and desire that I couldn't risk empowering it in writing. *So crazy to think how close it feels,* I wrote. *To remember the me who didn't want to do it. So abstract now. Someone else, I guess. I'm trying, I'm trying, I'm trying.*

I tried to explain this to the admitting doctor, how part of the reason I wanted to kill myself was because I wanted to stop hearing the voice in my brain telling me to do it. She stopped writing, let her clipboard fall to her side, and asked, with an alarm that betrayed a suspicion this might be more serious than she'd first thought, if I recognized the voice. Could I see the person saying it? Did I know them? But it didn't work like that. It was *my* voice, scared. When KC, Alissa, and I were discussing our approaching discharges, KC said he was nervous to leave.

"People out there, they don't understand," he said. "When I try to explain all the bad shit, they think I hear things or see things. I don't. It's just my thoughts."

I remembered the admitting doctor. *My voice, scared.*

When I look back on journal entries from those worst days, I don't see sadness as much as I see existential panic: Who am I, really? How much is a matter of pathology? How much does my fear of owning this darker voice hinge on a cultural insistence that it's unhealthy, even unnatural? What if I'm all of it?

* * *

"Don't let it win," Jordan said, but two years after his own hospitalization he was convinced that his depression was the victor.

"It's an objectively good idea for me to kill myself," he texted our sibling chat in the middle of a conversation about my cat's nicknames. "No one can provide me with a shred of evidence that it's a bad idea or that it isn't warranted. I'm not hoping for anything. Just because I have some people who have hope for me or who love a memory of me is no reason for me to suffer so much."

Danea, Dylan, and I regurgitated the same responses we always had: he was wrong, he couldn't see clearly, just because nothing had worked yet didn't mean nothing would work in the future. *Keep going*, we urged, we pleaded. There was some truth in what he told us, though. Each of those arguments was anchored by the same motivation—our deep love for him—and that made our efforts to persuade him away from suicide inextricable from our desire to keep him. We wanted him. We needed him. We told him to believe in himself, but really, we were asking him to think about us. It's a big request, asking someone trapped in his own thoughts, dogged relentlessly by his own pain, to dig up some empathy and put those who love him first. How much of our well-wishing is actually about our loved one's wellness, and how much is it about the impact of their unwellness on us?

Danea reminded Jordan that he was sick, that he just hadn't found the right medicine yet. His brain was distorting his thoughts. Dylan reminded him this was cyclical, that he'd had plenty of good days and weeks since he'd left the hospital; he just couldn't access those memories right now. But when it had gotten to the point that we were three years into the ebb and flow of his suicidality, my predominant response had become anger. I was fed up with what I saw as an active and stubborn refusal—he had always been so stubborn—to get better. Treatment had worked for me, though I still didn't know the how or why of it. Couldn't that be enough for him? Enough to make him believe that something would work for him, too? Why couldn't he just admit that there were treatments that had helped him in the past? That he'd been happy or, at the very least, that he had cared about something?

"You were happy when Theo was born," I said.

"I was pretending for you. I didn't feel anything."

I didn't buy it. *What about your tears when you held him for the first time?* I wanted to say. *What about, in the back seat of Mom's car, when you grasped his tiny hand for the forty minutes it took us to drive you back to the hospital, a trip we'd taken so many times I'd lost count?*

But we were wrong, he insisted. Those "good days" we swore we had shared with him were fantasies we'd mistaken for reality. Medication hadn't worked, shock therapy hadn't worked, nothing would ever work. Something inside him had cracked, and it couldn't be fixed. We were refusing to accept this fact, and he was the one being punished for it. Better didn't exist for him.

"There is no fix," he said. "It only gets worse and harder and more pointless."

"You think because you had three bad years you know some big truth about life?" I asked. "Who do you think you are?"

Jordan was certain he was anomalous—that there was something inside him that made him impervious to intervention, incompatible with life. Why couldn't we just concede that? His conviction was understandable; after all, his diagnosis of "treatment-resistant depression" had done little to inspire confidence. But resistance isn't outright rejection. Resistance implies friction, some force acting against us, but it doesn't completely block forward motion. Agency still exists. From a generous point of view, this could be a source of hope; we aren't doomed. But if we approach it with the cynicism that stems from cycling through countless failed solutions, those failures can lead us to isolate the defects in ourselves rather than in the treatment methods.

"You're all just talking in buzzwords and cliches," Jordan said, and I knew he was right. The buzzwords had never been strong enough to pull me out of my strongest desire for suicide, so how could I ask more from him? The insistence on a vague, better future; the cheerleading from the sidelines; all of it well intentioned but feeble, easily annihilated by the draw of nothingness. Jordan was trying to persuade us that he would be better off dead, but his arguments were based on years of convincing himself of the same, years of building a case that he was broken, exceptionally so. From that isolated perspective, the rest of humanity can become a blurry mass rather than a multitude of individuals, and their apparent ease of living can be taken for granted. How ironic it is to imagine a reality others live in just to assure ourselves that we don't; to invent an innate humanness we'll never possess; to prevent our recovery by working so hard to convince ourselves that we were cursed from the start. Perhaps we must believe our existence to be aberrant in order to end it.

* * *

Osamu Dazai, a prolific nihilist writer in postwar Japan who drowned himself with his lover six days shy of his thirty-ninth birthday, makes this presumed aberration explicit in his autobiographical novel *No Longer Human*. The novel's protagonist, Yozo, presents a sort of avatar of Dazai himself, and Yozo's belief in his monstrosity and the suicidality born from it are at the core of the story. His certainty that he is incompatible with life is rooted in disgust, directed at himself as often as at those around him. Sometimes he is subhuman; other times he's certain that the human being is one of the world's basest creatures; regardless, he is an other in a world built for the rest. "I can't even guess myself what it must be to live the life of a human being," he writes in the imagined found notebooks that make up the novel, but his evidence is faulty. Yozo is exhausted by the work of being human, but he fails to infer that others might be, too—that such upkeep might be a key component of being human, at least within a society that requires the performance of wellness to maintain the smooth-running machine of life.

Yozo discounts his connections with his peers because he feels they don't come naturally; if others find him charming—and many do—it's because he has deceived them. He believes that others have access to a kind of purity, an unmanipulated personhood, that is immediate and spontaneous. He finds relief in making people laugh, and he's good at it, but then he berates himself for what he deems as ignoble clownery. He's suspicious of every kind thing he does for another person. He assumes the absolute worst of his every action and intention. Any affection is unearned; those who like him are "half-wits." His desire to be loved makes him unworthy of receiving it. "People talk of 'social outcasts,'" he writes, ". . . denot[ing] the miserable losers of the world, the vicious ones, but I feel as though I have been a 'social outcast' from the moment I was born." The epilogue's final line, delivered by one of Yozo's oldest friends in conversation with the unnamed man who finds his notebooks, presents an alternate judgment, staggering in its distance from Yozo's self-appraisal: "[H]e was a good boy, an angel."

No Longer Human is distinct from much suicidal writing because of the hatred that seethes beneath the text and because of its significant, explicit focus on societal factors of suicide. Yozo has more than enough reason to condemn the absurdity of the world we've created and the cruelty of those within it: After being sexually abused as a child by a woman working in his home, he decides it's not worth telling anyone, suspecting he'd likely "be argued into silence by someone in good graces with the world, by the excuses of which the world approved." His depression fluctuates with his poverty, and he's rightfully incensed by the notion that a person should have to earn the right to live. "Nothing was so hard for [him] to understand, so baffling" than the "commonplace" idea that a person must work to stay alive. Still, his conclusion is always that *he* is the crazy one, that *his* version of being human is deviant. He sees suffering all around him—"Practical troubles, griefs that can be assuaged if only there is enough to eat"—and is driven "to the brink of lunacy" by the fact that the rest of the world can apparently "manage to survive without killing themselves." He assumes that he, not society, must be broken, and he is so ashamed of this brokenness, so terrified it will be discovered, that he keeps the assumption to himself, allowing him to harbor the misguided belief that he is alone in his fear. It's no wonder he is plagued by the misapprehension that he is "the only one who is entirely unlike the rest."

Better

Yozo's suicidality is more obviously linked to external factors than is that of those—say Plath, Woolf—whose desire to die is inextricable from melancholy. His first suicide attempt follows his fall into poverty after dropping out of school. He drinks to the point of addiction to dull the pressures and expectations of corporate life. Perhaps it isn't one's overwhelming desire to die that makes a person incompatible with life within our current society; perhaps it's our current society's incompatibility with life that makes a person want to die. This reversal—this sort of chicken-or-egg approach to suicide—is more than a philosophical supposition. Considering different causes of a problem tends to inspire different perspectives on how to provide a solution to it. If alienation comes first, the problem isn't completely internal. If alienation comes first, what in society—the strict requirements of survival, the epidemic of loneliness, the deliberate institutional quashing of systems of community and welfare—is causing it?

Chapter 6

Wait

When Theo was three years old, a close friend of the family died suddenly, shockingly, from an opioid addiction that no one, not even her husband, had suspected. It seemed cruel to have to introduce Theo to death when he was so new to life—I'd wanted him to have more time enjoying existence without having to bear an awareness of its inevitable end—but there was no getting around it. Annie had been a consistent presence in his life, had babysat and FaceTimed him and gifted him some of his favorite books, and her absence would need to be explained. Neither Brendan nor I am religious, but I was raised Catholic and carried on a vague Christianity until my early twenties. Within that world, mortality was explained with a mollifying simplicity that I still envy. I don't remember a time before knowing I would die, because I don't remember a time before knowing I would go to Heaven—before, indeed, I looked forward to my time in the clouds with not only Jesus but also everyone I'd ever loved. How can anyone who believes be afraid?

During that first conversation, I intended to stick to the facts—no euphemisms, no metaphors, just as all my research on child psychology and development instructed. I told him that Annie had been sick and her body stopped working. I told him it meant that we wouldn't be able to see her anymore. I told him it was very sad, and we would miss her very much. I asked if he had any questions.

"Where did Annie go?"

"Well," I explained, "no one knows for sure, and people believe lots of different things. What I believe is that she left this world and now she's somewhere else."

"But where?"

"Somewhere like . . . space. And I think while she's there she can still love us and we can still love her. We can even still talk to her and she'll hear us, even if we can't see her or hear her."

But children are literal creatures. He couldn't get past the body. If Annie's body stopped working and her legs couldn't move, didn't that mean she would be stuck wherever she died? And if so, did that mean if Theo was at his grandparents' home (his favorite place) and got hit by a car (the danger we most stressed) he could stay there forever? Wouldn't that, in fact, be great?

I abandoned the rational advice to be as clear as possible, to stick to the harsh facts. We deserve a cushion. I couldn't bear telling him that our bodies fall apart, that quite often we put them into boxes and place them in the earth, where they stay, deep beneath the ground, until they, too, are dirt. So I told him that they disappear, like magic. This was enough, but not for long. His obsession with death began to intensify and continues to; the questions grow more frequent until they've become an expected part of our daily lives.

Usually he asks without affect, in pure curiosity. When we're listening to a new song: Is this singer alive or dead? When we're feeding some pigeons: Will these birds die?

Sometimes it's funny, like the time he ran ahead of Brendan after school pickup, burst through the door, and yelled to me on the couch, "Are you going to die soon, or *what?*" Then there was the lazy Saturday morning, the two of us lounging on our respective ends of the couch while Theo's favorite Nintendo streamer played on the television.* Apropos of nothing, not even diverting his gaze from the screen, he told me that, actually, he knows where we go when we die. I girded myself for the possibility of a difficult navigation.

"Oh, wow! That's cool. What happens?"

"Butt World," he said, with the terseness and tone of an eye-rolling teenager, as if the phrase he'd dropped warranted no further explanation.

"Butt World? Like . . . butts, not attached to people?" I laughed, and his stoicism broke in a stream of giggles. But he didn't give me an answer, so I continued, "Okay, so I die. Then what?"

"A butt saves you and brings you away, out of sight, where nobody will find you again."

I repeated the scenario back to him for confirmation, which he provided with growing glee.

"Interesting," I said. "Why is it called Butt World?"

"Because butts live there."

"Just by themselves?"

"Yeah."

"Oh, boy," I said. "I don't know if I'd like Butt World."

---

* We are a family of rabid Pokémon trainers.

"You would. Because you can see what happened in the past. The butts show you what dinosaurs looked like."

I gasped, opened my eyes wide in exaggerated delight. "Whoa! Okay, yeah, that's pretty cool. Maybe I *would* like—"

"And then you get pooped on."

Thank god, I thought, *for these reminders. Thank god he is still a little boy, my little boy, my perfect, silly, baffling, gross-out little boy whose worries aren't so big as to leave no room for butts and dinosaurs and poop.* How grateful I was, in that moment, for the poop. Because more often than not, the questions are dipped in worry, relentless in the dark of his bedroom as I try to ease him into sleep: Who will die first in our family? When? Do we have to? What will happen? Recently, he's taken to maneuvering around death as a whole, excitedly explaining to me his solution: When I'm about to die, he'll save me, and then I can do the same for him, forever.

For nearly as long as Theo has been alive, my family has noted his and Jordan's similarities. The same stubborn scowl Jordan wore at five years old, the intensity of his attention, the hypersensitivity: they are there in Theo, undeniably. As any close-knit family is wont to do, ours has lore we never tire of repeating, and Jordan's primarily revolves around his youthful seriousness, the rawness of his emotions. We revisit those moments in sentimentality, without his participation. Jordan stands alone among a nostalgia-obsessed family, in a disinterest in the past that borders on resentment. But still, the rest of us can't deny the resemblance, especially now that the pair are so close, gleefully bonding over Pokémon stats and Super Mario strategies. My parents are in the living room for their weekly visit, and my mother and I are watching Theo in a rare moment of solo play. And we recount: Remember when we were watching MTV, and that Michael Jackson video was on, and Jordan cried and ran out of the room because it showed an elephant dead on the ground?* Remember when he crawled under the backyard deck to help that crying kitten and we couldn't convince him to come out? Remember when he got suspended for fighting that bully? Jordan still carries that hypersensitive boy inside him, and I know it's as much a gift as it is a curse. Would he be able to hurt so much if he didn't feel so much? I doubt it. Is the good worth the bad? I see Jordan in Theo, and I'm both overjoyed and afraid. What in his body, his mind, his soul, his genetic makeup connects them? Where and how do they split?

* * *

Three weeks into his hospitalization, Jordan still wasn't getting better. The Effexor hadn't worked. Neither had the Wellbutrin. Then came the electroshock therapy, but it only made him feel hazy, depleted, vaguely aware that with each session he was erasing memories with no guarantee they would return. He had no faith in the proposed medications and treatments; they brought him no optimism. I'm familiar with the exhaustion that comes from carrying a stymied desire to die, as well as the exhaustion of the mental and physical adjustments that come with each new intervention. At least the former is a known entity, a stasis. Why would anyone feel motivated to embark on a slight variation of a plan that had failed so many times already? How can they do so, knowing that they might be subjecting themselves to the devastation of adding one more item

---

* "Earth Song," from 1995. The elephant, which has apparently been hunted for its ivory, comes back to life and regrows its tusks at the end, which, unfortunately, Jordan didn't stick around to see.

to the growing tally of failures? How can they interpret this as anything other than a winnowing of their chances to get better? There was no pause in Jordan's daily begging us to let him die, to accept that he had to die, to understand that refusing him our blessing and asking him to continue living in anguish was an act of cruelty.

Still, I held on to the hope that I could use something of what I'd learned after my own low to pull him out of his, to challenge his resistance to treatment and his refusal to believe it might work. Everything I'd gleaned from the research I'd been doing in the year since my hospitalization had seemed so promising because it had happened in conjunction with a period of wellness. My recovery had yet to show signs of faltering. Couldn't it be the case that these new theories were the reason for my recovery's success? The idea was far more compelling and comforting than it—recovery—being a matter of luck. I'd amassed notebooks full of observations about the dangers of romanticizing the past; of conjuring up suicidality or its attendant mental illnesses with horrific, hateful imagery; of excoriating oneself for succumbing to it.

When I sat with Jordan in the sunny common room, leaning in to pinpoint his voice within the buzz of visiting-hours conversations, I tried to demystify what he was feeling, to make it small, logical. Okay, he wanted to die. He felt nothing. Well? So? I didn't tell him that this was because his brain wasn't working right; I didn't insist that he was a warrior. Rather, I asked, couldn't he understand that his chronic suicidality might be the effect of the rigid, misplaced standards he'd been holding himself to? But the damage was done, he insisted. Somewhere along the way he'd failed to adjust to life in the way the rest of us had. He didn't know how to be close to people; he had no desire to succeed according to our society's definition of the word. He had no desire for life because the life he wanted was impossible. All he'd ever wanted to do was to hang out with his friends, he explained, to chill at home and play video games, and of course that could never happen. But it can, I told him. We need to create the life we want. People should be able to live like that, people do live like that, just in the margins; he had to find them. He could have the life he wanted if he was willing to forgive himself for wanting it. Didn't he see how there was no separating the inwardly psychological from the outwardly interpersonal? Didn't he understand how simple this could be, how it was the only way to be free? And if he couldn't join me in my excitement over the long-term potential held in this revelation, couldn't he at least be relieved by it? Why couldn't he see that he just had to shift his thinking about his place in the world, about what suicidality is, and what life without it could be?

But all these rationalizations were powerless against his immediate, steadfast need to die. I was terrified of my brother's enduring wish for death, and intellectualizing it subdued that fear. That was all it did. Abstractions and hypothetical exercises failed to move Jordan even an inch. What good could they do for a mind overcrowded by despair? What solace can the vision of a gentler, more forgiving future provide a person who can't fathom any future at all? I had come up with ideas that I thought were philosophically interesting, concepts my English-major brain liked tinkering with, but if they had any use, it would be only in times of wellness, when one has the luxury to devote time and resources to cultivating a more ideal, durable mental hygiene. Any evidence-based theories about cognitive and dialectical treatments or long-term habits of maintaining good mental health might offer guidance when we're out of the proverbial woods, but they are laughably inconsequential—potentially overwhelming, infuriating, and alienating—for someone whose immediate priority is staying alive. We must figure out how to live before we can figure out how to live well.

Better

"For me, the question of suicide is not really or even remotely an academic issue," the contemporary philosopher Simon Critchley writes in the introduction to his stirring tract, *Suicide*—which, for much of its robust sixty pages, approaches suicide as just that. Critchley is referring to his intimate, personal history of wanting to die, but the book as a whole, to its benefit, complicates such a clean separation from academic engagement with suicidality, even one's own. This isn't a flaw in the premise, nor does it undermine his arguments; if anything, it emphasizes the impenetrability of suicide's basest reality. Suicide is tangible, carnal, but incredibly difficult to examine with both feet on the ground. It can't be separated from our greatest mysteries, so we drift into our heads without meaning to, returning again and again to the theoretical. More simply, though, it's tough to talk about because so much of it just doesn't make sense. Even our theories resist neatness, tangling with one another and folding in on themselves, snarling and tightening into a Gordian knot. These conversations abound with contradiction, and that fact is key to Critchley's study, which contends that conversations about suicide and autonomy are "doomed to severe conceptual confusion." That confusion isn't quite so limited. Just five pages after assuring his readers that "[t]his book is not a suicide note" he admits that the statement "is perhaps not to be trusted."

Most writing on suicide—indeed, the bulk of this book—arrives, and is possible, only in moments when the writer has reached a place of safety, lacking the immediate and full access to the urgency felt within the state of suicidality it is examining, and so it is weakened by distance. These perspectives necessarily tend toward the philosophical, spiritual, scientific. Outside of the danger, we have the advantage of time and mental fortitude to hypothesize about optimal methods of treatment, to challenge foundational beliefs about suicide's causes, to examine our cultural perception of suicide within the context of thousands of years' worth of recorded ideology, testimony, and direct experience. I have to imagine that the people who have the will to seek out and read these works are doing so from a similar distance.

As it became clear that my ideas were failing to move Jordan enough to want to survive, my conviction weakened. I began to rely on hope, which inevitably turned into fear. Jordan was discharged but almost immediately the texts resumed—"I want to die, it didn't work, please understand nothing will"—and they continued for over a year. By that point I'd reverted in desperation to all the tactics I'd thought I didn't believe in, maneuvers that felt like so much flailing. I called and texted my mother daily, telling her to take away the sleeping pills, lock up the knives, the razors, any would-be nooses. Track his location; remove the bedroom door. I trusted no one else to do what needed to be done, imagined holding him hostage in my apartment under constant surveillance. I pleaded with him: Go back to the hospital. It will work. Because it had to work. I needed to believe it would work. Because what if he just stayed sad? What did that mean for him, for me, for anyone else whose life had been reduced to daily waiting for the opportunity and gumption to kill themselves? Jordan hadn't wavered even for a day in his insistence that he had the authority—and more than enough reason—to choose to die. Could it be possible that he was right? Was the idea that anyone else could change his mind or stop him simply our own delusion?

In the midst of all this, an old friend, Billy, texted me from his home in Nashville to see how Jordan was doing. For whatever reason, probably my exhaustion, maybe the physical and figurative distance between us, I responded immediately with what I hadn't yet allowed myself to say to anyone, including myself: "If a person wants to kill himself for two years straight, is it not cruel to stop him?" I asked. "Feels sort of, to me, like the equivalent of forcing a sick person to live in pain."

Better

Billy asked if I really believed that Jordan had wanted to kill himself for the entirety of those two years, and I said I did, because though I never would have admitted it to Jordan at the time, I knew that any respite from his suicidality had been too brief to be meaningful. It had become the overarching theme of his life, any moment of happiness a trivial blip.

"You can't give up hope even if that's what's happening right now," Billy wrote. "I assume he's on meds and talks to a therapist twice a week?"

But no, he wasn't. He'd stopped, decided it was pointless, and I couldn't convince him that that was a mistake. "He doesn't listen to me," I said.

"Okay come on," Billy said. "You can't say it's selfish to make him continue to suffer if he's not actually putting in the effort to fight it."

We were saying what felt taboo, what shouldn't be said, but what I needed to say and needed to hear. We were saying what I knew was both true and contradictory: Jordan couldn't be blamed for his suicidality, and also he was choosing to refuse treatment. It was impossible to say that he would never get better, and also it was impossible to say he would. Killing himself before exhausting all possible treatment options would be short-sighted, and also he was justified in disregarding an unknowable future when his present was bogged down by grief.

"I'm so, so angry," I said.

"Well, you're scared," Billy said. "You love him."

What else was there to say?

I was angry with Jordan for being stubborn, but I was being stubborn, too. Neither he nor I could see the both/and of reality. We couldn't grasp the fullness of it or reconcile the contradictions of the situation. Each of us was stuck on our side of the sentence. The difference was that I was the one who wasn't constrained by current suffering. Billy's sentiments were iterations of the appeals everyone had been sharing with Jordan: "You need to fight it"; "You can do this"; "It's going to get better." I knew, for Jordan, that those messages couldn't and wouldn't stick—not because they weren't meaningful or well intentioned but because this is precisely what suicidality does to the brain: it blocks the light. Those overtures couldn't help him in that moment, but they did help me. Of course Billy was right. Of course there was hope. Of course my anger and nihilism were based in both fear and love. Jordan was rooted firmly in his depression, but I could still be moved. I already had been. Jordan was trapped in a doom loop, but I had the capacity to hold the hope of his survival hand in hand with the validity of his desire to die. Perhaps doing so was crucial to providing meaningful help. We were all asking him to carry too much.

"You don't have to believe you're going to get better," I texted Jordan that night. "You just have to wait."

In the moment closest to suicide, the only way to survive, the only requirement of survival, is inaction. The implicit plea: Do nothing. Sit still. *Wait.* Don't leave the house if you don't want to; it's fine. I will sit with you there, and when you wake up one day and decide you want to leave—and yes, I believe you will—then I'll get up and go with you. Both Jordan and I are blessed to have people who can, and want to, sit vigil. Their attention, and ours for each other, has functioned not only as a practical preventive—it's quite difficult to kill yourself on someone else's watch—but an emotional one as well. Whether or not the suicidal person resents the loved one's dedication in the moment, it is undeniable proof of their worthiness to be loved, of the fact of their being loved, or at least of their not being alone. For some people, this can be another source of pain; for others, it might be an item in the "Pros" column of the list guiding the decision to live or die. More likely, it's both at once. Jordan didn't need permission to kill himself, but his persistent requests for our acquiescence meant our denial was one of the few remaining hurdles between him and death. Jordan was furious that we were so committed to staying with him, and I was furious that he was so committed to leaving us. It felt wrong to show him my anger, to throw guilt on top of his misery, but I still believe that honesty is preferable to the alternative. Infantilizing him, stripping him of his autonomy, invalidating his experience of his own life, felt wrong because it *was* wrong—detrimental to his sense of agency when he most needed to believe in it.

"We were enemies who loved each other," Miriam Toews writes in *All My Puny Sorrows*, her 2014 autobiographical novel based on her sister's suicidality. It is a veritable master class in the persuasive efforts between a suicidal person and the person who loves them, each desperate to bring the other to their side. Toews's stand-in is the narrator, Yoli, a mother and writer whose sister, Elf—the enemy she loves—is determined to die. Elf is ethereal and well loved, a brilliant, wildly successful world-traveling pianist, but none of this is enough to make her want to stay. She tries to explain to Yoli that she wasn't made right—"she'd never adjusted to the light, she'd just never developed a tolerance for the world, her inoculation hadn't taken"—but Yoli's is a desperate, buck-up kind of love and she dismisses the claim. Yoli doesn't hold back her anger, but underneath the anger is a message, legible in the sisters' shared language: *This is how much I need you. This is how much I love you*. The two pass fluidly between anger and love, and though Yoli's visible frustration fails to push Elf to get better, that doesn't mean it doesn't help. In that rawest period, Elf hungers for honesty, and Yoli gives it. It's a reciprocal process, a tense exchange of respect—fraught and difficult but also an act of honoring their relationship by refusing to deny what's at stake: "Just stop lying to me about what life is," Elf says after Yoli tries to convince her that she can cancel her professional obligations without feeling guilty. "Fine, Elf," Yoli responds. "I'll stop lying to you if you stop trying to kill yourself."

I wonder if, at the very least, this transparency inspires emotion during a time of nothingness, even if that emotion is anger. It forces an honest and emotional interaction with someone else, an externalized focus, during a time when we're lost in ourselves. The act of persuading someone not to die is its own psychic breakdown. It's an attempt to ensure not only the suicidal person's survival but also one's own; surviving someone else's suicidality is a private mania. It comes from profound love, but that love can look desperate, mean, insufferable, antagonizing, and overbearing. It is either selfless or selfish; it depends on which side of the love you're on. Probably it's both. It is imperfect love, but it is all we have. But still, of course, it can fail. Elf refuses to cooperate in what her husband describes as her "journey to health" with her "team," sneering at the suggestion with well-earned contempt:

> *Elf was up in arms, gnashing her teeth against the smarmy self-help racket that existed only to sell books and anaesthetize the vulnerable and allow the so-called "helping" profession to bask in self-congratulation for having done what they could. They'd make lists! They'd set goals! They'd encourage their patients to do one "fun" thing a day! (Oh you should have heard the derision in Elf's voice when she said the word fun . . .)*

For anyone ruminating on suicide, talks of plans and toolboxes are often laughable. This is especially true for those who have been there before; their being suicidal again means that those plans have already failed. The focus on these tips and tricks isn't just frustrating but also detrimental. Society's insistence on—and my wavering hope for—a universal possibility of recovery that we know how to achieve carries the sinister implication that a person's failure to maintain wellness comes from their lack of commitment. The institutional assertion that we must return to the tactics we know have never been enough carries a damning latent message: *This time, do it better. This time, do it right.*

Our internalization of this message—and it's a deceptively empowering one—cuts whether we believe in it or not. In 2017, I failed to get help until I was at a crisis point because I was certain I had the power to right the ship myself, that if I just started going for a daily walk, waking up early, going to bed early, brushing my teeth, establishing simple routines—if I could just stop fucking it up; why couldn't I just stop fucking it up?—I could get better without needing anything so drastic or overwhelming or expensive as finding a new therapist, starting new medications, and asking for help. Jordan, on the other hand, didn't believe in the power of these methods or his ability to implement them, so he was fundamentally at odds with anyone trying to help him who insisted otherwise.

If we close our eyes to the reality that these efforts can and do fail, we forestall any chance at making a meaningful connection with the person who's fed up with them. There is no chance of extending gentleness, empathy, without plainly considering and inhabiting the reality in which the person lives, and to give credence to—or at the very least, not to dismiss out of hand—their conviction that their suicidality is terminal. To affirm, not belittle, the suicidal person's understanding of their suicidality is to affirm their already fragile sense of humanity. Fear is understandably at the heart of conversations between those who are suicidal and those who can't fathom losing them, but it is fear that makes those conversations sterile, alienating, superficial. By allowing into the mainstream the notion that suicidality isn't necessarily illogical, that certain cases of it might even be malignant, and by refusing to use our fear and deep-seated, inherent rejection of suicide as an excuse for condemnation, we can finally meet the suicidal person where they are and engage with them in earnestness. We might say, "Let's be afraid together. Let's be angry together. Let's figure this out together. I won't let this be another way in which you are alone."

We need only look to the people who've been in the trenches to understand the impact of such acceptance. Responding to a video in which a woman asked suicidal people to consider those who will suffer from their death before acting, TikTok user yayatizz, a woman who speaks frequently about her suicidality and failed attempt,* explains that knowing you are surrounded by people who love you and *still* wanting to die is among the most painful aspects of suicidality. She goes on to share, tearing up, what she wishes someone had said to her when she was at her worst:

> *I am so, so sorry that you feel this way. Life must be so overwhelming . . . that you don't want to be here anymore. I can understand why that's so hard. . . . I wish forever that the whole time I'm on earth that I share it with you. . . . That doesn't mean you should stay alive, but that does mean you should feel loved. In this moment where . . . you feel lost, I still love you here, and I'll still love you when you're gone. If there's a way that we can get you to a place where you don't feel like this anymore, I'd love*

---

* Though words such as *success* and *failure* are discouraged when talking about suicide, a great many people who are or have been suicidal use them, including yayatizz in this video.

to try, if you'd give me a chance . . . but no matter what, this is
your life and your choices, and I want to be here with you.

To date, the video has more than a thousand commiserators thanking this otherwise stranger for validating their experience.

In *All My Puny Sorrows*, Elf goes a step further by asking Yoli not only to accept her suicide but also help her do it. She begs Yoli to take her to Switzerland, the only place where she'd be able to go through assisted suicide, contending that her affliction is terminal. This is the moment Yoli's empathy breaks through her anger. She can't deny the potency of Elf's underlying argument. She'd been into and out of the hospital after multiple suicide attempts. It certainly seemed that she would keep trying until one worked. Not until she's faced with Elf's heartfelt request to help her die peacefully does Yoli consider, fearfully but in good faith, the possibility that Elf was "cursed genetically from day one to want to die." She wonders, "Was every seemingly happy moment from her past, every smile, every song, every heartfelt hug and laugh and exuberant fist pump and triumph, just a temporary detour from her innate longing for release and oblivion?" Could Yoli's greatest act of love, counterintuitively, be letting Elf die and holding her hand as she goes?

When asked if the book was "a sustained argument in favour of assisted dying," Toews, whose sister and father both killed themselves, said yes, absolutely—that her greatest regret in life was the fact that she hadn't granted her sister's request to take her to the Swiss physician-assisted suicide organization Dignitas. "When I think about how she died," she said, "violently, alone—absolutely [I regret it]." Spalding Gray expresses similar regret in one of the journals he left behind, regarding his mother's death. He mourned her suicide until the day of his own, but what haunted him specifically was "guilt for not having come back . . . to help [her] die."

I want to sit for a moment in the discomfort this presents and resist, however briefly, the deeply ingrained evolutionary instinct toward survival. If we earnestly consider that a person might be justified in killing themselves, that indeed there is logic in their decision, that doing so might even be good for them, and that it is their right—if we dare to suppose that refusing someone in misery the chance to end their lives in peace and dignity is inhumane—which paths unfurl from this line of thinking? By and large they are avenues of validation. If mental illness is indeed an illness, then of course treatments can and do fail, and when they do, those suffering treatment-resistant depression cannot simply will themselves into being cured. Or if suicidality is a sensibility, a debilitating emotional rawness that leaves a person especially vulnerable to manmade cruelties, then medical intervention will never be sufficient. And when we are accounting for the worthwhileness of a life, doesn't the quality of the years lived count more than the quantity? Might there be a more ethical imperative than prolonging a life by any means necessary? That assisted suicide for the terminally ill is increasingly gaining legal and public approval in the United States means a large swath of the country supports a person's autonomy and right to end their own suffering. This social and political progressivism is undermined, however, when we designate a type or level of pain one must reach before being able to enact that right.

All these considerations encircle a core fear: If we agree to destigmatize and accept suicide—not just suicidal thinking but the completed act—aren't we undermining all faith in prevention and recovery? Aren't we encouraging those suffering to stop trying to get better? In other words, if we tell depressed people that it's okay to kill themselves, aren't they going to do it? Well, sure. Maybe. But people are already killing themselves without approval. It's likely at least one person has done so in the time between your starting this chapter and arriving here: data suggest that one suicide occurs every eleven minutes in the United States. We can assume that there have always been, and will always be, those who will never rid themselves of their suicidality—those whom Toews described as "built to self-destruct"—as well as those for whom life might be possible. For the former, the benefit of accepting suicide as a valid option is obvious: They are allowed the dignity of directing their fate, and they don't need to spend their last moments alone and ashamed. But shifting the conversation toward acceptance also benefits those whose suicidality might not be chronic, because whichever camp that person falls into, their suicidality *in that moment* is dire.

This is a terrifying, alien, unnatural thing to consider, so antithetical to the belief in life's sanctity that it's quite likely—understandably so—that a suicidal person's loved ones might never support their suicide even if they can sympathize in theory. Still, it's a worthwhile shift in our thought processes, fertile ground for exercising empathy, regardless of where we ultimately land. It's an unsatisfying solution, because there is no satisfying solution; the best we can do is get as close as possible. Ultimately, a person who wants to kill themselves will always be able to do it. But there's good evidence backing up the theory that even the simple act of acknowledging this reality with the suicidal person—that they will always, eventually, have the power to kill themselves—is a powerful form of support in itself. The suicidologist Stacey Freedenthal advises clinical providers to begin by engaging honestly in the suicidal person's desire to die and finding "the part that makes sense"—the conditions in which suicide becomes a "logical response"—and admitting as much to the patient. There is a line between understanding and affirming, and though walking it can be scary it's also necessary. "Validation is evidence of empathy," she writes, "not agreement."

As it turns out, when Jordan met our mother's request for a list of reasons to live with a complementary list of reasons to die, he was intuiting a fruitful therapeutic method. My mother dismissed the latter as a script from his disease—why wouldn't that be the impulse, and how would she know to do otherwise?—but even though it seemed as though Jordan was pushing back against help, he was in fact extending an invitation to help from a different angle, whether consciously or not. In 2001, the psychologist Haim Omer and the philosopher Avshalom Elitzur coauthored "What Would You Say to the Person on the Roof? A Suicide Prevention Text," a practical guide for helping the suicidal person out of crisis. Shortly thereafter, their peer Israel Orbach published an argument to shift the focus in his response paper "How Would You Listen to the Person on the Roof?: A Response to H. Omer and A. Elitzur." Orbach, also a psychologist, finds the paper objectively useful but elucidates one flaw in the authors' version of empathy: it is based on the assumption that suicidality is broadly knowable, that other people "understand the essence of the suicidal person's pain" based on their own experience of, and education in, suffering. This entry into empathy—as Orbach writes, "presenting the pain of the person on the roof from the perspective of the person below"—will never succeed. In his own therapeutic practice, Orbach asks his patients to "actually 'convince' [him] that suicide is the only solution left," so that he can interact with the suicidal person as a "companion" rather than an adversary. Jordan offered us an opportunity to do the same, but none of us accepted it.

"I never wanted to die," Donald Antrim writes. "Have you wanted to die?"

It strikes one at first as a preposterous statement by a person describing years of suicidality. But then again: Have I? Antrim holds tight to his contention that his ideation and near attempts were never driven by a yearning to die but rather by a certainty that he *had* to die. His experience of suicide was as a compulsion. This makes sense to me. Decades ago, a realization that broke through my subconsciousness—I am in pain, but I can stop it—returned frequently enough to become a nag, a devil on the shoulder. "I did not want to die, only felt that I would, or should, or must," he writes, "and I had my pain and my reasons, my certainties."

Functionally, what is the difference between a person who wants to die and a person who thinks they should—a person who thinks they must? It's tempting to write the question off as a matter of semantics, but addressing these states as related but fundamentally distinct deepens our understanding of suicidality. Desire, compulsion, shame, fear: they are a Venn diagram of motivations for suicide and their respective approaches to survival. Does the suicidal person want to die, or do they want not to live? There's flexibility in the latter. It's so close to the crux of the issue, the key question. If only we can find the empty space, fill in the implied but absent qualifier that I can't help but hear: Does the suicidal person want to die, or do they want not to live *like this*? And from there: Not "How do we get them to stay?" but rather "Why do they want to go?" Trying to determine the former is useless without understanding the latter.

* * *

In the wee hours of November 6, 1971, forty-seven-year-old Michael Valenti called into the underground New York City talk radio show *Radio Unnameable* and, after making a light dig at the wait time, asked host Bob Fass, "Are you a gentleman?" It was a strange question, but strange was the norm on the overnight show. Fass zigged, eluding the question by saying, "I don't know what a gentleman means." The caller zagged: "I'm in the process of committing suicide." Fass kept his cool, maintaining the conversation as he would with any caller after silently directing staff to get help. He asked Valenti* about his life and why he wanted to end it; Valenti explained that his life "is in a total mess at the moment, both as far as jobs, [his] girlfriend, [his] so-called friends." By the time of making the call, Valenti had already taken sleeping pills, which is evident as his voice begins to slur. Still, Fass kept him on the line. For forty-five minutes they talked, despite Valenti's jumpiness—he was terrified of being stopped—and despite Fass's refusal to promise *not* to try to stop him.

About halfway through the conversation, Fass invited Valenti to make an argument—not to convince him that Valenti himself should die but that *anyone* should. "I mean, if dying is so hot," Fass goaded, "why don't you try to talk me into it?" Valenti refused. He didn't want Fass to die, after all. Maybe he didn't really want to die, either. Through a concerted effort of the *Radio Unnameable* staff, its listeners, the New York Telephone Company, and the NYPD, police were able to find Valenti in his Upper East Side apartment, unconscious next to empty pill bottles. He survived. In an interview with Sean Cole of *This American Life*, Fass explained, not without apparent discomfort, that their communication had made sense to him because he had felt a connection with Valenti. "Without going into it too deeply, I had been severely depressed at one important point myself," he told Cole. "And I recognized that it's possible to come back." Years later, Valenti called Fass again, off the air, to thank him.

Whether or not Valenti was consciously looking to be saved, he was undoubtedly looking for company. He chose to spend what he intended to be his final moments seeking connection, reaching out

---

* On the call, Valenti identified himself as "Stanley Kauffmann"—who was, in fact, a former *New York Times* drama critic.

for the host, and also, through him, an entire audience. As it turns out, this has happened often enough on call-in radio to qualify as a trend. Suicide notes, too, support the idea that even when the suicidal person has determined that they've lost everything, they maintain that most basic desire: to be understood. They reveal one final, tiny gesture of hope. Maybe the suicidal person spent their life feeling unseen, but they can make one last attempt to fix this in their death. It makes sense, then, that suicide notes are unique in allowing access to the most intimate explanations of a person's desire to kill themselves; there's no reason to hold back or self-censor as one might with doctors, family, or friends.

Why does the suicidal person try to bridge the gap between themselves and their loved ones? Are they looking for permission to leave or a reason to stay? If our concern for those who love us is the last remaining tether to a life we want desperately to leave, then perhaps these gestures really are just attempts at finding peace before going. But is that all these pleas contain? Our tireless endeavors to persuade others that our suicide would be a good idea are far more likely to inspire intervention than agreement. We must, on some level, know this. Removed from the context of justification, these defenses are simply efforts for communion. Building our efforts from the premise of suicidality provides a level of protection; a flicker of hope, otherwise so vulnerable, hides within the insistence that we've long since hardened against it. What does the suicidal person want? Antrim asks us to start from a positive assumption, to examine the suicidal person's actions and impulses within the context of their wanting to live. It's an exercise in gray areas and nuances: "I want to die" becomes "I want to live, but I can't."

Recalling the day he had "scrambl[ed] from fire escape to rooftop and back," certain he had to make it to the top to jump, Antrim describes a series of false starts—almost falling, pulling himself up, and then doing it again. If his neighbors witnessed the scene, he wonders, how had they interpreted it? What had they seen? "If they had known the man's troubles, had known the man, would they have understood that he was about to die?" he writes. "Or would they have imagined that he was trying to live?" The slip and the catch, the floating, the living death—these spaces reside in the overlap between trying to die and trying to live. The cycles, liminalities, and in-betweens seem interminable, but really, they exist because the person living within them still has something, even if seemingly trivial, to live for.*

This is often apparent in a specific genre of suicide notes: those written by teenagers. In the early 1990s, while writing about young women living in a Manhattan "crackhouse,"† the sociologist Terry Williams decided that "shedding light" on teenagers' plights was no longer enough; he wanted to spur change that would help them leave those struggles behind. Since the 1980s, as he had been creating ethnographies of teens surviving at the margins and in the underbelly—from "white, middle- and upper-class kids" finding community in rural and suburban goth and rave scenes to "kids who hung out on street corners"—he became increasingly aware of their painful alienation from not only society at large but also within their own families. He also realized that those kids (as he frequently referred to them) were willing, and even relieved, to confide in a nonjudgmental

---

* I think often of the absurdist poet Stevie Smith's macabre depiction of a man dying in plain sight in what is probably her most famous poem, "Not Waving but Drowning." Struggling in open water, the man says to bystanders on the shore, too distant to hear him: "I was much further out than you thought / And not waving but drowning."

† A term so linguistically weighted that it became the title of the resulting book.

stranger. So he pushed them a bit further, giving out hundreds of journals across the country and inviting teenagers to write their life stories. What were returned were essentially suicide letters from "child[ren] on the brink of the act" who didn't really want to die.

In his 2017 *Teenage Suicide Notes: An Ethnography of Self-Harm*, the culmination of this work, Williams presents the lives and suicidality of nine teens leading distinct lives across the US. They're queer and straight, religious and not, popular and ignored. Some later killed themselves; some only thought about it. Through their writing and interviews with Williams, we find recurring pain points: academic pressure, unforgiving body and beauty standards, fear of failure, lack of familial attention, external belittling of emotional and psychological pain. The letters, Williams explains, were methods of mitigating "the conflict between the self and an exterior imposition." The teenage suicidal fantasy he uncovers isn't so much about death or escape as it is, counterintuitively, about power and agency. It's a rejection of the expectations placed upon them, expressions of "anger, angst, disgust with life as it is lived." These teens didn't want to die—they wanted a different life.

* * *

What does the suicidal person want? What do I want? A guarantee that I'll never do it, a life free from obsessively questioning if I am, in fact, better? How can I know if I'm better if I don't know what I'm looking for?

One afternoon during our first year working together, I showed up to Elizabeth's office with no faith that any substantive progress would come from the session. I was doubting the possibility of substantive progress, full stop. I'd stayed home from work that day and quickly spiraled into a low, frustrated that I'd been on such a good streak and then sabotaged it. The misstep, as always, had pushed me back to zero. I was furious, and Elizabeth could tell.

"I guess I just don't understand what the fuck we're even doing," I said after some strained back-and-forth. I paused, but Elizabeth waited. "That's all. It's interesting to figure out what's going on in my mind, but what's the point? Why haven't you told me what to do, what to change?"

"I have an answer," Elizabeth said, "but I don't think you're going to like it."

"Fine."

"Keep coming to therapy. Right now, that is the most immediate thing to do."

She was right: I didn't like it. The directive stung especially because I'd been bailing on therapy almost every other week.

"When we started," she continued, "you came in and said you wanted to start a family. You wanted to get to a place where you felt ready. But that's *your* idea of where you need to be. What does it mean?"

In other words: What do you need? What do you *want*?

I thought, *I want to be normal. I want to function consistently. I want a year without the cycle of shutting down and rebooting. I want six months without scrambling to undo the minidisasters I created. I want to not feel like two different people, one successful and one stunted. I want to hold myself accountable. I want to let people help me without hurting them when they do. I want to believe that I'm going to survive. My entire adult life has been riding emotional tidal waves, but lately I wonder if it isn't my thrashing in the water that creates them.*

I said, "I just want to stop feeling crazy. And I don't know what to do with the fact that warning Brendan about these wild highs and lows doesn't really help, it just makes me feel like I have an easy out. Like, okay: How do I open up to Brendan without using that confession as a free pass to keep doing it? How do I just allow this to be an ongoing part of our lives?"

"I have one thought about that. Are you open to it?"

I'd been staring at the painting hanging on the wall across from me, a simple tower of teal, red, and yellow in a brown frame, just as I did every week, setting my gaze on it while I spoke, until the colors blurred. Now I turned to Elizabeth and nodded.

"All I'm asking—all I'm suggesting—is that you be open to the possibility that this doesn't have to be an ongoing part of your life, of your relationship, your family."

I nodded again, sat with it. "Okay."

"Are you just saying okay because that's what you think I want to hear?"

"Yes." I laughed, and so did she, and the tension eased.

"You don't have to believe it yet. Just be open to it."

I rolled my eyes; she smiled. "I guess I don't really know who I am without depression."

"I know."

Here I'd been thinking it was in my best interest to keep in close correspondence with suicidality so that it might become less jarring—that I might be less likely to kill it off if I'm less scared of its return. But maybe all this does is accommodate, even encourage, its return, making space for it in my home, my body, my brain. Even if I could save my life by keeping depression familiar, what kind of life would that be? Maybe the happy medium is in easing my grip on my imagined possible futures—refusing to double down on either a permanent *better* or a predestined defeat—and welcoming uncertainty, discovery. Maybe it's really a choice between agnosticism and conviction. The former, its expanse and possibility, strikes me as the obvious pick.

I turned back to the painting and tried to imagine it: leaving the office, going through the day without an underlying expectation and anticipation of failure; letting my history of suicidality disappear as it passes. Quicksand, sinking, behind me, without me in it. I felt it, I saw it, I tried to grab it, and it was gone, but now I know it's out there.

*   *   *

Theo and Brendan leave for Manhattan, where a Pokémon Go raid awaits. I give Theo my phone so he can play on our shared account, and he and Brendan head out to battle legendary Pokémon along- side anonymous players in either the virtual or physical vicinity. It's a common outing; sometimes I go, too, but it's nice to have the break. This time, within an hour of their leaving I feel the pull. I am alone, which is rare, and the thought occurs as out of nowhere. It doesn't matter that I'd been having a lovely day, a fine week. Still, there it is: I could do it. Right now, I could do it. But then: Theo, and my prom- ises to him that I'm safe. So I won't do it; well, not today. I won't do it, but that isn't quite a victory, not anymore, because I won't stop wanting to. When I left the hospital so full of energy, I wanted to prevent my eventual suicide, but it's the constant consideration of suicide that is unbearable. It's the wanting to die that's real and terrifying. I can't kill myself, because I don't want the people I love and who love me to hurt, but that doesn't mean the idea of oblivion doesn't provide a brief relief. It doesn't mean I've stopped returning to it. I don't want to be dead, not as I write this, but I'm not particu- larly committed to life. That's no longer enough.

"We must imagine the suicide wants to live," Antrim writes, and it is a radical, worthwhile sentiment, and maybe it's true of some who are or have been suicidal, but it falls just short of my reality. I am one step removed: I want to want to live.

Chapter 7

Artifacts

In the hours before I was escorted up to the psych ward in 2017, I sat briefly with a nurse whose task was to assess my risk level. He led me to a sparse office, the only pieces of furniture being two drab love seats facing each other. He motioned to one, and I sat. He lingered in the doorway.

"Usually we're not supposed to close these doors," he said, "but I can now, if you'd like."

It was the first of many instances in which a staff member would assume and imply I didn't pose a threat to his safety, that we both understood that I wasn't like the others, those who'd made the rule necessary. It felt wrong but also comforting. I didn't want to belong there. Regardless, I didn't care. I'd been through so many versions of that conversation already that day. I shrugged. "Either way."

"Let's do closed, then." He smiled and walked to the couch across from me. "I'm going to ask you some questions, and you probably have answered some of them already." He looked up at me and smiled. "Sorry about that."

"I get it."

"And we have to ask all of these questions to everyone, so don't be worried if some seem"—he laughed—"a little outside of your experience."

"I've done these before."

"Great."

We ran down the familiar list: my name, birth date, occupation, medical history, family history. What had brought me in today? What drugs had I done, and when, and how often? Was I a danger to myself or others? Did I feel safe at home? And had I ever known anyone who committed suicide?

I startled. It was the first time the question had been posed to me in a medical setting, and it took me by surprise. My eyes started to sting, and I looked up to the ceiling. "Yes," I said. "A friend. Alice. A few years ago."

I was embarrassed by what the question roused in me, such an immediate emotional and physical response. Even there, alone with a stranger, I felt I didn't deserve that grief. I knew how I'd mostly abandoned Alice in those final years, how, by the time she killed herself, it had been so long since she had been important to me. I suspected that I'd failed Alice, and I couldn't rid myself of the suspicion because there was no making it right. There was no closure, no alternate reality in which she had lived.

*   *   *

I spent the summer of 2010, my first summer in Portland following my first year at Reed, working full-time at the campus bookstore. A friend who was returning home for the summer had left me her bike, and the city opened to me in a way it hadn't during the school year, when I had been overwhelmed by work and reliant on inconsistent buses and expensive cabs in a pre-ride-sharing world. After seasons of rain, it was bright and fresh, and I sailed through the streets with minimal responsibilities and, for the first time in a long time, some cash to spend. I ran into a friend at a coffee shop one morning and found him sitting with Alice, petite with curly auburn hair, a broad smile, and bright pink lipstick that matched her floral 1950s-inspired dress; the kind of pretty that shocked. It was three years after the film critic Nathan Rabin named the "Manic Pixie Dream Girl" archetype, and Alice would often be counted among them, a designation she hated.* Our connection was immediate and intense, her existence in my life so potent, so dramatic, so obvious that it seemed strange that it had taken us twenty-four years to meet. We were party girls and gym rats, oversharers who were each as eager to hear the other's stories as we were to spill our own. We bonded over our respective mental illnesses, our crushes, dreams, and complexes about our beautiful older sisters. Alice was prone to non sequiturs, likely to ask strangers about their crushes or bathroom habits, and good at pulling me out of my shell.

So when she visited me during one of my shifts at the campus bookstore one August afternoon, I didn't clock her behavior as strange. She *was* strange. She was always a little more, a little louder, faster, more saturated. That day, she walked up to the cash register with a bottle of water and asked me, eyes wide and speaking rapidly, if I had gym shoes she could borrow. It wouldn't be the first time

---

* In her poem "Alice: The Ultimate Manic Pixie Dreamgirl"—which links Alice to her counterpart in Wonderland—Alice bluntly dismisses this category of fantasy girl: "In real life they commit suicide."

we'd swapped clothes. I grabbed my sneakers from the drawstring bag under the counter and passed them to her, brushed off her payment for the water, and told her to drop the sneakers back to me when she was done. I was planning to work out after my shift. But she never returned, and she never responded to the texts I sent while waiting for her. Annoyed, I went to the gym to see if she was still there and instead found my shoes next to her purse in a locker left ajar. I opened her bag and was alarmed to find a knife, but everything else seemed to be there, too: wallet, ID, keys. I debated taking the bag with me, but I figured she'd wandered off on a lark; maybe she'd run into a friend and followed them to the nearby pool hall. I assumed she'd be back to claim her things soon and would be more put out by my having moved them. Almost everyone treated those lockers like cubbies, anyway, and barely half were secured shut. I grabbed my shoes and changed.

Two days later, I still hadn't heard from her. I told myself it was nothing to worry about. She was flighty. Maybe we were simply past that initial can't-get-enough-of-each-other rush of new friendship and she didn't feel compelled to keep the conversation going. On the third day, a campus security officer came to the bookstore looking for me. Alice's housemate had reported her missing, and I was one of the last people to have seen her. Had she told me about any travel plans? Any usual haunts where she might be? But I had nothing to offer. I texted her again, suddenly feeling the distance between us. We'd been friends for what, two months? Could I say I really knew her at all?

Shortly after, I found out from our mutual friend that she'd been wandering the city in a psychotic break. Her parents picked her up and took her back home to Houston for treatment. Eventually she'd describe those days as stuck in a specific paranoia; she'd been certain, suddenly, that she was living in a real-life board game, and playing along required traveling through the city, looking for and dropping clues. That explanation would come much later, though. I didn't hear from her again until December, when she reached out via Facebook to tell me she'd be back on campus for the spring semester.

And then our friendship blossomed into a mutual obsession, the kind so intense it demanded evangelism, as if loving each other weren't enough—we had to announce it, and then again, and then again. We spent our days together and stayed up chatting online late into the night. All that remains of that period, however tangibly, is a history of Facebook messages that reveal an all-caps giddiness, our shared relief at finding someone who would never require that we close off any part of ourselves at a time when we both needed the acceptance the most.

February 21, 2011, 5:07 a.m., from me: "I called my mom yesterday and I was like, 'ALICE ALSUP HAS MADE MY LIFE SO MUCH BETTER.'"

February 25, 2011, 3:49 a.m., from Alice: "*Goes to inaccessible rooftop* (shouts) I LOVE ARIANNA REBOLINI!"

April 6, 2011, 4:01 a.m., from me: "hi, I like you lots"

April 18, 2011, 2:13 a.m., from Alice: "I miss you when we don't see each other!!"

For three months we were intoxicated by whatever it was that we had: I was in love but in denial about it; she was straight, or at least identified as such at the time, but generous with affection. We shared books, clothes, beds, code names for crushes, all-nighters in the library, dance breaks, morbid jokes, poems and essays, a vibrating and unbridled excitement about what we saw as turning points in our lives, and a frankness made possible by our mutually and deeply held belief in the strength of our relationship. When she asked me if a certain post she wanted to leave on a certain crush's Facebook wall would be a bad idea, I told her it would be weird and he might not be into it, but she was weird and he'd figure that out eventually. When I bleached my hair an unforgiving blond, she asked if I'd considered that my crush might hate it. I told her she was being unnecessarily negative; she apologized. Life was good after years of being bad, and each of us credited the other for the shift, at least in part.

Then, in April, my roommate Natasha's boyfriend—my friend—died suddenly from a cancer that wasn't supposed to be terminal, and everything else flattened. Alice's extravagances became nuisances; her honesty became mean. I was less generous with my time and patience. My circle closed. I took incompletes in my classes and went back to New York for the summer. I tried to forget everything about Portland. In September, I returned to Reed, but not to Alice. She had always been so much—together we'd felt like so much—but until then, we'd always allowed and encouraged each other to revel in our so-much-ness. Without warning or explanation, I turned my back on it. *So much* had become *too much*. I was embarrassed by it. What had I sacrificed, then, not just in Alice, but in myself?

That fall semester, she messaged me twice:

September 2, 2011, 12:16 a.m.: "Ari can I come visit you in not so long?"

October 27, 2011, 6:16 p.m.: "If you need to understand something from conference or the handouts or the notes, let me know. Good luck studying!"

I didn't respond to either, at least not on Facebook. Maybe I texted, but I don't remember, and those conversations disappeared a decade ago. Regardless, we stopped hanging out; we lost touch. That semester was her last at Reed, and by the time she decided to leave, we weren't even close enough for her to tell me. Still, I was glad to hear that she'd moved back to Houston and had found her place in the alt journalism and poetry community. I watched her thrive for the next few years from a distance. But one summer night in 2014, a high school friend who'd never even met Alice, who'd known her only through my gushing about her, called me to see if I was okay, saying he'd just seen the news about Alice on Facebook. I hadn't been online, but I didn't need to ask. Of course she'd done it.

* * *

If we're to take her at her word—and I'm inclined to—Alice didn't want to kill herself on April 11, 2014, when she sent me a Facebook message out of the blue. We hadn't communicated directly in two years, but we'd liked each other's posts here and there, and she'd shared some of the things I'd been publishing at BuzzFeed. "I posted your list of 12 things to do on your own, but my status sounded like a complisult so I deleted it!" she wrote. "It was so on point, and I feel like you bring it in all of your articles."

It was funny—true to form, a compliment from Alice would also carry some minor, unintentional jab—and I assured her that I hadn't seen it before she deleted it. I thanked her for her kind words, for wanting to share the article at all. I told her it was so nice to hear from her, and I meant it. I asked how she was doing. She told me she was fantastic, that she'd been blogging and interning for a thriving local culture magazine in Houston, doing poetry slams. She was "so happy and such."

I never responded, and I never saw, on May 30, her jarring Facebook status in which she asked, simply, "Favorite quotes from suicide notes?" The first comment is her own, sharing her favorite: Vincent van Gogh's "*La tristesse durera toujours.*"* Today, three responses

---

* Translation: "The sadness will last forever." The quote doesn't actually come from van Gogh's suicide note (he never left one per se, though he was carrying a letter to his brother, Theo, when he shot himself) but was relayed as his last words in a letter from Theo to their sister, Elisabeth.

from three other people remain; maybe there were more at the time that have since been deleted. I imagine it wouldn't have been the most popular thread. In a second comment, Alice assured everyone that she was asking solely for research purposes, regarding a poetry prompt. "Suicide is the worst," she wrote.

It's easy, years later, to resent the fact that this wasn't treated as an emergency, but warning signs always seem so blatant in retrospect. It's more difficult to grapple with the fact that a week later she posted another, more troubling status. The post apologized for one she'd previously made and subsequently deleted—one that I've never seen but have spent too long uselessly guessing at—explaining that it had been "narcissistic and poorly worded." The writing in the post is hard to parse, unusual for its grammatical errors, and mismatched in tone from the multiple daily thoughts she'd shared for years, whether serious or light. It's also rife with self-hatred. "I'm took [sic] attention seeking too far. I'm sorry, I'm falling into a pattern I need to get out of asap. I've having [sic] trouble . . ." As I write this, there are twenty-one comments beneath the post, some from Alice herself, explaining that she'd been too angry when she'd posted it and had acted without thinking, many others from friends telling her not to be too hard on herself. It's the final post on her Facebook page that's written by her. She would die in three days, and then the memorial posts, which continue today, would flood in.

Throughout those weeks, for those watching Alice post in real time, who wouldn't believe her—who wouldn't be desperate to believe her—when she said there was nothing to worry about? Who wouldn't be relieved, given permission to dismiss their concern as paranoia, when the person they fear might be in danger assures them that they're fine? Their disavowal of suicide is the result we go in hoping for. And then, too, who could believe that a person might crowdsource her own suicide note? That a person could be so flagrant? It would be such an unfathomable act of callousness, to turn friends into unwitting players in their death. Alice could sometimes be harsh; she'd never been cruel. Even her final post can be skewed out of the danger zone if it's read from a baseline assumption that she was fundamentally healthy—too strong, self-aware, and otherwise exuberant to be at risk. After all, she'd recognized the pattern and knew it was time to get out of it. Isn't that exactly the way it's supposed to go? And who am I to judge? I wasn't even there to offer support she could dismiss.

In a memorial published on *Free Press Houston*, Harbeer Sandhu, one of the few who'd responded to Alice's suicide note prompt with some of his favorite lines, described his rationalizations, all of which ring true: She was a poet, a "lover of words." Maybe she was working on a story, or maybe she "just had some kind of goth predilection." But also, I wonder if maybe the post really *wasn't* a warning that others had missed. Maybe Alice wasn't lying. Maybe when she said she was safe, she meant it. Maybe the poetry prompt was real, and maybe diving so deeply into the research had messed with her head, reminded her of the allure of oblivion. Maybe she was looking for ways to understand herself. Maybe those lines didn't make it into her suicide note; maybe she didn't leave one. Or maybe it was her sounding an alarm. Maybe it was a test for herself, for others.

The truth is that Alice was more on top of her diagnosis than most people I know—certainly more than I had been. When she'd returned to Reed after her psychotic break, she'd told me about the bipolar disorder support group that she had joined in Texas and was continuing through a Portland chapter. It had given her clarity about what she was living with, as well as the conviction that she was fully capable of managing it. I'd asked her to let me know if she ever felt her symptoms creeping up, if there were any triggers I could consciously avoid. Should I stop talking about my own struggles lest they pull her down?

"I'm too socially at ease to be brought into a bad state by most things anyone could do or say," she said, and it made sense. Alice was a lot of things, but self-conscious was never one of them. Messaging late one night, she recounted studying with a pair of freshmen who'd asked her what year she was in and how she'd told them she was supposed to be a junior but had gotten really sick and had had to take time off.

"It was the first time I didn't go into every detail, and it made me realize that that is still a totally truthful way to present what happened," she wrote. "Bipolar disorder is a sickness that creates chaos in your mind and life. But I'm totally managing it. I have this checklist of behavioral signs of good health/bad state symptoms, and if you'd like I could make you a copy and go over them with you. I think that once I start getting scattered and acting as erratic as I was last summer, that's when I'm in too deep."

I read that message now, and I wonder, not without anger: Alice, where was that list in your last months? Couldn't you see where you were heading? Did you refuse to use the coping tools you'd learned, or did they fail you? Or did you know what was coming but were too tired to do the work? Did you just think, *Enough*? Or had you fallen into another psychosis; could nothing at that point have reached you? If we could travel in reverse from that night, could we find a trail to follow, crumbs you'd left, that would take us to the moment that had set you on that path; could anyone have done anything to divert you? Alice, when you stood sixty feet above the ground all alone late in the night—Alice, was it windy up there, were you scared, did you mean to do it? Alice, in those last moments, those last seconds— Alice—what happened?

* * *

Shortly after Alice's suicide, her family published a collection of her poetry, *The Poet Walks Away*, but I didn't find out about it until after my hospitalization. As soon as I had it in my hands, it became an object of fascination; the pages are now barely legible with my underlining, highlighting, and marginalia. The book allowed me to separate myself from Alice and her death by considering both alongside Plath's poetry and Woolf's journals; it alleviated my painful obsession with her last moments by turning it into a more objective intellectual curiosity. She became her work, and her work became another repository of instructive artifacts left by people who kill themselves.

Alice's poems are, unsurprisingly, witty and charming, and though I recognized themes that continued from the poetry she had been writing when we were close—social anxiety, sexuality, frustrated ambition, alienation—the book held surprises. Only in the poems did I learn that she'd attempted suicide at least once before, by overdose, which she described in "Hope." The details of her overdose are affecting but brief, sandwiched between a swelling, anthemic opening declaration—"We came. / We came to. / We came to believe."—and her account of calling for rescue upon realizing that she was "shuffling off / This mortal coil with some unanswered questions."

There is a lot of pain, but most of it is cordoned off by the past tense: Alice "used to self-destruct"; her life "used to be [a] horror story." In "Lullaby," written at ten years old and then read at her memorial, the young, prescient Alice urged, "Remember there's always tomorrow / and today is moving fast." But if 80 percent of *The Poet Walks Away* is about Alice's pain, the rest is its polar opposite: vivid, sharp-tongued expressions of joy, wonder, sex, hope, the grand possibility of life. If she hadn't killed herself, the work would be read as triumphant, transcendent. We know this because that was the response she received when she was still alive. And now? Are they evidence of self-betrayal? Proof that she had never really been healed? A rueful account of a person who was always doomed? Was Alice building, for more than a decade, whether she knew it or not, one long, deconstructed suicide note?

It would be such a relief to think we could examine this work and derive a firm conclusion about the writer's wellness—or, more sordidly, her likelihood to kill herself—but art about suicide, and therefore our reading of it, can never be static. There will always be a fine, arguably imperceptible, line between catharsis and desperation—an exploration of a person's mind beside a testing of the waters, an attempt at connection beside a cry for help. The line between wavers like the tide, flowing and ebbing in relation to the writer's state of mind, their level of suicidality. The writing means something different in their life and their death, if that death comes from suicide. For as long as the author is alive and writing about suicide, their very existence will be appropriated as proof that others can survive, too. They become avatars of a cure that doesn't exist. Are those periods of wellness, those letters penned from within them, made meaningless for that wellness's fading? What do we do with their deaths; what do we do with their lives? As Simon Critchley notes, a person's suicide "produces a peculiar inversion of biography, where all of one's acts are read backwards through the lens of one's last moment." This reverse engineering is especially tempting when the subject is a public figure, but even then, still, it's precarious. The tenuousness of any meaning-finding mirrors that of the experience of suicidality itself.

I've never met any of Alice's family, but shortly after receiving *The Poet Walks Away*, I approached the publisher and asked if it might be willing to connect me with Alice's parents so I could let them know I'd be writing about her. They sent me to Alice's father, Mike, who I was relieved to find was eager to tell her story, volunteering any help he could provide. I shared my recollection of Alice's years at Reed and asked if he'd be able to confirm the timeline, along with sharing any details he thought would be useful in describing what had happened when she had gone missing. Mike laid out the events of that year as well as outlining Alice's psychiatric history and contributing factors to her eventual suicide, spanning as far back as her early childhood. He offered to share her paintings, her photographs, her college essays, videos of a play that her friends had crafted out of her poetry after she died. He explained that in April 2014, when she'd told me how happy she was, she had been in the "up, up phase of her bipolar cycle." In June, she was down. She was scheduled to return to a psychiatric clinic where, years prior, she'd spent six weeks going through what Mike described as a "pharmaceutical brain restart"—a "horrific experience for her"—but she killed herself the day before that second stay was supposed to begin. Beneath that enumerated list, Mike ended his email with a single sentence: "I should have caught her."

My data gathering was for this book, but it was more for me, and I couldn't help feeling greedy. It didn't matter that Mike was eager to talk about Alice, that he offered more than I'd requested or expected—wanting any of it, wanting more still, made me feel ghoulish. I'd long been consumed by a hunger for details about Alice's suicide and the events preceding it, but I'd always avoided looking that hunger in its face. Now there was no way to avoid it. I can say that the desire is largely based in the pain of knowing that Alice was suffering and the pain of losing the opportunity for a future reconciliation. It's the pain of knowing that that person I'd once known so intimately had become remote; of always wondering, if that hadn't been the case, whether I could have saved her. But it would be disingenuous to dismiss the grotesquery of my curiosity, too, the unavoidably macabre desire to make that knowledge incarnate.

In Diana Khoi Nguyen's *Ghost Of*, the poet grapples with her brother, Oliver's, suicide from a similar motivation. She undoes his "self-erasure" within the book, which is broadly built around family photos from which, two years before killing himself, Oliver had cut himself out. On the page, Oliver is both present and absent among poems in which Nguyen rages against this very paradox. In "Triptych," we see this process at each stage. First, there's the family photo from which Oliver has been removed; second, his shape remade out of words, surrounded by white space; and third, the inverse, his whited-out silhouette breaking apart the lines and words that wrap around him. These lines are streaming, desperate, confounding: "what has a form but no sound? there is no sound f / or everyone not eve / ryone has a sound there is no sound for there is no sound there for / everyone is there / anyone between the sound and the silence . . ."

It's an illustrated, multifunctional way of grappling with Oliver's absence, suggesting Nguyen's attempt to understand his decision, to place herself within it and literally and figuratively fill the gaps. In a later essay, Nguyen describes the shock and difficulty of having to "reconcil[e] with . . . the transmutation of [Oliver's] body" after his death and we can imagine the translation of his body, or its absence, into poetry as part of that work. This one, she controls. Oliver isn't there, but neither is the emptiness his death created.

These are endeavors toward understanding the person who's killed himself, but more fundamentally they're grasps at physical proximity, and for Nguyen they extend beyond the page. While pursuing her PhD, Nguyen received an assignment in a hermeneutics class to create a "radical eulogy," and she knew immediately that the project would focus on her brother—specifically "go[ing] in the direction of danger, of discomfort." In an interview with the poet Peter Mishler, Nguyen recalls trying to pinpoint "the most uncomfortable empathetic thing [she could] do" and landing on reliving, as closely as possible, his experience right before his death. "I could try to recreate and retrace my brother's steps leading up to his suicide," she decided, "and then build a coffin and then burn that coffin." And so she did.

Nguyen cites Frances Ya-Chu Cowhig's play *410[GONE]* as a source of inspiration, its main character also "trying to collect information about her brother's [suicide]." She wears his reading glasses; she eats his last meal, a burger, every night. She's desperate for answers and certain "a code [is] hidden between the wilted lettuce and processed cheese." Oliver also had a burger as his last meal, which Nguyen gathered based on the wrappers he'd thrown into his bedroom garbage can. That alone was a baffling detail, setting off a panicked spiral of doubt. "Did he eat McDonald's because it would facilitate the two bottles of liquid phenobarbital that he drank?" she wondered. "Or did we get it all wrong, not knowing him all along."

It's the coffin that tests the boundaries of propriety, challenging us in the audience to dive deep into the ugly muck of it without judgment. Nguyen built a replica of the cardboard box that had held Oliver, within the coffin, within the furnace that turned his body into ash. She kept the top open and lay in it for twenty minutes every day, talking to her brother, surprised to find the practice "cathartic [and] therapeutic" rather than "terrifying." Her goal, ultimately, was to create an empathy that could bridge life and death, an opportunity to "commune" with Oliver, and in this she was apparently successful. We are desperate to better understand the suicidal person as they were in the moments leading up to and beyond their death, and so we pore over the most minute details surrounding it. The idea that we might never understand this person we loved so dearly—that we may never have understood or even loved them as well as we thought we did—is too painful to bear. We didn't see the entirety of the suicidal person in their life, so we try to learn it in, and through, their death.

"I did not have language for what happened, or how I felt about any of it," Nguyen wrote, but her body, that ritual, made up for that lack. In *Suicide*, Critchley ascribes the "lack of language for speaking honestly about suicide" to a collective unwillingness to sit with something that is "at once both deeply unpleasant and gruesomely compelling." The gruesomeness—the "nasty, intimate, dirty details of the last seconds"—and our desire for it are cloaked in stigma. But probing that desire is key. A full understanding of suicide requires it.

* * *

The more I write about suicidality, the clearer it is to me that doing so is fundamentally an effort to stake a claim in a conversation dominated by fear and disgust. In *One Friday in April*, Antrim often uses the second person to bring the reader in and ask us questions. Only once does "you" become the actor within the story, the stand-in for Antrim himself. Its point of arrival, as Antrim walks us through the process of receiving electroshock therapy, is telling. Taken as a whole, his slim memoir can be read as a kind of manifesto, a protracted appeal to reimagining suicide. He never lets the reader forget that he has us in mind, never lets us get too far from the questions that concern him. Here, though, he brings us almost too close for comfort, forcing our participation. Describing one of the most extreme, polarizing, stigmatized, and misunderstood psychiatric treatments available, he moves the reader from audience to actor. It isn't enough to listen to his account; we must imagine ourselves inside it. How can the suicidal person make the rest of the world understand?

In *All My Puny Sorrows*, Yoli stands next to Elf in the hospital after her most recent suicide attempt, which has left Elf intubated and speechless. Sometimes Elf tries to use gestures to communicate, but Yoli doesn't know how to translate the messages. Though Yoli and her mother can speak to Elf, they go silent. "How many words do we have left?" Yoli wonders, and the double meaning is potent: How many words will they have time to speak before Elf dies? And how many words remain that haven't already been tried, that haven't already failed to persuade her to stay?

Are we running out of words? I've yet to land on a combination that accurately encompasses an experience so weighty and subjective. The instinct is to locate this ephemeral thing in the body, to find a place we can point to and say, "This is where it hurts." Antrim describes a deep "itch in [his] temple," "a weight . . . pressing in" on his chest; he wonders, "When had the light begun to feel like sand thrown in my eyes?" Plath's stream of vile self-criticism pours over her like an "icy flood." In my public and private writing, I've described my depression and suicidality as open wounds, expanding pressure, muffled hearing, static vision, and, like Antrim's, an unreachable itch. *The only way to describe it that even seems to make sense*, I wrote in the summer of 2013, a year after graduating from Reed, *is that the world flattens me. In the mornings I wake up thin, reaching, threadbare, frantic, unfamiliar to myself. Am I still so vulnerable, despite my job, my boyfriend, my plans?*

And what to do with the *pull*, the *low*, the *abyss*, all those nods to downward motion? The most easily intuited reading would suggest that they represent various dips in mood. I call my periods of depression lows, and it feels right. If I were to measure and chart my happiness, energy, hope, and will during those weeks and months, the lines would quite clearly plummet. But there's something in the physical orientation, the motion of it, too. Down below is darkness but also stillness, a cradle, earth. When we feel the *weight*, the *sinking*, must it be a harbinger of doom, or might there be something close to the ground that we need?

To what end does the suicidal person torture herself, trying to pin down the elusive string of words that might make her experience legible? How much of her pain must she be able to articulate, and to what level of granularity, in order to appeal to the arbiters of grace? It's one thing to explore for the sake of better understanding yourself; it's another to, consciously or not, build a case in defense of your own humanity. The latter is an unconscionable requirement of anyone, especially those whose illness, or whose treatment for that illness, can leave them working from a cognitive or energetic deficit.

In a journal entry during the low preceding my hospitalization, while I was considering calling a new therapist and already dreading the process of explaining myself, I wrote, *How can I reliably explain what I'm going through when I can't even think straight?* After the hospital, I began to notice that I was having an uncharacteristically difficult time thinking of words. Suspecting it was a side effect of one of my new medications, Lamictal, I turned to the internet to see if I was right or if I was just imagining things. I found confirming accounts from others taking it, too. Medication literature often refers to this side effect as "poor word recall," but in any of the many psychiatric medication forums I've obsessively checked over the years, it's put more bluntly: users describe becoming "dumb and dumber on Lamictal" or coming down with "a bad case of the stupids."

Brendan and I found ways to adapt. I'd get out of the shower, tell Brendan it was time for a new——hm. A new shower thing. I'd wave my arms up and down. A shower sheet, but it hangs up. Shower curtain. Once on our way to a party, I spent a good two minutes trying to explain to Brendan why he would like the venue. "They've got . . . you know," I said, holding my hands in front of me, thumbs extended at right angles. I wiggled them back and forth. Brendan shook his head and shrugged.

"No. You know," I said, frustrated, reaching. "You know! It's, like, a table. With lights."

"Ice hockey?"

I sighed. "No."

"It's okay! You can show me when we get there."

I closed my eyes. I wanted to be able to communicate this simple idea on my own; it didn't seem like too much to ask. I turned my right palm face up, made a fist, and yanked my elbow back, again and again. "It's got the marble and the lights."

It had taken a full block, but we arrived at the word: pinball. This was a relief, a victory akin to winning charades, though frustrating and alarming not to be able to get there on my own. As my Lamictal dosage has increased—and, surely a factor, as my age has increased as well—this loss of words has become both worse and more familiar. Now, at least, it doesn't send me into a brief panic. If I pause midsentence and take a beat, I'll usually find what I'm looking for, but the disorientation remains. On July 25, 2006, an anonymous user who'd just recently started taking Lamictal to treat bipolar disorder went to MetaFilter to ask for advice, or even simply commiseration, describing memory loss and "fuzzier thinking." The title of her post is powerful in its succinctness: "Am I losing my mind while trying to save it?"

Surely, we don't need to embody another's pain to trust that they feel it. Surely, we don't have to remake people into warriors to decide that their struggle is worth our attention. A person in pain can just be a person in pain; that is enough to warrant compassion and support. What could be more human? In "Floodgate," a poem Alice wrote the year before she died, she laments the ways in which people dehumanize her for her difference, making a modest but vital claim: "I'm pretty sure my heart works / the same way as theirs."

When I think of Alice's writing today—both in poetry and on social media—I can't help wondering if, art and self-examination aside, her explicit references to and discussions of suicide weren't in some ways a means of feeling powerful, of having a secret all to herself, of dangling that secret in front of others and then snatching it back. Antrim describes this as "hoarding death," the suicidal person's instinct to insist that they're fine even up to the moment of their death. "Is suicide our refuge?" he wonders, and I know my answer is, immediately and undoubtedly, yes. It is our refuge, and so we live in it, we indulge in it, we ruminate on it, and, if we are writers, we write about it. But writing about it requires a difficult compromise: there is no way to add our experience of suicidality to the public record without also losing some claim to it.

Two days after I left the hospital and blogged my confessional, I went to a party where a drunk-ish friend of a friend, Anthony, pulled me aside and asked if I'd be open to talking about "everything." I said sure; he was the third person to bring it up, and my responses had started to feel rehearsed, as if I were on a micro–press tour.

"What was it like there—like, was it scary?" he asked.

"Yeah, at first, but mostly it was boring. I played a lot of Monopoly."

"Are you glad you went?"

"Oh, definitely. I mean, it saved my life."

"Was it hard to write about it?"

"I know this probably sounds fake, but not really. I'm obsessed with writing about myself."

The longer we stood together and the more he drank, the wackier the conversation became. I was grateful for the disruption of our stilted formality and my self-deprecating attempts at keeping it light. We talked about projects we were working on. Anthony, a visual artist, was trying to be a better writer, and I, a writer, was playing around with drawing despite being hopelessly bad at it.

"I'm trying to get better at being bad," I said.

"Yes. Yes!" Anthony spoke slowly, with intention and searching eyes, as if he was sharing revelations as they appeared to him. He suggested we collaborate on a project: we'd brainstorm a story or "abstract concept" that he would write and I would illustrate. I said it sounded great, and we promised to hold each other accountable to the plan, both knowing that we wouldn't.

"Can I ask you something about your blog post?" His tone softened as he shifted his weight.

"Sure."

"Don't you think that everybody's sad?"

"Yeah, probably. Sad covers a lot of ground."

"But everyone's repressing it, right? And it's all just fucking hard."

I nodded. He drained his beer.

"This is weird to talk about, but when this is in me"—he shook the now-empty can—"it isn't, really."

"It's not that I don't think it's weird, I just feel like I have to do it."

"Can I get, like, way too personal?"

"Of course."

"You know how I drove across the country last summer, right? I had this moment in the middle of it where I realized how little I had waiting for me afterward, that I couldn't just do this for the rest of my life. And I'd just had this really bad breakup. She was supposed to be on the trip with me. And I don't know. I was in the middle of nowhere. It would've been so easy to do."

He paused and I waited, wondering if he'd regret all of this in the morning.

"It's, like, you're here." He thrust his left hand out as if to shake mine. "And you need to move here." Down came his right, connected at his wrists to form a V. "But then time is moving like this." He moved both hands slowly to his right. "So you never really get closer to where you need to be, even if you keep moving. Does that make sense?"

I wasn't sure, but I didn't think that mattered. "Yeah!" I said. "I think so."

"You know, I haven't read the whole thing yet."

"The blog post?"

"Yeah. I mean, I clicked on it. I heard about it, so I wanted to read it, but it's just been open on a tab on my laptop."

"That's okay, you really don't have to."

"No, I want to. It's cool that you did it, it's just really hard to read."

"I guess I'm surprised people are reacting so strongly to it."

Now it sounds ridiculous, but at the time it felt true. In my mind, the thesis of the blog post—the whole point of sharing it—was a declaration of victory. I was fine now. I was better! Why was everyone acting so serious? Anthony looked at me, scrutinized me, sharply. "Well, what did you expect, writing something like that?"

What did I expect? And was it reasonable? I'd told Anthony that writing the post was something I had to do, but that can't be the complete truth. If writing through the experience was a necessity, I could have done so in a journal; I've been running through diaries since I was eight years old. I needed that piece of writing to be seen. *I* needed to be seen. I needed a public record of where I'd been and how I'd survived it. I needed approval of, even praise for, defiantly claiming something I knew I was meant to hide. What I was after was a clean narrative conclusion. If others were able to feel less ashamed because of it, well, that would be a wonderful bonus.

Was that, too, what I had been chasing when, seven years prior to the blog post, during my first creative writing class in college, I had handed in an essay called "Reasons to End It All"? The first section was a stream-of-consciousness string of justifications I'd amassed in recent periods of wanting to die; the second, a straightforward re-telling of a story about me and my brothers exploring an abandoned recreation site. The essay began as a journal entry from earlier that semester: *If I killed myself tonight, what would be the reasons?*

I wrote the list as an unpunctuated burst of keywords:

revenge desperation weakness detachment ego boredom hopelessness defeatism fatalism isolation anger self-righteousness laziness self-centeredness self-pity exhaustion frustration sadness sadness sadness

I imagine the process of turning that late-night rambling into an essay was its own mode of therapy—writing myself into survival, my recovery solidified in ink, with the printed copies as a stack of tangible proof. But writing is no longer a solitary act when we invite an audience in to bear witness. It would be disingenuous to deny the provocation of the essay title alone. Now I look at it, and I think, *What audacity.* Whether consciously or not, I wanted to shock my classmates—stir them, awaken them—but whatever they did with that reaction wasn't my concern. Who knows what, if anything, I wanted from them in response? Certainly, if I was hoping for their worry, I didn't want them to voice it to me. Workshopping the piece, my classmates kept their notes and discussion limited to craft and technique, but my professor opened his feedback letter with a note saying he was torn between grading the essay and reporting it. I was vindicated; I was embarrassed. Someone—someone powerful, even—was worried about me. But had I scammed that person into misplaced concern? Had I manipulated him into missing what should have been so obvious—that I was fine? And now would I be forever changed in his eyes, forever fragile, forever seeking attention, unable to ask for it outright?

* * *

I don't remember a specific moment of first learning a person could kill themselves, but I do remember learning that it was something they could do wrong. For reasons I can now only guess at, my fourth-grade teacher explained that most people who slit their wrists don't end up dying. One must cut *along* the tracks, she explained, not *across* them. I've forgotten the details surrounding the sentence, but never the sentence itself.

As a young child I wasn't depressed, hadn't even heard the word *depression* in a medical context, but I was lonely and sad and angry about it. I was also a girl with OCD that would go undiagnosed for more than twenty years, nagged by sudden, distressing visions of violence that popped into my young mind out of nowhere. Walking with a friend, I'd see myself shoving her to the ground; standing next to my mother as she ironed, I'd imagine slamming the burning hot steel down onto her hand. I didn't want to do those things—I was terrified of them—but I was overcome with the fear that I would act on them regardless of my intent, as if those flashes weren't thoughts but premonitions. In those moments I'd sit on my hands or clasp them behind my back. I prayed every night, begging the god I still believed in, *Please don't let me become a murderer.*

The more anxious I was about what I believed to be my true, secret self, the more visible that anxiety became, manifesting itself in angry outbursts. And the more frustrated my mother became with those outbursts—losing her patience, yelling that something must be wrong with me to be so young and to already have such rage—the more I leaned into it, letting that rage simmer into provocation and cruelty. I tore up the Mother's Day card I'd made for her at school and left the pieces strewn across her bed. When she scolded me for fighting with my sister, I hissed that she didn't know what she was talking about because she'd never had a family. After she had a miscarriage, I told her I wished Jordan had been miscarried, too. I ran away once just to scare her but ended up horrifying myself after coming back to find my mother in tears.

Such viciousness rarely felt good for long and never solved my problems. I wanted to feel better, I wanted to believe I was good, but I didn't know how to do so. I probably wanted help, but I wouldn't have known what that help might look like or how to ask for it. I'm sure I wanted to be seen not just as a brat—which I was and in many ways am—but as someone who was confused and scared. So I focused on myself and remembered the tracks. One afternoon, I grabbed a plastic knife from the kitchen drawer and stood frozen with it placed at my wrist, waiting for someone to walk in and find me. That person was my father.

"What are you doing?" he asked as he stepped into the room, I imagine now more in confusion than alarm.

My cheeks warmed in embarrassment, and I suddenly felt foolish. What *was* I doing?

"Nothing!" I shouted, then shoved the knife into the drawer and ran out of the room.

My methods have evolved over the years, but this pattern of dangling evidence and then grabbing it back remains. In my senior year of high school, I wrote a suicide note on LiveJournal almost as an exercise, just to know it was there and ready to go if I needed it. I published it privately at first—it existed, but the only way to read it would be to log in to my account—but I quickly decided that it would be smarter to make the post public and simply hide it in the archives, backdating it to three years before I'd opened my account. Probably no one would find it there, but maybe they would. I liked the possibility, the outcome out of my control. Is this meaningfully different from when I posted a flippant "joke" about writing a will* on Instagram alongside an assurance that my talking about making a will wasn't a warning sign? By the book, it *is* a warning sign regardless of my protestations, signaling exactly what a loved one is supposed to look out for. It's a warning sign precisely for this reason; it accounts for the likelihood of my saying it isn't.

Long ago, I figured out how to experience the catharsis of sharing suicidality while avoiding the discomfort of vulnerability—recounting it only after it's passed, after someone else could have helped me out of it—and I've never dealt with mood shifts in any other way. There's a reason I am never more honest about wanting to die than when I'm sharing on a social media platform I know my loved ones use infrequently. Even if they do see it—and how many times has Brendan or Danea lamented having to find out how terribly I'm doing alongside thousands of other people on Twitter?—the medium is the message. I've offered no invitation to intimacy, sent no signals that such a gesture would be welcome. Maybe someone will reach out anyway; maybe I'll respond, or maybe I won't. I've done

---

* "Isn't it crazy how you get so deep into the outlining of your wishes that you're almost disappointed when you realize this weird alternate life for your child can happen only if you're dead?"

my best to relinquish minimal control. It's the only way to protect my complicated relationship with suicidality. How do you ask for help if you don't know that you want it—if you're afraid of receiving it? I'm open to communication as long as it's done through a one-way conduit.

Well, then. What's the point?

Chapter 8

Comfort

On Elizabeth's recommendation, Brendan and I have started couples counseling, and quite often those hours are spent with our therapist, Sara, guiding us as we try to dismantle the roles we've taken on in our decade together. Our relationship works because the pieces of ourselves—our goals, desires, strengths, and shortcomings—fit well enough together to create a sturdy-ish whole, but that means our deep-seated but defective coping mechanisms fit together, too. Somewhere in the course of Brendan's life he's learned that it's his responsibility to take care of everyone else, and that means he's more than willing to sacrifice his own needs for the sake of others'. I grew up unable to show anger or sadness without being made acutely aware of the detrimental effects on my mother—how my pain hurt her—so I've learned to funnel all my energy into managing my emotions before anyone else can see them. We complement each other for better and for worse—the latter enabling our respective self-destructive habits, cogs that interlock perfectly only to power a machine that's stuck. We slide easily and naturally into roles we both resent: I am the person who needs care, and Brendan is the person to give it. I am the person who is troubled, and he is the person on watch.

During a particularly intense session, Brendan describes frustrations I know are valid, which only makes them more difficult to hear. He can't help feeling like an afterthought while I write and retreat and prioritize alone time over family time. He's committed to being a team in supporting my work and my wellness, but when do we join forces to do the same for him? I thought I was getting better at this, but he's right on all counts. My heart rate and breathing quicken; my mouth goes gluey. I can't experience Brendan's account as anything other than a condemnation, proof that I am, in fact, bad, but I don't know how to say anything that won't make it worse.

"What's going on with you over there, Arianna?" Sara asks. "Where did you go?"

"I don't want to answer."

"Why?"

"Because if I do, I'll start crying, and then the focus is back on me." Panic is glowing in my chest. "I keep thinking I'm doing the right thing and keep finding out I'm getting it completely wrong, and I just don't want anyone to hear me. I don't want anyone to look at me."

Sara says that my perspective is important, and Brendan agrees, but the sobs begin. The air is tight, I feel as though I'm suffocating, as I repeat the same explanations on a loop: I don't want to say anything because I can't say anything without making it worse, and I don't want to make it worse—I don't want to make him worse, so please, can't we focus on what Brendan's going through, on helping him? I feel the familiar trap binding me, tightening. My depression affects Brendan whether I deny it or not. Either way, I am hurting, which means he is, too. The moment we decided to join our lives, we ceded the right to contain the effects of our moods, actions, decisions in ourselves. Since Theo's birth, this reality has only become heightened. It has never been more important for us to function as a team.

We have only two minutes left in our hour-long session, and Sara recommends that we continue talking after she logs off. Brendan pulls me toward him, and my insistences that, really, it's okay, I'm okay, are futile as they become muffled in his chest. I sit up and wipe my eyes. I tell him he's allowed to be angry—he *should* be angry— and anyway, he knows I cry over everything, but he draws me back to him, and now he's the one repeating that it's okay. Still, my body stays stiff against his. All I want is to not be there.

There was a time after I left the hospital—those naive months committed to uncompromising recovery—when I responded to Brendan's concern with comfort and positivity, desperately trying to convince him that he didn't need to worry about me. I did so not because I was bothered by his concern but because I didn't want *him* to be bothered by it. I wanted to protect him from the worries I was already managing—namely, that an irreversible change had occurred in our relationship the moment he discovered I was a person who had the capacity for suicide. Did a chasm open between us that morning when he rushed home from work, a distance we'll never quite bridge? I spent those first months thinking, *There's no way he gets past this. He will always be a little bit afraid.*

Antrim notes an almost imperceptible change in conversations pre– and post–psych ward. After the hospital, people "looked at [him] with skepticism . . . leaned backward rather than forward." When he wonders, "Was it safe? Was I safe?" it isn't clear whether he is posing the questions himself or imagining them in his loved ones' heads. In my experience, both points of inquiry can be torturous. So much of Brendan's and my anxiety surrounds the precarity of safety. He can't feel safe until he can trust that I am; I don't know how to feel safe without having the impossible guarantee that I'll never be at risk of killing myself again. More simply, I haven't figured out what being safe means, so the uncertainty runs underneath every action, every conversation, every day. The topic of suicide arises on a podcast we're listening to or in a show we're watching, and I tense up, wondering if he's thinking about me. Those nights when he held me while I cried about Jordan, when I was so scared we'd lose him, I knew I was also crying in fear that eventually we'd lose me, too. Did he also feel it? Was the fear contagious? Will *I* always be a little bit afraid?

It's a mess of doubt, a morass of unspoken questions between us, but their being unspoken means that I'm constantly assuming the answers. I've started checking these assumptions only in the past year of counseling, but I'm still reluctant to believe Brendan when he says that we're not in as bad shape—emotionally, financially, parentally—as I fear we are. There is no limit to my ability to invent someone's dissatisfaction with me, my stubborn insistence that I can discern resentment once I've decided it's there.

A few minutes after our session ends, my tears are drying and Brendan gets up from the couch, apologizing: He's late for a work call. I'm relieved. I'm humiliated. I avoid his eyes for the remainder of the afternoon, but then it's time for me to pick up Theo from school, and on the way home he pleads with me to go get some frozen yogurt and catch some Pokémon along the way. I concede, but we stop home first to drop off his backpack and pick up his scooter. I'm supposed to be on solo parenting duty tonight—Brendan and I claim one night each week so the other can get much needed recuperative alone time—but as soon as we walk into the house and he finds Brendan at his desk, Theo insists that he come along, too. Brendan looks at me questioningly.

"Your night, your call," I say.

"You want me to come?" Brendan asks, and I tell him yes, offering a smile that—I can tell by the weak smile he returns—looks as unnatural as it feels. We barely talk to each other on the walk up the street but finally start to warm up as we settle into the booth. I grab his hand and lean my head on his shoulder, watching Theo across the table, one hand shoveling a dripping spoonful of vanilla yogurt into his mouth, the other swiping Pokéballs on my phone in front of him. Later that night, after I've gotten Theo to sleep, I sit on our bed while Brendan works at his desk, and I tell him I'm sorry I'm like this; I don't know why I'm like this; I hate that I'm like this.

"I can't be around you without being constantly aware of every way I'm failing you," I say. "I can't get away from it."

He swivels to face me. "I don't mean this to sound rude, but I think you have this idea that I'm just sitting here every day resenting you, and that's not real. Like, in terms of things that stress me out, I'm not obsessing over the fact that you haven't done the dishes or laundry or whatever. I'm too busy worrying about work and my health and Theo. I just want you to be okay."

In other words, the only person obsessing about me is me.

* * *

"The depressed person was in terrible and unceasing emotional pain," opens David Foster Wallace's 1998 short story "The Depressed Person," "and the impossibility of sharing or articulating this pain was itself a component of the pain and a contributing factor in its essential horror." When I first read the story, I was deep in my own depression, and I had no idea who David Foster Wallace was, not to mention the impact his writing would have on my life. My English professor assigned it shortly after his suicide, which she'd announced to us, tearfully, the day it had come out in the news. The professor was a stoic woman to the point of severity; to see her so visibly moved by the loss floored me, as did the story.

Over the course of those eight pages, the depressed person—given the moniker in place of a name—flails while trying to get help from a circle of women who are more acquaintances than friends. She's in a period of clear crisis, but she wants to survive, which is why she continues to call these women despite her anxiety in doing so—something she discusses ad nauseam with her therapist. She wants to be better, but her belief in her inherent vileness gets in the way. She's hamstrung by insecurity and guilt, so she ends up undercutting the purpose of her phone calls with them—to be understood, to be cared for, to connect—with relentless self-deprecation. The main source of her self-hatred is her self-centeredness, which is a fair appraisal. She is always the talker, never the listener. She is stuck in a torturous loop of apologies for being an emotional and energetic leech, and the fix is so obvious it's maddening: *Just ask a question!* That the solution is obvious doesn't mean it is simple— this is a woman whose anxiety is both palpable and debilitating— but her ongoing utter failure to help herself in this way becomes torturous. The pain of witnessing it becomes more acute as the omniscient narrator slowly reveals, via lengthening footnotes, that the other women, and even the depressed person's therapist, are in dire crises of their own.

The depressed person is so easy to dislike—it's easy to suppose, even, that Wallace has written her with disdain—but it is impossible not to pity her. Those eight pages ascribe to her no redeeming qualities, but they do reveal a brambly, inescapable internal masochism as she tries with increasing frenzy to derive some emotional relief from her friends. Even the piece's accompanying artwork, interspersed throughout the text, portrays the depressed person's vision of the scene playing out on the other end of the line: We see an illustration of a woman in bed next to a sleeping partner, the bottom half of her face covered by a book but the top drawn in an image of exaggerated annoyance, one eyebrow raised almost to her hairline, her eyes dark slits. A rotary phone sits atop the bedspread, its receiver hovering in the air, literally ringing off the hook. Everything about the story pushes us toward the worst possible reading of the depressed person and her effect on others, but there's no textual evidence to suggest that this is anything other than her unreliable perspective. That she's unaware of her friends' pain doesn't necessarily mean that they resent her for it.

She's so effective at convincing us she's bad because she can't see herself any other way. But this isn't precisely what tortures her. If that alone were it—if she truly believed she was beyond hope— she'd have given up trying to get better. So much of her agony comes from not being able to see herself through another's eyes, in a perspective that, perhaps, might conflict with her own. She nurses a tiny, shrinking hope that she might actually be *good*, but it's easy for a person who believes she is inherently flawed to convince herself that any assurances of the opposite are simply proof that those assuring her don't know her deepest, truest self.

So there's comfort in the idea of confirmation; if someone else would admit that they hate her as much as she hates herself, she could stop wondering. This is why the depressed person's modest requests for her friends' honest evaluation morph into "begging shamelessly" for potentially traumatic feedback: "What terms might be used to describe and assess such a solipsistic, self-consumed, bottomless emotional vacuum and sponge as she now appeared to herself to be?" she asks. The story ends before we learn of any response, but the response is irrelevant. In some way, the depressed person wants to hear she's terrible so she can stop hoping that she's not. In some way, I want to kill myself so I can stop hoping that I won't. The hope, so easily ruptured, hurts, too.

*　*　*

As soon as I realize that I was misguided in assuming that Brendan was embroiled in resentment, I'm immediately pulled in two directions: relieved that he's absolved me of my guilt but also burdened by the knowledge that my self-castigation over not being a better partner has been preventing me from being a better partner. This could be a win—*should* be a win—but only if I can observe it as a fact and then set it aside. If, instead, I use it as an invitation to dive deeper into myself, pretending that such scrutiny is a necessary act of growth, I will only exacerbate the problem. I find myself powerless against the urge to give this revelation—that I was too focused on myself to see the reality of our current dynamic—weight and shape, to turn it into another block in this ouroboric tower I'm building out of reasons I should eventually jump from it. I could, instead, just leave.

It's tempting to decide that the best way to improve ourselves and our lives is to become experts on our emotional and psychological mechanics. We are the teacher, student, and subject; there's no one else to disappoint. Like most self-improvement projects, it starts from a fine guiding principle but turns poisonous when taken to the extreme. Is it self-awareness or self-destruction when our need to understand ourselves quashes our ability to connect with others, or when our richly developed interior world becomes the only one we trust? It can become a trap, and the suicidal person is particularly susceptible. Plath, for one, was often caught: "I have weapons, and self-knowledge is the best of them," she writes while "flooded with despair, almost hysteria," but that weapon fails her again and again.* In 2009, I wrote, *Being inside myself exhausts me*. Fifteen years later, I'm still digging in my heels.

Is it masochism, this raking ourselves over the coals of our pain, or is it a function of the belief that pain has inherent value, that it makes meaning, that it's productive? If our lives are so full of hurt, surely it must be good for something. If not, at the very least we can *make* it good for something, especially if we can turn it into a badge of honor or art. It becomes comfortable, too—even alluring. I'm trying to dispatch the idea.

Above my desk, thumbtacked to the wall, is a printed bit of dialogue from *Six Feet Under*, a show I've watched in full three times. In this particular scene, Michael C. Hall's David Fisher, suffering in the aftermath of a traumatic hijacking, stands facing a rainy window beside his dead father, Nathaniel Fisher, Sr.† Looking out at the loud downpour, David ruminates on the injustice of his experience, to which Nathaniel offers tough love:

---

* In social psychologist James W. Pennebaker's 2011 book, *The Secret Life of Pronouns: What Our Words Say About Us*, Pennebaker compares pronoun usage in published poetry from writers who committed suicide—including Plath—with work from those who didn't. Though both groups explored "negative" emotions, the suicidal poets used significantly more "I-related pronouns" than the others; Pennebaker suggests this reveals their being "psychologically close to their sadness and misery in ways that the nonsuicidal poets were not."

† As always, it's up to the viewer to decide if this is communing with a ghost or an imagined interaction. My reading is the former.

Better

NATHANIEL: You hang on to your pain like it means something, like it's worth something. Well, let me tell you, it's not worth shit. Let it go. Infinite possibilities, and all he can do is whine.

DAVID: Well, what am I supposed to do?

NATHANIEL: What do you think? You can do anything, you lucky bastard. You're alive! What's a little pain compared to that?

DAVID: It can't be so simple.

NATHANIEL: What if it is?

On July 17, 2017, one month out of the hospital and caught in a moment of exhaustion, desperate for a break from having to define the purpose of that stay, I wrote, *THERE IS NOTHING INHERENTLY MAGICAL OR MAGNIFICENT ABOUT LIFE AFTER FAILED SUICIDE.*

Can it be so simple?

* * *

The day after Brendan's and my counseling session, I'm debriefing with Elizabeth, trying to explain where my panic came from but failing to articulate it in a way that satisfies me. Yesterday I felt trapped because I had to react to Brendan's perception of me in real time, at the very moment that he was laying it out in front of me. I didn't have time to retreat into my mind and body, where I could juxtapose his description of my actions against what I imagined were my intentions. I didn't have time to figure out whether my reaction was valid, how I could defend myself; didn't have time to solve the problem on my own so that I could avoid sitting in ambiguity with an audience. Plath describes alone time as necessity—time when Hughes is away, when she can finally "make [her]self." Only then can she "build up

[her] own inner life, [her] own thoughts," in the absence of Hughes's questions, which make her "promptly and recalcitrantly stop think-ing and doing."

My commitment to, as Woolf calls it, "medicin[ing] myself" is born of anxiety and shame—I don't want to burden others; I don't want anyone to see me at my worst—but it also involves the partic-ular insecurity that my personhood might not be substantial enough to weather external interference, that my capital-T True self re-quires a purity that only solitude can provide. And there, too, is a fair amount of hubris, in no small part a defensive response to the above-mentioned shame and insecurity: How often have I gone into therapy confident in the belief that whoever is sitting in the chair across from me has nothing to tell me that I don't already know? How much of my getting help has meant doing only what I've de-cided I need to do and making sure there's a witness?

"It's the same reason I hate having this conversation right now," I tell Elizabeth. "I didn't get to prepare my answer—like, I want to be allowed to say, 'Let me think on this and get back to you.'"

"But why would you be required to come up with the answers on your own? Isn't that why you're here?" It's a fine point, but I still hate her for making it.

"Because I need to make sure the way I feel is the way I really feel. I know that sounds dumb, but it makes sense to me. I need to under-stand what I'm doing and how I'm feeling outside of the context of everyone else, and then I can come here and tell you who I am, and then you can tell me what to do about it."

Elizabeth is unperturbed. "Look. We all have different skill sets, right? I majored in anthropology, and then I went to med school. I love talking to people who can look at an essay or piece of litera-ture and analyze what's going on in there. I think it's interesting, but

Better

I can't do it myself. You can. That's your skill set. This—helping you work through these issues—is mine. It doesn't need to be yours. What's preventing you from accepting that help?"

I have no answer, and I'm not interested in finding one. Or maybe it's that I'm scared of finding one. Right now, it doesn't matter. I'm eight years old and stamping my foot. "I just don't want to."

Eight years ago, I showed Elizabeth a YouTube video that had become my go-to salve. Called *Jessica Meets Vanessa, and Assures Her She's Fine*, it delivers exactly what it promises. Jessica is a toddler meeting her newborn sister, Vanessa. Vanessa starts crying, and Jessica immediately shifts to hover over her, her little voice repeating "You okay, you fine" until Vanessa's crying stops. In just forty-seven seconds, it provides a more effective nervous system reset than most meditations or exercises I've tried. That repeated phrase—so simple, nonjudgmental, reassuring, kind. Taken out of its particular context, it isn't a rebranding or dismissal of struggle; it asks nothing of me. Firmly planted in the moment, it makes no promises it can't keep: *You okay, you okay, you okay; you fine, you fine, you fine.*

I'd watched that strange family's home video dozens of times. For months, I had called to mind Jessica's cheerleading when I most needed validation—walking to work on a morning when fear had almost kept me in bed, wrapped up on the couch on a night when I'd bailed on all the plans I'd really thought I could keep, standing at a party certain that everyone could see something was wrong with me. These were embarrassing admissions, but I'd written about the video in an essay that I then sent to Elizabeth—not even my therapist was exempt from my rejection of one-on-one discussion in favor of telling her to read something I'd already shared with the masses—and I was curious what she thought of the video itself.

"I have some thoughts," she said, "but first I want to hear what you like about it."

"Well, obviously, it's extremely cute. But also, it's so easy. Sometimes I just want to be able to tell someone that everything sucks and I'm hurting a lot and that all I need is to be told it's fine."

"Why can't you?"

"I don't know what kind of help I want beyond that. I feel like I have to figure that out before going to someone else, otherwise I'm just like 'Hey, here's a lot of sadness I don't know what to do with, can you hold it for a while?'"

"But isn't that what helping is? What if we agree, at least, that that's my job—to hold that sadness for you?"

"Maybe. I don't know. What did you think?"

Elizabeth smiled. "It's a beautiful video. I get it. It's comforting."

"Yeah. But then again, in real life I hate being comforted."

"Do you?"

"Yes." This—my squeamishness in the face of emotional intimacy—was so taken for granted that it had become a joke among those closest to me.

"Let me ask you this: Do you *know* how to be comforted?"

* * *

In *The Anatomy of Loneliness: Suicide, Social Connection, and the Search for Relational Meaning in Contemporary Japan,** the anthropologist Chikako Ozawa-de Silva describes "intersubjectivity"—i.e.,

---

* In her introduction, Ozawa-de Silva explains that *The Anatomy of Loneliness* didn't begin as a project about loneliness; she'd originally intended to investigate suicide in Japan at large. Only when it became obvious that loneliness was a key "critical underlying issue" did her focus shift and narrow. In other words, addressing the loneliness causing suicides became more urgent than addressing the suicides themselves.

the idea that "one is and becomes a self in relation to others"—in examining the existential consequences of interpersonal alienation. Broadly, the concept complicates the idea of individual personhood, but, to narrow the focus onto our concerns, it calls into question any argument *for* suicide that is based on personal autonomy. Debating the notion that such autonomy and "self-ownership" make a person's suicide unimpeachable, Simon Critchley challenges the idea that a person owns himself and denounces the individualistic worship of pure sovereignty. "Dependency is not a limitation of my freedom," he writes. "It is its condition."

How much of ourselves do we owe to others? The question works in two ways: How much of myself am I obligated to give to others, and how much came from them? If I am a mother, it's because Theo made me so. If I am a wife, it's because Brendan and I chose each other. If I am a writer, even, it's because other writers have guided my work; it's because you are reading it. If I am alive, it's because my friends and family have given me something worth staying for—whether that thing is my love for them, theirs for me, or both. But it's more than a matter of mutual care, of give-and-take. If subjectivity—which, Ozawa-de Silva writes, "includes a person's experience of themselves . . . , their environment, and their 'being in the world'"—is relational, then our sense of self will always be weakened by our isolation. In other words, self-awareness in a vacuum is insufficient; the disconnected person is incomplete. The suicidal person senses this, I think, within those panic-filled moments of feeling less than human. If a core aspect of selfhood relies on interactions with others, loneliness and isolation will literally make that person feel less real: another version of a living death. In September 2010, in the midst of what I described as *a sadness without foundation, abysmal melancholy*, I wrote, *I need someone to know me. To validate my existence. Tell me I exist, convince me. Please.* These days I wonder if healing on one's own is possible at all.

Shifting our focus outward is beneficial to recovery and general mental health both practically and existentially. For the former, and more immediately, doing so necessitates the mind's extraction from obsessive, hypercritical self-analysis. In the case of the latter, and less obviously, it strengthens our sense of self. We need to exercise our humanity with and among others to believe in it, to understand and define who we are. In surveying Japanese college students, Ozawa-de Silva finds that one detail that links the participants who rated their lives as "highly meaningful" is their reporting having close relationships. Often, those participants identified the "purpose and meaning of life" as "being needed." She notes the "intimat[e] connect[ion]" between "find[ing] an active and constructive role for oneself" and "recovery, happiness, and moral repair." It makes sense, and it bears out in mental health treatment environments. The medical and psychological anthropologist Neely Laurenzo Myers describes the vital importance of "social bases of self-respect" in successful psychological recovery, calling for care plans that would provide patients with a "sincere opportunity to be recognized as a good, accountable person by others." This requires our expanding the scope of mental health care beyond facility walls. The suicidal person, if only ever aware of themselves as a person needing help, can easily believe that that is the extent of who she is. We need opportunities to act upon and receive empathy in order to sit firmly within a sense of inherent worth. From this presumption, abstaining from seeking help is no longer something we're doing for our loved ones but in fact something we're *taking from* them. If the depressed person so clearly benefits from the chance to help others, it follows that others do, too. How shortsighted, indeed hubristic, it is to circumscribe another's capacity for care based on nothing but our own fear.

"We *are* burdens to our caretakers; we know this," writes Donald Antrim, outlining all the ways the suicidal person causes loved ones to worry, and I wonder, *Well, isn't everyone?* Note "caretaker" here as opposed to "friend." Note the clinical detachment, its association with work, its implication of the power imbalance between a custodian and their charge. But the most intimate, fulfilling relationships require taking and giving, and not only in terms of care. They require each of us taking up space in the other's mind and life. When examined through the lens of empathy, what resembles a burden transforms into an offering, an invitation, a sacred opportunity to foster community and, in doing so, fortifies both the helper's and the helped's sense of self. What is community, after all—what is the highest calling of humanity—if not the reciprocal carrying of others? Antrim admits that his friends had "reason to worry for [him]" but also that this worry "effectively compounded [his] own." Their worry acts as a detriment to his health. If we can rid ourselves of the idea that a friend experiences this worry as a burden, we might learn to see their worry as evidence of their investment in our welfare; we might learn to use it as an impetus toward recovery—or at least use it as a reason to stay alive—rather than as a tool for self-flagellation.

* * *

Still, we are lucky to have even a single relationship to fumble through. What of those who don't? Wallace's depressed person has a dire and obvious need for intimacy, but her "Support System"—consistently made formal, clinical in its capitalization—comprises "acquaintances from childhood or . . . various stages of her school career." The women live in cities far enough away to require long-distance calls; she hasn't seen them in years. It's a far-from-perfect group, but they're the only friends she has. What is she supposed to do? Her job separates employees into individual workstations; the social environment is "totally toxic and dysfunctional." On her therapist's recommendation, she musters up the nerve to attend church groups, local enrichment classes, and "community woodwind ensembles." Each attempt turns out to be excruciating, and sure, maybe it's her fault.* This would be easy to assume; she certainly doesn't seem like a person who, at least at this moment in time, would make good company. But, then again, trying to build "intimate, mutually nurturing relationships" as an adult *is* excruciating—even if you aren't depressed.

It's reasonable, then, that a depressed or suicidal person would seek virtual community among those who are intimately acquainted with the desire to die. Tucked away on Reddit is a forum called Suicide Watch, and it is the only community I've found that is guided by a true, evidence-based understanding of what support for a suicidal person should and shouldn't look like. A brief blurb on its home page describes its purpose as "Peer support for anyone struggling with suicidal thoughts." Primarily, it is a place where some users come to announce that they are about to kill themselves and others come to help them stay. It is a stark, often uncomfortable feed to scroll through, strictly moderated to maintain a tone of pragmatism that, to those who've been conditioned to equate mental health with unnuanced hope, might appear cold and withholding.

The community's moderators provide extensive resources to

---

* As the saying goes: If you run into a jerk in the morning, you ran into a jerk. If you run into jerks all day, you're the jerk.

explain, without judgment, which types of responses aren't allowed and why. Ultimately, these are guides to performing the delicate maneuver of empathizing with a person in distress without unintentionally inciting their suicide. The guide cautions against messages ranging from the more obviously misguided—"Your life can't possibly be that bad"; "Suicide is selfish"; "You don't really want to die"—to those that more likely come with the best intentions, most infamously, "It gets better."

The popularity of the community is particularly compelling in that it suggests both what the suicidal person wants and also, more valuably, what they *don't* want. Though it falls under the umbrella of social media, Reddit is more a hub of decentralized forums than it is a single feed, and it's unique in that the user's right to privacy is a foundational principle—meaning that a vast majority of its user base is anonymous. This anonymity, along with the subreddit's well-established ethos, ensures that a suicidal person can express themselves on r/SuicideWatch without fear of judgment and also without risk: responders can try to talk them out of killing themselves, but no one has the means to actually intervene.

On social media platforms with wider audiences and share options that encourage light-speed virality, this isn't the case. Depending on the account's reach, such a post on TikTok or Twitter might spark the frantic coming together of followers to find them, to alert someone close to the suicidal person who might be able to intervene, or, at the most extreme, to call 911. These are understandable and, to varying degrees, appropriate responses, but they are also terrifying and potentially harmful. There is safety, or at least some sense of it, in knowing that one can express an intent to die and then decide against it without repercussion, without being forced into a treatment plan they might not be ready for, and without permanently altering their relationships with those who saw the announcement.

It is, perhaps, the only way for a suicidal person to be vulnerable without losing autonomy.

Studying early websites in Japan created specifically for those planning to commit suicide, Ozawa-de Silva wonders why people not only wanted to share their pain with strangers but also to literally die with them. Often, the sites' visitors made plans to meet in hard-to-find locations just to have company when they go. Sometimes it would pan out, sometimes it wouldn't, but the risk of being stopped was always low. The phenomenon emphasizes two directly opposed but deep-seated desires, encapsulated in a comment left by one user called Boa: "I want to be alone, but I wish someone were there by me."

It stands to reason that even a community forged in apathy is nonetheless a community, and one that serves many at that. Just because the majority of people don't understand it doesn't mean it's inherently misunderstandable; for some people, the strangeness is the point. Here, though, the question of what we owe one another is magnified. Our influence on one another is stronger and the stakes are higher. In a conversation with Slate writer Amanda Hess, one r/SuicideWatch moderator, identified only as Laura, noted that some visitors confess being helped by *giving* help. They occupy a uniquely powerful position from which to help. Laura continued, "If you're standing on the edge, the person who can reach out a hand to you is not standing that far away."

But when we're simply venting, when we're not in active or explicit crisis, one person's commiseration can become another person's backslide. Are we supporting one another on the way to getting better, or are we indulging one another in staying down? When does our mutual acknowledgment of how awful life can, and does, become turn into nihilism? There is a mutual understanding between friends who are suicidal: eventually, either might do it, and the surviving friend will not hold it against them. But still, there's the chance that the survivor will see their leaving as a reason, or permission, to go. I look at the pact Kay Redfield Jamison made with a longtime friend, which she recalls in the opening to *Night Falls Fast*. Over dinner, the pair promises each other that if either decides to kill themselves, they will first call the other and give them a chance—over the course of a week at a remote lake house—to talk them out of it. "We thought we knew how we could keep it from being the cause of death on our death certificates," she writes. But when she hears, years later, that her friend has shot himself in the head, she's not surprised that he didn't stick to their vow. Suicide, she writes, is "not beholden" to our best intentions; it has the "ability to undermine, overwhelm, outwit, devastate, and destroy." I'm not angry when I hear that one more friend or colleague or beloved artist has committed suicide, and neither am I inspired to turn around and do the same. There's something in between, a weakening akin to losing a member of the team who, whether actively or simply by existing, compelled you to stay. I can't help appropriating the loss. We're only rarely aware of a person's decision *not* to kill themselves, meaning the data is skewed so that a person keeping track finds nothing but a tally of those who looked at the same options they do daily—live or die—and chose the latter.

What I am trying to pin down—what, at this point, dogs me as much as my need to understand the tendency toward suicidality—is why I, and so many of my friends, have had brushes with it. A majority of the dearest, closest people in my life have traveled through periods of self-harm, hospitalization, addiction, and/or suicidality, often in cycles. With them, the foundation of our relationships is our ability to help each other survive while knowing how often we don't want to. In writing this book and talking to dozens of colleagues and acquaintances about it, only one person responded by saying they were interested in the topic because it was so foreign to them; they could only imagine the desire to die, and they were eager to better understand it. I wanted to say, *I was starting to doubt that people like you existed. Thank god you do.* In private conversations, emails, and direct messages on social media, friends and strangers have shared details with me about their past attempts and ideations or their grappling with the loss of friends and family members who'd killed themselves. Each time, they begin with apologies for possibly overstepping a boundary—or, as the concept has expanded in the zeitgeist, for trauma dumping. Sometimes I am able to engage; other times I can't. Every time, I've mourned the fact that their coming to me means they couldn't go to someone else, someone more connected to them in daily, physical life. I often wonder if, simply, we find each other. It's a romantic notion, but more likely the reality is that countless people are living with a silent but profound despair and waiting desperately, constantly, for an opportunity to release it.

* * *

Do I know how to be comforted? Do I believe it's possible? I've long known that my most compelling reason for staying alive— the reason that has consistently kept me here—is the fact that I have people in my life whom I love and who love me. But love on its own isn't comfort. In my most desperate moments, I've invoked that love in solitude, a unilateral experience. Two days before going to the hospital, I wrote, *I could do it tonight. (I won't.) I could call someone for help. (I won't.)* Rather than contacting any of the people I knew who would certainly want to help, I built myself a sort of shorthand argument for staying by listing their names in one uninterrupted

Better

stream: *Brendan Nena Dylan Jordan Mom Dad Emily Andrew Melissa Katie Natasha Annelyse Rose Juliet Caitlin Jackie Marcy Mila everyone everyone everyone everyone everyone.*[*]

These people are among many who have saved me, possibly without even knowing I was close to death. Still, this is love as fact rather than process, stripped of its function. I've used people as counterarguments to my desire to die, but the key word here is *used*: by turning real human beings into items in my tool kit, I alone control my access to their love. The key word here is *alone*. I've decided that this is all I need of love, and I've insisted upon it for so long that I've come to believe I'm incapable of accepting anything more. It's a skill I never learned, I insist, or maybe it's a human ability I wasn't born with. I explain this to Elizabeth, I explain it to Sara, and each reacts with skepticism.

"You keep insisting you don't know how to be in a loving relationship, that you weren't made for it," Sara says. "I don't buy it."

Elizabeth says, "I'm not convinced it's that deep."

For most of my life, I've found comfort in my freedom to abandon anything at the first sign of impending failure, as a response to guilt, fear, or simple discomfort. Each time I've only made the situation worse. I've quit jobs without notice because I'd been late too many times; I've dropped out of college after missing a few classes, fleeing abruptly and tanking my GPA because I couldn't face the bureaucratic process of officially withdrawing. I've bailed on friendships because I took too long to respond to a text; I've ghosted therapists because I feared I'd revealed too much. I've tried and failed to run away twice, putting a deposit on an apartment three states over when I was nineteen years old and then ignoring the landlord; then, two

---

[*] It's worth noting that this list includes my cats.

years later, packing up my car in the middle of the night only to call my best friend sobbing on the Throgs Neck Bridge when I realized I had no idea where I was supposed to go.

"You set up your life like this intentionally," Elizabeth says. "You chose a life—a partner, a child, a home, a community—that would root you in place, that would make it very hard to leave, and now it's working exactly as you wanted it to. And you're really, really struggling. I feel for you. You've separated yourself from your escape routes."

I want to leave, but I'm boxed in. I know I should stay, but I'm feeling for the cracks. I'm claustrophobic and thrashing. If the only help I accept from someone else is their barricading against suicide, then inevitably I will rage against them. Inevitably I will hate them for standing there. I will hate myself for having asked them to. It's an unsustainable strategy, but I haven't mastered the alternative: the active, ongoing support, the thing that might preclude the crisis that would make the last-ditch effort of crisis survival necessary. The safety mechanism is valuable but insufficient, unreliable. Crash into those barricades enough times, and surely they'll collapse.

This, of course, is the answer I keep avoiding. I want to define and then solve my problems on my own because part of that process requires reminding myself that I can always flee. Sometimes it has required following through. Maybe the escape is suicide, or maybe it's blowing up everything I've built. It's the only thing I've ever known how to do. Brendan doesn't deserve to hear, numerous times a year, that his wife is desperate to escape, but instead of trying to get out of the cycle, I've decided that the solution is to shut up about it, sitting alone with that desire until it passes, always risking the possibility that this time, it won't. My most immediate source of discomfort isn't that I can't die; it's that I can't hide. Antrim is troubled by his conviction that "only lonely rooms are safe"—this being the "one feeling [that] has defined [his] life"—and when I read the sentiment, it resounds mournfully in my soul. I built a life that I hoped would keep me here, but I didn't realize that its success hinged on my leaving this belief—leaving my lonely room—behind. Am I willing to?

* * *

Before Brendan, I'd never told a partner about the extent of my depression, but it forced its way into our lives when I checked myself into the hospital. That I can't control his reaction to this fact is maddening, not least of all because I don't know what I want that reaction to be. When he commiserates with me, I feel as though he's dismissing the reality of what I'm going through, as if the subtext is "Everyone else survives this, why can't you?" When he asks if I'm okay in the way I know means that he suspects I'm not, the idea of responding with earnest vulnerability is, well, icky. Most of the time I respond either with disingenuous denial (I know I've been staying up until 3:00 a.m. playing video games in the dark, but I'm fine and truly have no idea why you'd think otherwise?) or irritated nihilism (*Obviously* I am not okay, just like you're not okay, just like everybody is not okay, so what the hell do you want me to do about it?). In both cases, the message is clear: *Don't ask.*

During our first year navigating this new dynamic, I'd create entire arguments in my head where he'd tell me I was selfish, and I'd tell him he couldn't fault me for mental illness; he'd say I wasn't doing anything to help myself, and I would insist he was expecting too much from me. I played both roles because I believed both sides. One afternoon I sat on Elizabeth's couch venting about these hypothetical fights in which I finally told Brendan how awfully I was doing and he finally left me, and she asked, simply, why I couldn't tell *him* all of it.

"Because I know he'll be mad at me," I said, "and then I'll have to deal with all of that. Telling the truth is not worth the aftermath."

"Are you sure?"

I wasn't. So I tried the following week, on a particularly bad day. I'd woken up late and missed an important meeting. A story I'd pitched during a brainstorm was rejected. I wanted to cry, but I refused to do it at the office. I opened Brendan's chat window with the intention of sharing my frustration, but doing so made me furious; why did it make me so furious? So instead, I performed an attack on myself and turned him into collateral damage, spraying a barrage of DMs he wouldn't be able to keep up with, messages that I knew would scare him. I wanted to scare him:

fuck this

fuck everything

i'm done

i'm quitting my job because clearly i can't handle anything and clearly i'm not better which means i never will be

and i know i'm letting everyone down but what do any of you want from me

please tell me

i don't know what else i can do

He told me it was okay, asked if I was going to be okay, and I calmed down and told him never mind, I'm sorry, I overreacted, don't worry. I went to therapy that afternoon and cried on the couch, asking Elizabeth why I kept taking my sadness out on Brendan. I didn't want to be alone in my panic and anxiety—why, outside of this room, did I treat intimacy like mutually assured destruction? She didn't have an answer, but instead asked again, "Why don't you tell him all of this?"

I went home and apologized. I edged into the kitchen while he was washing the dishes I was supposed to have done the night before. His hands were busy; I could talk to his back. Maybe, if he knew me as I hoped he did, he wouldn't turn around. I told him that I'd been talking to Elizabeth about everything and she'd helped me realize that he's right, I'm not doing well. I told him that having to be close to someone—not just emotionally but physically in this one-bedroom home—while going through a low made me feel as though I was running out of air. I didn't know how to be so absent, so worthless, next to someone who rightfully expected a baseline of interaction from me, and, because of this, the sadness roiled and churned and turned to acid in my guts. While I spoke, he scrubbed the pots filled with hardened oatmeal and refried beans, the mugs ringed with evidence of coffee left standing for days. This mess; my mess. He turned off the water and I expected the worst, but the worst didn't come.

"I just want to help," he said, turning to face me, "but I don't know how."

"I don't really know, either," I said. "I'm trying to figure it out."

"If you need time to be alone, you can tell me. That you're going through something and you need to check out for a bit. I just want to know what's going on."

"Okay," I said, trying to imagine what it would look like. "Maybe." Solitude in the past had always devolved into a complete shutdown, an entry point to self-destruction. Perhaps, with this openness, with validation, such a thing could finally, simply, be a break. I haven't yet figured out the balance. I don't know that I've really tried. Part of me is scared that if I stop treating solitude like a kind of martyrdom, I'll lose my taste for it completely.

What do we owe each other? Empathy is the easy answer, but beneath that, and equally important, is trust. When we're lost within an overwhelming sense of our worthlessness, we must trust that the person insisting on our value is right. When we are on the other side of this dynamic, when we are well, we must trust that—despite our potential resistance—our support is powerful enough to break through, understanding that it might not. When we're struggling, we must trust that others want to help us effectively; when we have help to offer, we must trust the struggling person's level of discernment and buy-in. This trust is a requirement of respect. Of course, the risk remains that we will miscalculate. The friend we've texted for help never responds, or maybe—as happened to Antrim—the friend overreacts, overestimating the risk and calling authorities. People make mistakes; people disappoint. At our best we are braving innumerable leaps of faith and course correcting wherever we land. I'd been trying to build a wall around my depression and telling myself it was a way to keep Brendan safe, but maybe it was a way to keep myself comfortable. Either way, it wasn't working. It still isn't working.

That day, I wrapped my arms around his waist and rested my head on his back. "You're the first person I've ever been this close to," I said, but what I meant was: *You're the first person I've ever loved.*

Chapter 9

Real Life

One Sunday evening in the early days of February 2021, I sat on the bathroom floor and watched Theo, five months shy of his second birthday, as he lined up dozens of toy vehicles along the rim of the tub. Only the top half of his face was visible from my vantage point: his brow furrowed in concentration, his bright hazel eyes laser focused on the procession of miniature vans, convertibles, trucks, race cars, and excavators, each connected by a dripping trail of bathwater and soap bubbles. Theo was quiet and intent on the task, organized by a principle only he understood, and I wondered at the emerging features of his distinct identity, the unique mannerisms, opinions, and ideas we were discovering together.

For months he'd been deep in his most intense fascination: city buses. All the parenting guides and developmental timelines told me that, at nineteen months, Theo was likely working with a roster of thirty to fifty words, but "bus" undoubtedly got the most play. We were, and are, a family who loves to walk, and we are blessed to live three blocks from a bus terminal. Stand at the right corner, and it's a veritable feast: blue buses, white buses, old buses, new buses, each papered with a rotating array of colorful advertisements. For months, I spent daylight hours steering Theo up and down the main drag in his red push car, pausing every few blocks to watch the passing traffic. His communication those days was mostly tonal: "Bus?" lilted upward in question meant that he wanted assurance some were coming; it fell in a whine when he was frustrated that they were taking so long to arrive. When the word came in a quick succession of breathy, staccato bursts, it meant he'd finally spotted one: *Bus! Bus! Bus!*

That afternoon, after thirty minutes and more than twenty bus sightings—not to mention the occasional ambulance, fire truck, and even a cement mixer—he'd thrown a tantrum when it was time to go home. It didn't matter how bitterly cold it was growing as the sky darkened; his hunger was never sated. I mitigated his frustration by turning on the TV and playing his favorite video, circa 2016, from the niche but prolific YouTube community of public transit fans we'd recently discovered: forty-five minutes of uninterrupted hand-held camera footage capturing traffic at a busy Queens intersection.

As Theo became entranced by the video, and I moved on to cleaning and making dinner, a familiar malaise crept in. I tried to focus on an audiobook but kept having to double back, inevitably realizing well into the chapter that my mind had wandered into anxiety about work. We were nearly a year into the pandemic—still two years from when the World Health Organization would demote covid-19 from its status as an international public health emergency—and I had, fortunately, survived BuzzFeed layoffs. Growing factions among the American population were becoming complacent, with some of those who were lucky enough to be largely unaffected by the virus simply deciding that it was time for covid-19 to be over. Skepticism and conspiracy theories about the validity of the disease itself, not to mention its treatments, pushed groups further into extremes. Schools were reopening, people were unmasking, and much of the palpable early-pandemic concern for workers' well-being had disappeared.

It didn't matter; it had been lip service, anyway. When the Buzz-Feed offices had shut down in March 2020, management had sent out a tips-and-tricks guide to working from home—a jaunty diagram with bright yellow text boxes dancing across the pages and scattered emojis complementing tidbits such as "TV? BE MINDFUL: If you wouldn't do it at the office, don't do it at home"; "GET DRESSED: If you don't get ready for the day, your day never really starts"; and "GO OUTSIDE: Be sure to get fresh air." It was cheery and optimistic, but any implicit encouragement weakened in the following months of layoffs and pay cuts. Loosened expectations tightened again even though countless workers were still caring for children or loved ones. In the wake of George Floyd's murder and the international uprising it inspired, leadership sent out a companywide email assuring staffers of their sympathy, support, and commitment to prioritizing our emotional and psychological health. In practice, such lenience had an unspoken limit; namely, it was available only up until the moment it put a deadline at risk. In my corner of the market—the book world—we were trying to figure out how to best support the books and writers we loved at a time when stores were closed, unemployment was up, and the vital in-person book launch was a thing of the past.

One afternoon, barely making a dent in my workload between bouts of crying, I reached out to my manager to explain the lag. I was struggling to get out of my head, I told her; I couldn't look away from the news and refocus. Maybe I wanted permission to take the rest of the day off—indeed, we'd been allotted one "mental health day" per month—or maybe I simply wanted reassurance that I wasn't in trouble, that my struggle was justified, a perspective check reminding me that nothing we were doing was an emergency.

"Well, there's a lot of work to do," she said instead. "It would be really helpful if you could grab an essay to edit as soon as you feel like you can."

I felt chastened and angry, but not entirely with her. Our poor performance as a team would become her failure, and her job at the time was only marginally safer than mine. There are so many protective layers between those who make the rules and those who suffer most from them. Middle management's sliver of power is easily revoked and swiftly betrayed; in the C-suite's shrine to profit, they, too, must bow. I was covering three people's jobs—or, more accurately, failing to—and regularly insisting on the unsustainability of the setup, asking for relief. Instead, I was assigned a student intern who was promised guidance I couldn't provide nearly as well as they deserved. On my side, it was another weight atop a pile of work—presented with increasingly false urgency—that seemed to be squeezing the air from my lungs. I knew that what we were doing was important and necessary, insofar as culture and its spaces are important and necessary, but in the context of the world's many overlapping crises, it wasn't *that* important. We weren't saving lives. Yet every Sunday night brought that familiar souring.

On that Sunday night in particular, the souring had grown so subtly that before I could even notice, let alone stop it, it had me sitting on the cold tile floor, catching errant splashes and running through reasons I should die: Come to think of it, when was the last time I *didn't* feel this dread? Even today, hadn't I been losing patience with Theo too quickly? Shouldn't a mother—wouldn't a *good* mother—be able to put work stress aside or at least be better able to manage her moods? Didn't the fact that I kept returning here, to this sadness, mean that I was already failing, had already failed? Wasn't I—let's be honest—playing pretend, just as I'd always feared would be the case? Wasn't I doomed? And didn't this pull toward suicide, right here, right now—this dark distraction keeping me from joining Theo in his game at this precious moment during this precious time that I was constantly told to appreciate before it disappeared—didn't it mean I couldn't love him as I needed to, after all? Just as I'd done on that morning in 2017, I picked up my phone and googled overdoses of each medication I had immediately available, trying to ascertain their lethal doses, the likelihood that I wouldn't simply get sick.

I'd been suicidal at various times since Theo was born and more frequently in the past few months, but this felt different. I imagined Theo's and Brendan's happiness in my absence, leaning into my despair by indulging in a vision of Theo raised by a different woman, whomever Brendan would end up with. Surely she'd be generous with her affection, so selfless, so kind. Surely she would succeed where I'd failed. She would have a seemingly bottomless well of patience. She'd never scare Theo by raising her undoubtedly mellifluous voice. Maybe she'd give him a sibling or two, which would be fine because she'd have the kind of natural proficiency in motherhood and domesticity that would ease Brendan's stress, but she'd never consider Theo as any less her own. And though she wouldn't be able to fathom my decision to leave him, she'd withhold judgment and help him, even encourage him, to accept my suicide with compassion.

And in that case, wouldn't I be doing him a favor by going? Couldn't my leaving, considered through this lens, be a gift? It was a relief. Now the comfort of suicidal ideation, previously stymied by Theo's existence, came from imagining how he would thrive without me. And if I were to do it, shouldn't I do it now, or soon, before he settles into who he is, before his memories start taking root and his identity gels? Shouldn't I do it now, or soon, so that he'll more or less forget me? How long would it take before I became a stranger? Wouldn't that be easier? Still, there remained a tiny nagging, a thorn piercing through the delusion: Easier for *whom*? My child in this hypothetical future or myself in this moment, trying to invent a guiltless departure?

* * *

A few days later, I emailed Elizabeth and told her I'd reached a point of intermittently planning my suicide. It had been four months since we'd last met, when I'd decided I wanted to take an indefinite break from therapy. Our conversations had started to feel useless against the backdrop of covid-19, despite the onslaught of corporate and po-litical messaging about the importance of maintaining good mental health. It wasn't that I'd been feeling *well* when I'd told Elizabeth I wanted to say goodbye—or at least "See you later"—but I recog-nized the limits of any potential successes. The work we were doing within those forty-five-minute visits couldn't fix the most immedi-ate cause of my distress, i.e. my having to bear witness to runaway death and destruction. Talking about my mom or my body or my work, seemed silly. Talking about everything else didn't, but it also couldn't bring about any material improvements. Ultimately, I didn't care about my moods so much as I cared about what caused them, the devastating circumstances over which I had no power. I sensed myself talking in circles, repeating myself half-heartedly. Elizabeth saw it, too. So we paused, with the understanding that I'd reach out whenever I needed to.

One week before I started researching overdose possibilities, I'd taken my frustration to Twitter, as I often did at the time. Desperate for a sanity check, I posted:

> *so basically everyone I know is depressed, every conversation*
> *I have with a close friend is a check-in like "ok so how serious*
> *is YOUR desire to die" and we're all just supposed to like . . .*
> *keep . . . working? like this isn't happening? still gotta clock in*
> *those 40 hours?*

After close to a decade spent in public-facing work, I'd gathered a modest following of just over ten thousand Twitter users, but my tweets rarely surpassed a hundred or so likes, a dozen or so retweets. This one struck a nerve. Forty-three thousand users tapped that heart, and close to six thousand shared it with their followers. Responses streamed in, tinged with disillusionment, bewilderment, profound despair, and simmering rage, each *yes-and*-ing the injustices laid out above it:

"Everyone just acts like it's business as usual, nothing abnormal here. I'm trying to keep a modicum of sanity while not shouting 'do I look like I give a f*ck if the oven isn't spotless.'"

"And your employer wants to cut your pay if you're working from home. Please also install the surveillance malware. And also pick up the slack for your coworkers who burned out and left."

"Not to mention your employer 'being here for you in these unprecedented times' is a load of garbage."

"Really tired of living in this dystopian apocalypse where your choices are work or die. Oh wait, pandemic, so work AND die."

"I work at Amazon. It's Hell. I already used up all my vacation time cause I can barely get out of bed. All I think now is how long I can make it for."

Certainly, there is comfort in finding your pain articulated by someone else, to be reminded that you aren't uniquely weak or flawed for struggling. But that mutual recognition of pain can't alleviate the pain itself; even the sense of comfort fades once it becomes clear that both sides are getting worse. Those struggling to stand can't very well prop up others. "Ask for help," "Tell someone," and all such similar dubious, anodyne messaging works only when we have people who are well enough to help us. Or, as user @crazyquantum responded with perfect bluntness, "It's getting increasingly difficult to reach out because everyone is having the sameish shitty time." Those who related to my original post were able to only because they, too, lacked the power to improve the conditions causing our shared despair. This impotence is doubly devastating. Practically speaking, it means we're barred access to, at worst, survival necessities and, at best, tools that demonstrably improve our quality of life—everything from health care, housing, and livable wages to time and the freedom to use it as we wish. But powerlessness brings existential degradation, too: without massive wealth or meaningful political influence, we are denied the basic dignity of self-determination.

But the world continued. Employees clocked in, logged on, and worked. What else could we do? We still had to pay rent. We still had to eat. I, like hundreds of millions of other people around the globe, found distraction and solace on TikTok. In the early days of the pandemic, we'd used social media to panic, grieve, and lament, but many of us still believed that the world would return to normal, and soon. We'd commiserated and joked, shared pop culture recommendations and lifestyle advice. We were inventive: Zoom happy hours and movie nights; quarantine raves featuring livestreamed sets by famous DJs; virtual celebrations and cultural events. That period benefited from novelty—in both experience, playful and promising, and concept. Novelty signified human ingenuity, resilience. It puffed us up even if we suspected that we were fooling ourselves.

By the year's end, though, lockdown content seemed to experience a broad energetic shift. On February 17, 2021, TikTok user Aria Velz posted a fifteen-second video comprising just two shots. In the first, a spare, melancholic piano swells while Velz, sitting in an office chair with a bed behind her, stares to the side in a daze. The text above her reads, "I haven't seen most of my friends in almost a year and my career goals are dead and this pandemic has destroyed my sense of joy and no one knows when it will end." Abruptly, the melody brightens into a ragtime tune, and Velz shakes her head as if to refocus, turning to type on the laptop now visible in front of her. "Remembering I'm in the middle of a staff meeting," the new caption reads.

The video captures the tone that emerged once it became clear that America wouldn't be adjusting its priorities in favor of true society: society as in fellowship, as in collaboration, as in people. Never in modern history had there been a more obvious and crucial opportunity to reimagine our institutions and inspire widespread investment in community, equity, and mutual care, but those in power had decided instead to uphold our most alienating and dehumanizing systems.* Social media content reflected this failure in videos emptied of any gestures toward comradery, any hints of faith in change. If all of it—the global shutdowns, the makeshift morgues in trucks, the bodies piled on the streets or buried en masse, the brutalities against

---

* A particularly deadly example being incarceration: In 2020, people in prison died at three times a higher rate than did those outside. Despite most governors having the power to pause or shorten sentences, no such actions were taken on a large scale.

Better

Black Lives Matter protestors, the job losses and union busting, the violence against Asian Americans, the decimation caused by California and Oregon wildfires, the attempted coup of the US government, the proliferation of conspiracy theories that spurred said coup—weren't enough to dissolve the status quo, what could? The videos slipped into nihilism, but sometimes even that categorization was too forceful, implying more emotion than existed. Often, they revealed more of a hollowness, a deadening, a clear and comprehended abandonment—a giving up.

I emailed Elizabeth that morning not because I believed that something had changed that would enable therapy to make me feel better about a horrific world; I did it because I needed help navigating a horrific world without killing myself. We resumed weekly sessions, which provided some relief. The very act of admitting my suicidality was enough to diminish it, at least momentarily, but the fantasies still came and went in waves. Elizabeth asked me why I didn't want to go back to an inpatient facility, and the whirlwind of emotions the question stirred in me was so dense I could hardly pluck out one reason: Because part of me saw it as a failure. Because I didn't want to believe things were that bad. Because I still wasn't entirely convinced that it was the hospital that had saved me last time. Maybe it was and maybe it could again, but now I had a partner and a child for whom my absence would be devastating, not only emotionally but also logistically. The idea of going back to the hospital was no longer scary, but now it felt impossible, even cruel. Whether we want to admit it or not, whether it is fair or not, our illnesses don't exist in a vacuum; they affect those around us, and those effects are valid. But it was clear that I was stuck and that something needed to change. Four months after I started half forming a plan to kill myself, two things set that change into motion.

*   *   *

On June 22, 2021, Amazon's annual Prime Day began, which, as anyone who has worked in commerce journalism knows, is a period[*] of great import. The preceding weeks are spent brainstorming hundreds of themed shopping articles to capitalize on Amazon's whirlwind of limited-time sales and promotions, countless lists of the "We Found the Best Deals So You Don't Have To" variety, all of which comprise thousands of affiliate links. This urgency is warranted when such links bring in hundreds of millions of dollars in digital media revenue.[†] But Prime Day is also notoriously contentious among those who are wary of supporting the corporate behemoth, especially in 2021—and especially at BuzzFeed. Its news division had been actively reporting on Amazon's egregious warehouse conditions and its alleged violations of workers' rights throughout the pandemic and in the years preceding, alongside the numerous damning reports coming from other outlets. Current and former Amazon employees were coming forward to expose the company's retaliations against workers who began organizing employees for collective bargaining or filed internal complaints. External investigations revealed unsafe, inhumane, and exploitative working conditions throughout the entire

---

[*] Lasting, in fact, two days.

[†] In BuzzFeed founder and CEO Jonah Peretti's 2020 missive on BuzzFeed's business model, he shared that shopping content had made up 21 percent of the company's 2019 revenue and that BuzzFeed had brought affiliate partners more than $425 million through "directly attributable transactions." (He did not disclose what percentage, or percentage range, of those transactions had been kicked back to BuzzFeed.)

supply chain, from corporate and customer service to fulfillment and delivery. Amid increased focus on the billionaires making bank while millions of people suffered layoffs and wage cuts, Amazon founder Jeff Bezos, then the wealthiest man in the world, was a particularly compelling villain, having increased his net worth by more than half during the first year of the pandemic—from $113 billion in March 2020 to $178 billion in March 2021, to be precise.*

But Amazon plays a uniquely adversarial role within the publishing world thanks to its near monopoly on the industry, having edged beloved independent bookstores out of the market and used its massive pool of user data to reduce taste to algorithms. Amazon's "death grip on the book market," as *The Nation* writers Sandeep Vaheesan and Tara Pincock describe, allows it to wield a scary amount of power over a book's—or publisher's—success. No publisher is too big for Amazon to marginalize should that publisher upset them, and those "retaliatory games" (like delaying shipping to customers or falsely claiming a book is out of stock) have demonstrable financial repercussions. But this wouldn't necessarily be apparent to most consumers or readers, people who love good books but aren't deep in the weeds of the industry. With that in mind, I pitched some Prime Day counterprogramming—specifically, a list of places to buy affordable books without supporting Bezos and his speed-obsessed supply chain, once so eloquently described by the lawyer and podcast host Peter Shamshiri as "a Rube Goldberg [machine] of human

---

* Compare this to other Americans' coinciding experience: In 2020, we saw the first statistically significant decrease in household income in nine years, and in the year after covid-19's onset shot unemployment up to 13 percent, we still hadn't returned to the prepandemic rate of 3.8 percent.

suffering." The post would offer alternatives to Amazon while also explaining the reasons to go elsewhere.

I knew the answer would be no, but I needed to hear it. I needed an acknowledgment of the hypocrisy, the untenable systemic absurdity, in publishing investigations on corporate corruption with money made by driving that same corporation's sales. News leadership assured us of the sanctity of our ethics, that our journalism wasn't influenced by our funding and vice versa, but of course that can't be the case within a profit-driven business that is beholden to its shareholders. I needed management to draw the line we were readily told did not exist, because I was tired of hearing people in power espousing progress they were actively working against. I emailed an outline of the idea to the culture team that morning, received enthusiastic messages from my fellow editors and, from my manager, instructions to wait until we could talk about it over the phone. A few hours later, I listened as she explained that she had discussed the matter with our executive editor and the pair had decided that the negative framing wasn't necessary. I agreed to publish the article without mentioning Amazon: a recommendation list that would hide the determining factor on which it was built. My resistance during the phone call was feeble, so I was angry with myself, too, when I decided to write about the experience in my newsletter that evening, trying to understand what about this day had felt so urgent, why I'd spent the night crying over an outcome I fully expected.

"I'm trying to hone the despair of this moment, to better see its shape," I wrote. "It's not that I believe that these things I want to do—publishing a post about alternatives to Amazon, omitting Amazon from BuzzFeed Books full stop—could put any significant dent into the Amazon empire. It's more that I feel very helpless, even frantic, looking around like, *Aren't you angry? Aren't you terrified?* It's more that this tiny stance, one with such minimal consequences, still has to be a fight, and one I am, again and again, losing."

June 22 was also the day I told Elizabeth I felt as though I was losing my grip on my sanity and we decided it was time for me to take a medical leave.

* * *

In 2014, Princeton economists Anne Case and Angus Deaton embarked on an investigation into potential links between reported happiness and suicide, attempting to determine if "unhappy places" around the globe saw higher rates of suicide than their counterparts. Their research uncovered a piece of data that so shocked them that they changed the framing of their investigation entirely: around the year 2000, after thirty years of rapid decline, the death rate of middle-aged white Americans* began to rise. How could that have happened? There had been an increase in suicide in those years, but not nearly enough of a hike to explain the shift. Upon closer inspection, suicide was indeed a *piece* of the puzzle—namely, it was one of the three causes behind the fastest-rising death rates, along with drug overdoses and alcoholic liver diseases. Altogether, Case and Deaton saw a clear theme and named it: these were "deaths of despair," and after years spent deciphering the conditions that had

---

* For clarity, the death rate, or, as Case and Deaton define it, "the risk of dying," is inversely related to life expectancy: the greater the risk of dying, the lower life expectancy is, and vice versa. In recent history, the life expectancy data have been even more distressing than the mortality rate, having decreased annually from 2014 to 2017 among the US population as a whole—the first three-year decline since 1933.

created this uniquely American crisis, the pair laid the blame firmly on capitalism.[*]

In their resulting 2020 book, *Deaths of Despair and the Future of Capitalism*, Case and Deaton illuminate capitalism's sometimes deadly effects on one demographic: middle-aged white Americans, especially those without a four-year college degree. Indeed, suicide is broadly understood as a majority white male issue, and there are some data to back this up. As of 2022, the most recent data available, white men accounted for over 68 percent of US suicides. But this statistic is potentially deceptive, not least because the requirements for naming suicide as cause of death are imperfect and leave potentially large swaths of communities uncounted.[†] In particular, Case and Deaton's data set has one glaring, egregious omission: Native Americans, who, in fact, have experienced the highest rates of midlife deaths of despair since 1999. Still, their findings are worth extrapolation. Capitalism's failings are universal among the working class, even if the felt effects of those failures vary by demographic, and Case and Deaton's analyses offer valuable points of entry into the forces behind suicide in more vulnerable populations.

The keystones of Case and Deaton's theory of deaths of despair are close examinations of the causes and effects of increased pain, low income, and the lack of meaningful work. This last item, pointing in part to the societal scourge that the late anthropologist David Graeber referred to as "bullshit jobs," is particularly compelling, because for it to hold value, we must allow that work can be and has

----

[*] Case and Deaton are explicit in their support of reformed capitalism, rejecting the notion that its exploitation of the working class is inherent and inevitable. I disagree.

[†] The CDC goes so far as to present this most recent report with a warning that racial and ethnic data should be "interpreted with caution."

been a source of pride and meaning. I couldn't help but resist the notion when first considering it. All I've come to understand about survival and well-being requires centering community and care, and all I've come to understand about work is employers' easy sacrifice of both. If the responses of employers at large weren't enough to completely disabuse me of the notion that workers were managed from a baseline of respect, sitting in on negotiations between BuzzFeed's lawyers and the recently acknowledged BuzzFeed News union succeeded. My job not only failed to provide me with meaning, but it had also made it increasingly difficult to look for meaning elsewhere, thanks to the company's outsized expectations and unsustainable hours. But that wasn't always necessarily the case.

Looking specifically at Americans without four-year college degrees, Case and Deaton describe the loss of this work, broadly, as the loss of "attachment." Whereas once such workers could reliably develop a mutual "long-term commitment" with their employer—a relationship that provided "structure and significance"—they are now left trying to hold on to precarious positions with no opportunities for camaraderie or growth, if they haven't been ousted from the work force entirely. This is particularly the case for workers in "low-ranked" (i.e., service) positions: cleaners, drivers, and customer service representatives who were once employed by the corporations using their labor are now managed through whichever business service firm the corporation outsources to—a firm that will undoubtedly pay far lower wages and offer fewer benefits than the big boss company would. And what of their sense of belonging in the shared work mission and culture? Case and Deaton refer to the illustrative distinction made by the economist Nicholas Bloom in 2017: "When it comes time for the holiday party, the struggling contractors are nowhere to be seen."

Previous generations of workers also benefited from more widespread unions, which have seen a rapid decline in membership since the mid–twentieth century. Those unions not only gave workers leverage in negotiating for "higher wages, better working conditions, and more benefits" but also created unity. With unions came the union hall and the built-in social circle, but more fundamentally, they brought the confidence of knowing you belonged to a team that was as concerned with your job and your rights as they were with their own. They codified social support with benefits that spread beyond the workplace: union membership has a demonstrable, positive effect on workers' satisfaction in life and psychological well-being as a whole.

To put it bluntly, your job can shore up your self-worth. It's a surprising conclusion to draw alongside an argument based largely on disconnecting from external validation and material success, but in an ideal system, work wouldn't be so precarious as to require a constant, panicked proving of your worth. Doing the work would be enough. In Chikako Ozawa-de Silva's exploration of the psychological and emotional benefits of being useful, there is no caveat about the venue of that use. One can feel needed, as in "Her best friend would be lost without her" but also as in "She's the only person on her team who knows how to fix the espresso machine." Both are valid sources of satisfaction and pride. There's a flavor of condescension in the resistance to deriving pride from one's work. Just as a wealthy person who insists that money isn't everything belittles the real, measurable harm of poverty, so, too, does the left-leaning college graduate who disparages corporate ambition belittle the person whose success in the corporate world was never a given. Disillusionment arises when the self-respect we garner from getting promotions and raises and progressing through our career isn't met with the same level of respect from our employers. And the system in its entirety becomes toxic when professional achievement becomes not simply a possible component of someone's value but synonymous with it.

None of this is to mention possibly the most significant factor in suicidality: financial insecurity. If we're talking about the suicidal person's pain points, money is everywhere. We can see evidence of the connection between poverty and suicide by looking at suicide rates in 2020—but not for the reason you might suspect. Despite layoffs and wage cuts, increased cash benefits from the government meant that many of the poorest Americans were receiving more than they would have through the usual welfare services. Poverty *decreased*, and so did the suicide rate.*

That more money correlates with fewer suicides is consistently shown in research from around the world using varying metrics. Children especially are vulnerable to the effects of poverty; studies in the United States have shown that children ages five to nineteen are 37 percent more likely to kill themselves if they live in "high poverty" communities; in Sweden, children in families that are receiving welfare benefits are about twice as likely to die by suicide than those in families that are not. Even just the forecasting of a national economic downturn spurs a spike in the suicide rate. Particularly interesting is the finding that *relative* poverty is a better predictor of suicide than absolute poverty: as the sociologist Sylwia J. Piatkowska put it, "People are likely to commit suicide when they have less than

---

* That might have surprised Émile Durkheim (1858–1917), the father of sociology and the first to develop a theory of suicide, who argued that "Poverty protects against suicide because it is restraint itself"—or, the poor benefit from their lack (both of material resources and "of power") because they've learned not to expect more and therefore won't be disappointed when they don't receive it. That Durkheim remains a prominent resource in suicidology is a testament to the need for upheaval in the field.

what is expected or what is considered normal" within their society, even if they have enough resources for basic survival.

The US health care system is the subject of Case and Deaton's greatest vitriol, deservedly so. Allowing for the fact that health care is expensive around the world and that wealthy countries *should* dedicate a large proportion of their money to it, they mince no words when asserting that "America does this about as badly as it is possible to imagine." Strong evidence of this statement comes from the fact that even though Americans are paying for the most expensive health care in the world, we are also, as compared with other wealthy countries, in the worst health. Case and Deaton discuss the failures of a capitalist health care system in terms of its financial costs—to both the individual and employers, which is then recouped via low wages and fewer jobs—as well as its proliferation of the opioid crisis, but what about its direct connection with the suicidal person? Americans without medical insurance have higher rates of suicide, but even among those who are insured, half can't access mental health care treatment. How does the medical insurance machine block them out?

In August 2024, ProPublica published an extensive report on the paucity of therapists who accept health insurance, which uncovered a detail that might be surprising to anyone who hasn't tried to obtain psychological treatment through the system: though medical insurance companies are required by federal law to provide access to mental health care, they do so with a wink and fingers crossed behind their back. Technically they cover therapy—but good luck finding a psychologist who is in your network. Mental health treatment, it turns out, is not a robust source of revenue, which means that medical insurance companies don't want to insure the people who need such care. As one former contract manager explained, medical insurance companies look at therapy patients and providers and think, first and foremost, "I am never going to make money on them."

Better

For a long time, I focused my anger about the exorbitant cost of mental health care on the practitioners setting the rates and widely refusing to accept insurance. I've softened since coming to a better understanding of the ways medical insurance companies back them into a corner.* Through interviews with five hundred psychologists across the United States, the journalists Annie Waldman, Maya Miller, Duaa Eldeib, and Max Blau discovered people who had set out in the field with righteous goals to help struggling communities, only to be squeezed out of network by the insurance giants. Troubling themes emerged. Some had left the network because insurers "interfered with [their] patient's care," such as Eugene, Oregon–based Melissa Todd, who was subjected to challenges by UnitedHealthcare, demanding proof that her patients' treatment was necessary. Some had left because they were losing hours on the phone with insurers to appeal claim denials. Some had left because insurance companies simply weren't paying them enough to survive. Across the board, insurers pay mental health providers a fraction of what their "medical" counterparts receive, so it's in the therapists' best interest to guide their patients through their insurance company's out-of-network reimbursement policies rather than working directly with the insurer. This, from the patient's perspective, or at the very least from one patient's perspective, is not ideal. Allow me to lift the curtain.

---

* Still, though, skepticism lingers. When Elizabeth raised her rate from $350 per session to $600, the increase didn't affect me because, either way, I was meeting my out-of-pocket maximum cost. But this isn't a universal experience. She explained the change as keeping up with the market rate, and I can't help feeling the same as I do about landlords: a rise in the market rate means they *can* get away with charging more, but it doesn't mean they *must*.

My family is insured with UnitedHealthcare[*] through Brendan's employer. Since Brendan and I are both chronically ill, the most cost-effective plan turned out to be the most expensive. It costs us roughly $3,000 per month, taken from Brendan's pretax income. I try my best not to think about this. In exchange for that $3,000,[†] we have lower-than-average annual deductibles and out-of-pocket maximums: In regard to providers who accept this plan and who provide services that the plan covers, we must each pay $500 before our individual coverage begins,[‡] and if either of us reaches $2,500 paid, that person's care will be covered in full for the rest of the year.[§] But neither Elizabeth nor Sara accepts insurance. What then? Let's look at out-of-network coverage, i.e., reimbursement. I must pay $2,000 before receiving any reimbursement, at which point I receive 30 percent back per visit. Once I've spent a total of $6,000, I receive 100 percent reimbursement for the rest of the year.

Here is where it gets tricky.[¶] Though it isn't disclosed in the

---

[*] To be precise, UnitedHealthcare Oxford Direct, not to be confused with UnitedHealthcare Oxford Freedom, UnitedHealthcare Oxford Liberty, United-Healthcare Choice, UnitedHealthcare Choice Plus, UnitedHealthcare Select Plus, UnitedHealthcare Empire, UnitedHealthcare Options, or UnitedHealthcare Community Plan, among others.

[†] For simplicity's sake, relatively speaking, we'll keep this snapshot focused on financials, acknowledging that doing so fails to examine a large chunk of coverage details (e.g., what sorts of doctors and procedures are covered, how many visits are allowed, and so on).

[‡] This doesn't include prescriptions, which have a separate $100 deductible.

[§] By comparison, 2023 data on employer-sponsored coverage for individual plans (in network) showed a national average deductible of $1,992 and a national average out-of-pocket maximum of $4,346.

[¶] Bear with me; we're about halfway through.

summary of benefits and coverage, insurance providers determine the allowed amounts for out-of-network services, which are hidden until after you've already received them. Regardless of the providers' rates, you will be reimbursed a percentage of the *allowed* amount, and anything you pay beyond the allowed amount does not count toward your out-of-network out-of-pocket maximum. Again, with real figures: In 2023, Elizabeth charged $600 per session and UnitedHealthcare allowed that rate, so I paid $6,000 for a year of mental health care, as expected.* In 2024, with no notice, UnitedHealthcare decreased the allowed amount for the exact same service to $459.43, meaning that I would be paying, in addition to the $6,000 annual out-of-network out-of-pocket maximum, $140.57 per visit.†

Twelve years ago, I stood huddled in a closet at the BuzzFeed office on the phone with my then insurance company and tearfully tried to understand why my claim for therapy reimbursement had been rejected, despite my choosing a plan specifically for its mental health policies. The allowed amount was to blame. I couldn't afford it. I emailed my new therapist and told her I wouldn't be back. I've since made it my business to become an expert in medical insurance red tape, but it's a luxury to have the time to do so. I've spent countless hours on the phone, mostly on hold, with customer service representatives, as well as filling out reimbursement claims. I've memorized diagnosis and procedure codes. I've filed a complaint with the New York State Attorney General because of UnitedHealthcare's failure to send my $10,000 reimbursement. I've had family members and

---

* Not counting medication costs.

† Thankfully, Elizabeth works on a sliding scale and agreed to lower her rate to match this.

friends hand over their insurance cards so I could log in and decode their precise mental health care benefits. I am happy to do it. When it comes to insurance providers and their literally banking on users' not understanding their rights, I am electric with rage. I have all the energy in the world.

Sometimes, though, time and energy are not enough. After Theo's pediatrician recommended that we book an evaluation with a pediatric psychologist, I knew better than to expect any of the clinics or doctors on her referral list to accept insurance. I spoke with each provider and requested the individual procedure codes and respective rates that we'd be responsible for, so that I could take them to UnitedHealthcare and find out how much, per code, we'd be reimbursed. They were happy to oblige, sending over codes for services ranging from $400 to $6,000 per session. The process seemed reasonable enough to me: rather than filing a claim after the service and discovering what UnitedHealthcare would cover after I already owed it, I would simply provide all of the information up front so we could determine which services, if any, would be feasible. The proposition, when presented to UnitedHealthcare customer service, proved to be bewildering.

I had the initial request clear and rehearsed: "My son requires care from a mental health provider that is out of network. I need to find out what your allowed amounts are for each procedure code, which they've sent to me."

"I'll be happy to help you with that," the first customer service representative said in a tone so bright that I believed her. She returned after a quick hold. "I've looked at the details of your plan, and it will cover thirty percent of the out-of-network rate, after a $2,000 deductible."

I thanked her and, wishing for a world in which I didn't have to, explained that that wasn't quite what I was looking for. I repeated the initial request, but she, understandably, seemed confused. The confusion is by design.*

"I'm so sorry," I said. "I know this is probably a weird request, and maybe I need to talk to someone in the claims department? Basically, I want to know how a claim will be processed before receiving the service, so I can know if I can afford it."

The woman apologized for misunderstanding and for having to put me on another hold while she looked into it. She returned to say that she wasn't allowed to give that information. One hour and twenty minutes later, after being successfully transferred to someone higher up and then being told by that person that the information I wanted was impossible to determine before receiving a service; and after telling them to humor me, to *pretend* that I've in fact received the service and am now filing the claim, and then being told that they would need *more* than just the codes if they were to do this, that they'd also need the address, the tax identification numbers, and the type of the facility; and after telling them that in fact, I had that information as well, I finally received the allowed amount for one of the six codes. The doctor charged $400, and UnitedHealthcare would allow $180. I hung up, exhausted. It was time to pick up Theo from school.

* * *

---

* As a former manager at Cigna told ProPublica, customer service is regularly outsourced to employees who don't have access to the "full claims system" or fluency in the medical terminology for a reason: "The idea is if you make it so frustrating for providers to follow up on claim denials, they're just going to give up and the insurance company is not going to have to pay out." The effect on patients is the same.

Let's stay, for a moment, with children. Let's consider the fact that when we refer, vaguely, to youth suicide, that range begins at five years old. Five years old, as in a kindergartener, as in just a baby, your baby, my baby, as in Theo. When I've imagined, or tried to stop imagining, the possibility that Theo may one day find himself suicidal, I've calmed myself down with timelines. We have years to prepare, I've reminded myself, to build him up solid, so that he can weather the crashing winds of adolescence, never questioning his support at home. Reading that range—"children aged five to eleven years"—in a study about the critical rise in suicide rates among Black youth was a walloping.

This age group complicates theorizing because intention is hard to parse. This category of suicide, for example, includes the child who makes the tragic mistake of playing with their parents' gun. Who can know what they meant to do when they picked it up? What does a five-year-old really know about death, about finality? About risk and consequences? Lately, when Theo is at the peak of a melt-down, he's taken to shouting that he's going to kill himself. He'll get mad that we have to go grocery shopping, leave my parents' house, or stop playing a game, and he'll whack his face and yell, "I'm going to hurt my body, I'm going to hurt myself, I'm going to kill myself, I'm going to die!" Do I think he wants to die? No, not really. I think he's scared of death, so he guesses that I might be, too. He knows that his death would make me sad because we talk about how sad death is, so he knows that it's likely an effective way of communicating whatever distress he's in. But I know, too, that he's fascinated by dying, will ask me when we're standing next to any barrier over-looking any kind of drop, what would happen if he fell. *Would I die or just hurt my body?*

So I sit on the floor next to him and dismiss the rules that say I'm not supposed to scare him or threaten him, and I tell him, "When you're mad, you can punch your bed, you can scream, you can even hit your leg, I don't care. But if you do the things that you know are dangerous, like running into the street or jumping from something high up just to scare me? You will die. And dying means you are gone. Forever. And we will never get to play or hug or anything again. Do you understand?"

And he nods silently. I'm sure I've handled it wrong. It's something to discuss with the child psychologist, whenever we get there. Theo is not at a point of crisis—maybe he never will be—but for parents whose children are, the impenetrability of the medical insurance machine can be catastrophic. See Arizona mother Denise, whose fifteen-year-old son, Jake, killed himself less than three months after his insurance company deemed his stay at an inpatient psychiatric facility no longer medically necessary, despite Jake's team of doctors insisting otherwise. See Rochelle and Michael of Ohio, who paid out of pocket to continue their fifteen-year-old daughter, Rose's, treatment after their insurer cut coverage—despite doctors' insisting that she wouldn't be safe at home—until they ran out of money after two months, having spent more than $40,000. Rose was sent home, where, a few weeks later, she again tried to kill herself. She survived.

For Black families, there is another barrier to care, albeit more nuanced: the therapy industry is notoriously lacking in cultural competency. More bluntly, most therapists are white. According to the American Psychological Association's most recent data, from 2021, only 5 percent of those working in psychology are Black. Many of the rest are ill-equipped to help Black patients—especially Black youths. Upsetting the long-held belief that suicide in the United States is a white issue, it is now in fact Black children who are twice as likely to kill themselves than their white peers, and that rate is increasing faster than within any other demographic. They're being failed by a system understood through a white lens, built on theories of white pain. Caregivers are missing warning signs, because they've been given the wrong set: depression in Black youths often presents as anger or irritability, as opposed to the more melancholic symptoms of white teens, as seen in almost all mainstream media depictions of suicidality. Even when presenting similar symptoms, that same issue is more likely to be assessed as a behavioral problem in a Black child, rather than a mental health concern.

Risk factors vary, too. Black children are unique in that their suicide attempts are less likely to be preceded by ideation than by a recent crisis, usually domestic—meaning that risk assessment questionnaires focused on thoughts of suicide and self-harm are less likely to serve them. In an interview with the *New York Times*, the mental health advocate Jordan Burnham recalled his parents discovering his stash of alcohol the day he jumped from a ninth-story window and survived, but not without suffering injuries that would leave him unable to walk for four years. He was eighteen at the time and feeling "like an outsider as one of the few Black students at a mostly white school in suburban Philadelphia" but said he wouldn't have even recognized the urge to commit suicide if someone had asked him that very day.

These suicides, alongside suicides in LGBTQ communities and the Native American population, involve an amalgam of unaddressed social concerns, in large part because research on suicide within these marginalized communities is underfunded. More than half of the country's LGBTQ youths have either seriously considered or attempted suicide, but those who live in what they describe as "very accepting communities" attempt suicide at half the rate than those who don't. Of those who have attempted suicide, more than half have been either threatened with or forced into conversion therapy. Native American LGBTQ youths are the most likely to commit suicide, but that's because Native American youths as a whole are more likely to commit suicide than youths in *every other* racial and ethnic group in the country.

It would be impossible to isolate a single root on which to direct our focus. If poverty increases the suicide rate, we must consider that Native Americans have the highest rate of poverty, with the Black population close behind; Native Americans have about a quarter of their population living under the national income average, as opposed to less than 10 percent of white Americans.* Having a four-year degree increases one's income,† but Native Americans receive those degrees at roughly half the rate of the national average. Speaking of education, men whose education ends after high school are twice as likely to kill themselves as are those with a bachelor's degree, but even the lowest tier of tuition—for in-state students at public schools—costs an average of eleven thousand dollars per year. Racial discrimination increases both suicide attempts and ideation; 75 percent of Black adults in the United States report being discriminated against, some regularly.

I don't mean to go astray, to get bogged down in the numbers, but feeling that density is important. To talk about suicide is to talk about despair, which means—not to hyperbolize—every aspect of it. You'll find that most of them are connected. And so I want to return to Case and Deaton's working-class white Americans, particularly working-class white American men. In a patriarchal society built on white supremacy, sympathy for white men in general—especially

---

* To put this into clearer perspective, a family of four in 2024 would have needed to have a household income of less than $31,200 to be counted among those in poverty.

† Yes, still.

young, impressionable straight white men—can be sparse. Work that devotes resources to improving the well-being of these men, a demographic that is demonstrably favored in Western capitalism, invites scrutiny. But in untangling the web of suicidality, it is crucial to approach masculine despair in good faith. White men aren't exempt from rigid gendered ideals, nor are they safe from punishment and ridicule if they fail to uphold them. Such consequences are largely more dangerous for women and non-gender-conforming individuals who reject their assigned roles, but I hesitate to dismiss or assess male pain—or any pain—based on a system of interlocking qualifying factors. I've seen and grieved too much of it up close.

Watching Theo—his gentleness and sensitivity, his enthusiastic affection—I preemptively mourn the day he'll be told that whole chunks of his personhood are wrong. But perhaps that day has already come and gone. When Theo was three, watching me paint my nails, he asked me if I could paint his, too, and I did, without hesitation. The next day he came home from day care and said that nail polish was actually for girls. It was his teacher who had told him. When he was four, he fell in love with *Frozen*. We watched the 2013 film, inarguably a cultural phenomenon, once a day at minimum. He wanted Elsa's dress and hair; he requested a *Frozen* backpack and lunch box. When I picked him up from preschool, one of his classmates told me that boys couldn't like *Frozen*.

"But Theo's a boy, and he likes it, right?" I said. "So that can't be true!"

I'd kept my voice light and warm, made sure to smile. That girl adored Theo, shouted his name from across the street if we happened to pass each other. To her, it wasn't a matter of criticism; it was factual information. She was letting us know. It starts so young. And though the details now seem so inconsequential—a kids' movie, a favorite color—these incidents around them are the beginning of a lifetime of erasure and erosion, small violences against a child's whole self. I see Theo's confusion in such moments, and I see everything I know will come. Or maybe everything I think will come. I hope I'm wrong.

I tell him these ideas are so silly whenever he repeats arbitrary opinions stated as facts at an age when he hasn't learned that there are people and beliefs he can't trust. "You like wearing necklaces,"* I'll say, "and just because someone says you're not supposed to, that doesn't suddenly mean you don't!"

What I'm trying to communicate, sometimes explicitly but also in underlying messages, each becoming increasingly urgent: *Nobody can tell you who you are. Nobody can tell you what life you must live.* The latter is more of a wish.

* * *

The relief I felt after setting up my out-of-office email response and logging out of every work account was immediate and total. Elizabeth had me commit to a plan—having therapy twice a week, leaving the house every day, picking Theo up early for dedicated no-device play, and allowing Brendan to contact her if he has any concerns—with the caveat that if I failed to maintain the plan, I agreed to go to an inpatient facility. But I wasn't concerned, not really. The pain wasn't so dire now. I was eager to begin. I got out of bed and started going for long walks. I listened to audiobooks; I became a regular at a local café—I learned the baristas' names, and they learned mine. I started meditating; I reconnected with friends. I gardened, and then I joined a forum for local gardeners and found a neighbor who wanted

---

* Or having long hair or wearing makeup or singing songs from *Moana* and *Frozen*.

to do a used-book-for-fresh-cuttings swap. I set up a Little Free Library in front of our house. I didn't want to die.

Most days, I picked Theo up from day care, and we explored not just the neighborhood but the city as a whole. He was learning the different letters and numbers of the trains and buses and could now name our stop. One day, after some swinging and sliding at the playground, I decided we'd get dinner out. Brendan had to work late, and I hated cooking; plus, it would kill some time. We meandered up Fresh Pond Road, getting a little lost, but not in any real sense, never so far astray that simply opening the map on my phone couldn't bring us back home. When it began to rain, we got onto a bus and headed to a diner in the neighboring town, which we'd been to once before. That time it had been something of a disaster even with Brendan there to help, ending with my carrying a thrashing and crying Theo out the front door while Brendan rushed to pay and apologize. Now I had no toys in my bag, no in-case-of-emergency diapers, not even Theo's water cup, but I was committed.

I held him on my hip with one arm and used my free hand to grasp a pole as the bus lurched forward. His face next to mine, I whispered, "This is an adventure. An adventure is when you're not really sure what's going to happen or if it's going to be good or bad. But I think that's fun, right?"

He repeated the word quietly: "Adventure."

This was a relatively new phenomenon, having a conversation, something I hadn't thought would be possible so early. I hadn't accounted for our mutual knowability, the effect of years of wordless communication, a language that long predated his first echo of my standard greeting: "*Hi, babyyy!*" But now I could ask him questions about his day—in the bath, at the dinner table, while falling asleep—and I'd get to watch him consider them, really consider them, before providing his one-word answers. At the diner we shared silver dollar pancakes and bacon, every second that passed without his crying a miracle. Whom had he played with at school? Noah. Had he seen any trucks today? Yes. Had he read any books? No. When we asked for the check, our server brought it with a free to-go cup of cherry Jell-O and Theo's eyes widened at the glistening, wiggling mass on my spoon.

The rain had stopped by the time we stepped out to the sidewalk, so we walked along the bus path home, testing the limits of his little legs. As we walked, Theo sang—sometimes familiar tunes and words, sometimes a kind of freestyle—and I thought, *This is exactly what I always dreamed it would be.* Brendan was home when we got back, so I handed Theo over and took a shower. When I got out, all of the doors in our railroad apartment were open to accommodate one long pillow and couch cushion obstacle course that Brendan and Theo were racing across, laughing wildly. So when I say I lived for those moments—watching Theo grow, how the world is filtering through him, how he's reshaping it as his own and presenting it back to me and Brendan—I mean it literally.

I didn't want to die, but more important, I wanted to keep living, until inevitably I'd remember that my disability pay would soon be up. I'd remember the nine thousand unread emails I had left plus however many had piled up in the month since. I'd remember the fights with management, the traffic, the engagement, the spreadsheets, the algorithms, the anxiety of having to prove the value of a job I had specifically been hired to do, the maddening bind of being asked to build something profitable without the resources to make it *good.* So I quit.

I write this now, and I think of the response I might have had when I was younger, before I was so lucky as to meet people who are smarter than me and willing to teach me otherwise: So you'd be happier if you didn't have to work. Well, sure, but that's life. Deal with it. When Melissa, in our first year at Reed, told me she didn't believe that a person should have to work if they didn't want to, my mind blanked out for a second. Melissa, who had grown up in the foster system and spent some time homeless—how could I disagree with her? I *did* believe that everyone who worked should be able to easily survive, but let's not get carried away. To have a home but not to have to work? Well. But! It wouldn't be fair. Right? Then no one would work. It would be chaos. Right? I couldn't fathom the idea that a person could simply live, has the right to live, without having to earn it. I mistook the absence of a system that would allow real freedom as evidence of its impossibility. I was wrong, and thank god for that. Quitting my job didn't solve my suicidality. I still have depression and I still live under unchecked capitalism. But it helped.

* * *

Donald Antrim categorizes suicide as a "social disease" birthed by "trauma and isolation . . . violence and neglect . . . [and] the loss of home and belonging." He wonders if his suicidality wasn't actually "an expectable expression of a global sickness," rather than a personal affliction. If this is the case, it isn't the suicidal person who is irrational but the world in which he lives. How can it be that life, what we call "real life," is what makes me want to die? Am I not really depressed, just unsatisfied? If disillusionment ends in suicide, does the distinction matter? We can manage the individual symptoms, learn ways to healthily cope with and survive despair, but what if, also, we could live with less despair? What if we, as in all of us, as in this country, as in this world, could be better?

Chapter 10

Touching Death

It's a Sunday afternoon, and we're in the car on the way to the grocery store. It's Danea's car, but she lives in Manhattan and parking is expensive and she almost never needs it, so for a while it was Jordan's car, and now, for a while, it's ours. It's fifteen years old, and the air-conditioning works only on the highest setting, but it is a luxury. Grocery shopping has been one of the most surprising benefits. I'm driving, so I don't get carsick, and Brendan is in the back next to Theo, in case he gets carsick. Brendan's stomach, in the car, is safe.

We're listening to Theo's three-hour playlist of Pokémon soundtracks, when suddenly he shouts over the music, "Hey, Mama!"

I lower the volume. "What's up, bud?"

"Can people only have dreams at night?"

"Kind of," I say. "You really only have dreams while you're sleeping, but you can sleep during the day, too, right?"

"Oh, okay," he says, looking out the window. I sneak glances at him in the rearview mirror. "Thank you for that advice."

I turn the music back up and then, after about ten seconds, turn it down again. "Why do you ask?"

"Well, I heard something during the day but no one else heard it."

I make eye contact with Brendan, who smiles, and I smile, trying to suppress a growing panic. It feels like a betrayal. Why can't I join him in his delight? What an active inner world our son has, what a brilliant little mind. Perhaps he has an imaginary friend! What a gift, surely.

"Oh, yeah?" I ask. "What did it sound like?"

"I can't say." He's looking down at his lap. I work to keep my voice airy, with a smile.

"Oh, okay! You don't have to tell me, but you can if you change your mind!" Against my better judgment, after a beat of silence, I add, "Was it scary?"

"Yeah," he says, but he doesn't sound scared, more matter-of-fact. I'm leading the witness, I know. He'll follow my train of thought. He loves to worry me; he loves the attention. He's admitted as much numerous times, and Brendan has reminded me of the fact even more often. "It was bad."

"When did it happen?"

"Umm . . . sometime, like, last week. Last . . . Tuesday."

He's being silly. He's making it up on the spot. It's fine. Of course it's fine. But what if it isn't? What if he isn't?

*　*　*

I spent most of Jordan's hospitalization and the year preceding it angry at my mother. Every frustration I had regarding his stubbornness, his treatment, the impossibility of ever knowing whether we were making the right decisions, got funneled into blaming her. She was failing him, I was certain of it, and I hated how hard it was for me to extend any grace to her. I was angry at some amorphous, elusive thing, but I couldn't be mean to my father, lest he start to feel bad; and I couldn't be mean to Brendan, because he already felt bad; and I couldn't be mean to Jordan, because what if it hindered his improvement; and I couldn't be mean to Danea or Dylan, because, well, we just weren't mean to each other. I wouldn't know how.

My mother isn't depressed or suicidal, even though, if depression and suicidality were strictly objective, hers would be the most warranted out of everyone in my family. She was born in Brooklyn to a single mother, Frances, who was raised in an orphanage after her mother, an Italian immigrant, died at twenty-six years old. Her father abandoned the two of them, and my mother spent years living with her aunt and uncle while Frances worked. There, for the bulk of her childhood, my mother was sexually abused by her cousin—a man who would eventually spend a decade in jail for rape. When she was eleven, she and Frances finally moved into their own studio apartment, where they spent Sundays slow-cooking tomato sauce and hosted sleepovers where Frances allowed my mother and her preteen friends to play dress-up with her luxurious nightgowns and lace robes. On Saturdays, my mother would go with Frances to the Cookie Jar, a baking factory where she worked, to sample the wares and chat with the other women working there. The pair had three years in modest, lower-class bliss until, at thirty-nine years old, Frances was diagnosed with breast cancer and died one year later. My mother was fourteen. She spent the rest of her childhood living with a neighboring family who were kind but, perhaps unwittingly, never helped her feel like anything other than an outsider.

I look at my mother, and I think about everything I've learned about suicide, and I realize it's a miracle she's alive. Her anxiety is all-consuming; her hoarding, at its worst, turned our home into an array of overflowing piles and stacks of unopened boxes; and I still can't get her to stop counting calories in front of me, but she is alive, and she has achieved her one dream: to have a family. It is a beautiful family. I wonder why all of this context can't translate into more kindness, more patience, from me to her. But our relationship has always been strained, largely, I'm sure, because I aligned myself so strongly with my father and his depression at an early age.

I went home frequently in the months before Jordan's hospitalization, and at that point, the house was as bad as it had ever been. During one visit, I arrived to a flurry of information—my mother explained that she'd been so tired, too tired to work on the house, she'd taken herself off her third antidepressant without letting her psychiatrist know, and now she was taking some kind of supplement, but she was still so tired, and she was worried that maybe she had a tumor. She was a machine of perpetual motion while she spoke, picking one tchotchke off the bookshelf and pushing it into a cupboard and then taking something from that cupboard and putting it elsewhere, but I knew that that didn't mean she was lying about being tired. She was always tired and she was always moving.

"You don't have a brain tumor," I told her, grabbing a fun-size Crunch bar from a glass jar on the kitchen island. "But you probably do have a vitamin B_{12} deficiency. Or vitamin D. Maybe both."

"I'll get bloodwork done," she said, reaching above one of the cabinets and pulling down a different glass jar, this one dustier from having sat up near the ceiling for who knows how long. It was filled with different chocolates of the vaguely fancy variety found in the mysterious grocery aisles in Marshalls. "Eat these. It's the good stuff."

We ran through some checking in before getting to Jordan. I'd signed my parents up for a meal kit delivery subscription, which she had canceled, which made me angrier than the news warranted, especially since I had at least two bags of rotting vegetables in my own refrigerator at that moment.

"It was too much pressure," she explained.

"But you have so much time now." She had recently retired. "Just set aside an hour to cook one good meal every now and then."

"I have so much time?" She threw her hands up and outward, gesturing at the space around her in exasperation. It had been the family party line for years, that my mother was always working on getting the house into shape, despite all evidence to the contrary. "What do you think I'm doing all day?"

"Ari's kidding," my father said from the kitchen table. "Right?" He eyed me over a small mountain of notebooks and the papers he was grading.

I sighed. What I wanted to say was "Okay, but moving photographs from one small box into tens of frames isn't helping anything." Or "Okay, but why is there a new green dresser just sitting in the kitchen?" Or "Fine, but please, for the love of God, just let me throw away these three bins of dish towels."

Instead, I put my hand on her back, hunched as she leaned over the island. "I know. I know. It's hard."

The year before, my siblings and I had staged an ad hoc intervention based on our discovery of her new abuse of both Adderall and resale apps. "We just want you to get better," we'd said. "It's not your fault." We'd booked appointments with a psychiatrist and at an addiction outpatient program, and then, for six hours, we'd filled twelve industrial size garbage bags with clothes and dropped them at local donation bins. A week later, in a group text, she'd explained that she didn't need the appointments we made, that they were for serious addicts, not people like her, that they were too far away, that our father agreed with her appraisal. Years before that, we'd had a similar intervention with my father, whose depression had become so concerning that for the first and only time, I asked him if he was going to kill himself.

I want my mother to be better, and I want my father to be better, and that day I wanted Jordan to be better, but I was certain that my mother was enabling his depression. The same way she'd decided she didn't need help, she was letting him decide he didn't, either. The hospital was scary, and she could take care of her son. She couldn't very well force him to go. Those conversations ended in fights, usually with Jordan sleeping just a few feet away in his room. I would yell that he was going to kill himself, and my mother would cry that we were on the same side. I would go to leave, and my father would tell us both to take a break and calm down. When Jordan finally ended up at the hospital, my mother was there every day; it was her life. But still I was at a distance.

On one of those days, I told her I'd come by the hospital for a visit, too. Jordan had begun electroshock therapy, which wasn't any less upsetting for its potential progress—there was no getting around the sheer violence of it, and Jordan hated having to do it. We wanted as many people as possible to keep him company. I ended up arriving just at the end of visiting hours, when my mother and Jordan were playing rummy. The plan was to all leave together, walking downstairs with Jordan and the nurse to the ECT ward as visiting hours ended, but the hospital schedule was running behind.

"Just head to the lobby," Jordan's nurse told my mother. "I'll call you as soon as it's time."

"But we'll walk down with him, right?" my mother said. "I want to make sure we walk down with him."

The nurse smiled. "You will. Don't worry."

So my mother and I went to the lobby. I got a corn muffin and a coffee; she got a blueberry muffin and a tea. We played a half-hearted round of rummy. She was anxious, checking her phone again and again. It was taking too long.

Finally, after about forty-five minutes, she noticed that a call had gone straight to voicemail. It wasn't her fault; service in that lobby was notoriously dodgy. But she'd missed it, and it didn't matter that the nurse sounded calm when she said that the procedure was over, everything had gone fine, and we could come down to find Jordan in the recovery area. It didn't matter, because for even one moment he had been alone. And in that moment, he might have been scared. My mother was crying immediately, pushing the cards into her bag and rushing through the hall and down the elevator while I tried to keep up. She was torturing herself—he wasn't supposed to be alone, he must have been terrified, he needed to know she was there waiting—and I repeated, "It's okay, it's not your fault."

When we got to the appropriate waiting room and the nurse ushered us to the recovery beds, Jordan was there, fine. The sessions always left him in a dream state, not dissimilar to coming out of anesthesia for any procedure, only in this case he lost more memories than just those upon waking, and sometimes for good. He didn't remember the nurse having taken him to the procedure without my mother because he didn't remember anything from that morning; he looked at me and asked when I'd arrived. My mother grasped one of his hands, and I grasped the other. There was nothing worse than seeing him like this.

When it was time for us, again, to leave, I hugged my mother in the parking lot, and we cried. I softened that day, but it shouldn't have taken so long. I softened because it had been easy to dismiss her pain when she was in power mode: endless energy, aggressive positivity, this was just Jordan's depression, it was going to get better. It was easy for me to dismiss her pain because I'd convinced myself that she was expressing it wrong. She was doing it all wrong; she didn't understand. She didn't understand it the way I understood it, the way my father understood it. But to watch her running down that hall crying only up until the moment she was standing in front of him, making sure he wouldn't see her tears: *We* didn't understand. This was her baby. He was her baby. She'd carried him then; she holds him still. His heart came to life through her blood. She listened for its rhythm beneath her skin. I understand it now, I think.

*   *   *

The person who kills himself "does no harm to society," wrote the eighteenth-century Scottish philosopher David Hume. "[H]e only ceases to do good." All this time, all those years worrying about having a child, worrying now that Theo's here, my fear has been focused on the active effect of my suicide, what it would create—which is to say, its harm. In an already too painful world, my suicide would give Theo a trauma he'd carry until he died. I hadn't considered the opposite, the ceasing of good: not what I would do to Theo but what I would take from him. There's something helpful, deceptively positive, in the switch.

Watching Jordan want to die was scarier than wanting to die, because I could know only what he told me. *I wish I could take it from him*, I wrote after visiting him at the hospital. *Please, give it to me. I trust myself more.* And now, even though he is well and has been well for years, I'm still afraid. What if he and his girlfriend break up? What if he loses his job? What if something happens—maybe someone is rude, maybe something embarrasses him—that makes him hate himself? Does he hate himself? What if this world he's so sensitive to, its injustices, its cruelty, the billionaires, the bigots, the violence—what if it becomes too much? What if, as Joey said, standing with the blade against his neck, facing a police force he knew would either shoot him* or take him back to one holding cell or another—what if it all just hurts too much? And what if, despite my conviction that a better world is possible, that it's coming—what if everything is only worse by the time Theo is the age Jordan was when he was admitted?

I tell Elizabeth that I'm so scared, sometimes I can't look at Theo without worrying that he's going to kill himself, that I know he's going to be just like me, and she says, "Even if that were the case—we can't know if it is, but even if it were—you didn't die."

These days I look at Theo and I feel equal parts joy and despair, wonder and loss, a premature mourning or regret. I look at his body, and I want to burrow inside. His body, which used to live inside mine, separates from me more every day. As his navigation and mastery of it grow, so does our alienation from each other. As time passes and I become less of him and he becomes less of me, I worry: Will it only become easier to leave? Is that how it works? Is that how a mother makes peace with it? Did Sylvia feel as though she'd done enough to prepare her children for the rest of their lives? Did she love them as much as I love Theo? If I can convince myself that she didn't, am I allowed to relinquish my fear?

Cuddling on the beanbag one night, just after smothering him with kisses, he grabs my cheeks with delicate hands and says, "This time I give *you* a kiss." Very deliberately, he drops quick little kisses all over my face, each time announcing the destination: "A kiss for your cheek"—*smack*—"A kiss for your other cheek"—*smack*—"A

---

* In their decade of tracking fatal police shootings in the US, the *Washington Post* has found that one in five victims—2,046 victims, to be precise—were experiencing a mental illness crisis when killed.

kiss for your nose"—*smack*—and so on. Then he asks for more kisses from me to him, directing me to his fingers, one at a time, and then his toes. What I struggle to explain is how embodied my love for Theo is and his is for me, how it feels feral, primitive, close to the ground. How could that not be the case? I grew him; he lived inside me, was an extension of my body, only five years ago. He spent the first month in the world not even realizing we'd been separated, assuming that *I* was an extension of *his* body. How can we describe this phenomenon with unabashed honesty within a Puritanical culture so discomfited by physical intimacy, so determined to sexualize and condemn it, and so eager to criticize mothers in general?

Early in motherhood I found on TikTok a video of a mother lamenting the fact that her son had gotten old enough to no longer allow her to smell his feet. I cringed then, and I cringe now; I was vicariously embarrassed and a little bit disgusted, as were most of the users lambasting her in a flood of comments. Now, though, I also get it. It's not the act so much as the nearness. It's the feet themselves, the bodily symbol of the child's agency and autonomy, carrying him through the world, hardening against the ground as more ground is covered, equipping him with thick enough skin to make it on his own. Where will those feet take him? When will he go?

I think I will always be afraid, but not just for Theo's or Jordan's or my dad's or my own suicide. There are countless risks, so many ways to hurt, so many ways to die. Maybe I will always be afraid, but maybe that's just me, or maybe that's just motherhood, maybe that's just love. I'm learning to see the fear, name it, feel it, and then let it drift from my mind like a cloud. My mother is crazy and my father is depressed, and they raised us before our culture started to develop a growing awareness of mental health as a concept, but Jordan didn't kill himself, and neither did I. We're alive, and they helped us get here. If Theo does end up like me, I'll be here to help him live, too.

* * *

In thinking about all of this, about bodies and birthing and motherhood, I find myself on Maggie Nelson's doorstep, seeking out her description of labor in *The Argonauts*: "It isn't the pain that one forgets. It's the touching death part." By the time I arrived at labor, I'd already been through ten months of hell. When the nausea cropped up one week after the positive test, I maintained my sanity by counting down the days until the second trimester, telling myself that it would pass. But the second trimester came, and it didn't pass; in fact, it got worse. By the third trimester—after months of throwing up multiple times daily, missing weeks of work, relying on IVs for hydration, and having one desperate, terrified conversation with Brendan about whether I could make it to the end—I'd come to terms with the fact that the nausea would leave when the baby did. Friends and family joked that, karmically, I was ensured a smooth delivery. I believed this, cautiously.

But one thing after another went wrong after my water broke, and suddenly I was getting prepped for an emergency C-section after twenty-four hours of labor. Theo's heart rate was dropping with each contraction, and I asked Brendan if he thought the universe was punishing us, if I wasn't supposed to be having a child. I was delirious and catastrophizing, imagining a rapid deterioration that would lead to Brendan having to choose between my life and Theo's.

If I was touching death in labor, it wasn't mine. I felt it as a thread binding around his heart. I worried that it was his death I was touching, but the only way I've ever managed a fear of death—both my loved ones' and my own—has been in a refusal to forget its presence, in a constant reaching for it. I've done this my whole life with suicidal thinking, but I also spent my pregnancy obsessed with Theo's death. I kept death close for nine months, staying up late at night reading about all the ways he could die. It wasn't enough to worry about it; I had to envision it, to feel it, and then to remind myself that it wasn't real. This book is also a way to maintain contact, to keep death close. What can I let in when I let go?

* * *

I'm in bed with Theo, and we've been here for nearly an hour. We've read books; we've had some talking time; I've turned on the seven-hour YouTube video of calm instrumental music that plays over a looping animation of cartoon fish swimming across the screen. I'm tired and impatient, wanting to be on the couch playing video games but trying to be present, reminding myself that one day I'll be desperate for the chance to fall asleep next to him again. Finally, he's silent for long enough to make me think he's fallen asleep, but then the familiar question comes in a voice so tiny but so assured. "What will happen when you die?"

I repeat what I've told him before: We go to a place we can't see, where we find all the people we love who died before us. We get to hang out with one another for as long as we want, until we decide we'd like to come back to Earth and start again. He is especially partial to the idea that on our next go-around, I could be his baby. This time, though, he's looking for the nitty-gritty—the details, the procedure. "But what will happen to your body?"

"Well. My body will stop working. You remember when you were learning about all of your body parts?"

"Like my intestines," he says. He loves the intestines for their proximity to the butt.

"Right," I say. "So when I die—"

"I'll cry a lot," he cuts me off.

"Yeah. That's true. It will be very sad. But you'll be okay, because you'll have a lot of people around you to help you feel better. So my body will stop working, which means my heart won't send blood around my body anymore and my brain won't have thoughts."

"And that's bad."

"Yeah, that's bad."

"So when you're dead, can you walk?"

"No, you can't really do anything."

"What happens then? Does your body freeze?"

This is the farthest we've ventured into the physical practicalities of death, and I take a moment to strategize, trying to avoid anything that will give him nightmares.

"Are you sure you want to talk about this now, bud? Sometimes I don't like thinking about it right before bed, and we can talk more tomorrow if you'd like."

"No, I want to talk about it now."

"Okay, well. When your body stops working it sort of . . . falls apart." I grimace, imagining this horrifying image from his perspective. "Okay, no, think about this. You know how the leaves fall? And they change color, and they kind of—okay, actually, no . . . compost. You know how we put all those different things in the bin for the wormies and after a long time all of that food and grass and everything turns into dirt? That's kind of what happens. We put the body into the ground—"

"What?!" he screeches, and I panic.

"No, but it's okay! Because your soul is somewhere else."

"What's a soul?"

"It's just. The thing that makes you, you. It's your love and your feelings and your thoughts and your personality. Does that make sense?"

"Yes."

"Okay, so we put the body in a nice bed, and we decorate it with all the things you loved, and that goes in the ground, and you say goodbye to your body, and everyone else says goodbye to your body, and you go on to the afterlife."

"And then I see you."

"And then you see me."

"But how do you do things in the afterlife if you don't have a body?"

"Okay, yeah, that's a good question. You have . . . a different kind of body."

"So then we can still lie down next to each other."

"Yes."

He's appeased, and I'm ready for the conversation to be over, not only because it's getting dangerously close to deflating the beliefs I use to keep myself calm but also because I'm tired. I need him to go to bed. Another concern arises. "What age will you be when you die?"

"Nobody knows that, but it will probably be a very long time from now."

We pinky-swear once again to try our very hardest to live for a very, very long time, to be safe, to be healthy. He promises that he will listen when Brendan and I tell him to get down from some precarious ledge he's found, to stop walking as close to the street as he can get, to hold my hand on the subway platform. I know he believes in this promise as certainly as I know that tomorrow he will be making his best effort to turn the mundane into an extreme sport. I ask if he has any other questions; he wants to know how people know what color the dinosaurs were. We're in the clear, for now.

Theo turns to me, burrows one arm under my neck and drapes the other over the top, touches his face to mine. I know this phase will end, and probably soon, but for now he remains ravenous for my body. No amount of touch is close enough, but he'll settle for what physics allows. I wrap my arms around him and squeeze; our grooves shift into place. We're almost there, I can tell by the lengthening of his breaths. Soon, sleep.

"I'm not letting go of you," he whispers. "Are you gonna let go of me?"

I believe it now, and all I can do is hope that I always will. Tonight, it is the easiest answer to give, a visceral, thunderous certainty deep within my bones.

"No, my love. I'm not letting go."

Acknowledgments

When *Better* comes out, it will have been just shy of eight years since I began writing it. Eight years is a long time to keep a project in mind, even if it's sitting at the very back, and one of the ways I maintained some level of connection to (and general faith in) this book was by keeping an ongoing list of the people helping me along the way. Eight years is a long time, and this will be a long list.

Thank you first and foremost to Ian Bonaparte, my shrewd and often hilarious agent extraordinaire who so clearly saw, understood, and loved the book that was hiding within the mess of my original proposal, and who then helped me carve it out. Thank you to my brilliant angel of an editor, Rachel Kambury, whose patience, compassion, and unwavering support is the only reason this book made it to publication, and whose editorial instincts made it beautiful. Your name should be on the cover next to mine. Thank you to my powerhouse publicist Kathy Daneman for taking me on despite the state of the "manuscript" I submitted.

I'm immensely grateful to Karen Rinaldi—whose enthusiastic support from the first meeting meant the world to me—as well as

Acknowledgments

Rachel Molland, Milan Bozic, Jessica Gilo, Frieda Duggan, and any and all copy editors, publicists, marketers, producers, sales representatives, associates, assistants, and interns who had a hand in bringing *Better* to life at probably half the pay they deserve. A huge thank-you to Wudan Yan and her sharp, expedient fact-checking team at Factual, including Andrew Rosenblum, Simi Kadirgamar, Adam Smith-Perez, and Beatrice Hogan. You are lifesavers.

Thank you to the genius editors who worked on and published various portions of this book, especially Matt Ortile, Tajja Isen, Rachel Sanders, Tomi Obaro, Karolina Waclawiak, and Isaac Fitzgerald. Thank you to Beth Herstein, Sara Theiss, Ricki Schecter, Adrienne Wong, Erika Bartolini, Melanie Lynn Danza, and Eve Mastro for your invaluable early insights: Let's get the gang back together. Thank you to the champions who've kept the faith in me and my work throughout all the times I've lost it, especially Michael Taeckens, Jaime Green, Shayne Terry, Lydia Kiesling, Kiyomi Shimada, Julia Furlan, Shannon Keating, Kimberly Burns, Cecilia Majzoub, Kristin Chirico, Brian Bernatzky, Erik Kindel, Nikki Georgopulos, Amelia Newburg, Lindsay Myers, Kelly Hoffer, Alicia Parter, Rebecca Munro, Grace Lieberman, Elise LaChapelle, Lindsey Adler, Alair Southerton, and Maya Seligman. To my story pals: you genuinely make my life better.

A massive thank-you to the Kimmel Harding Nelson Center for the Arts for giving me the precious gifts of time, space, community, and a vote of confidence; thank you, also, to Hannah Demma for facilitating the best first residency a girl could dream of. To Kermit and Azadeh Westergaard and the Woodward Residency, I can't thank you enough for your generosity and support. I send much love to the many other scattered establishments in which I wrote *Better*, but especially the Ridgewood Public Library, OStudio, the Millay Arts barn, and Erika's Worcester Airbnb.

I'm endlessly grateful for the teachers who instilled in me a love not only for literature but also for, simply, education. A few are responsible for setting me on the path to *Better*: Michael Nolan, thank you for recognizing something in me that I wouldn't see for a long time, and also for planting the seed of my Samuel Beckett obsession. Carol Rosen, thank you for letting me enroll in your master's class on English and Irish playwrights, and for being the first person to ever introduce me as a writer. Pancho Savery: I can't overstate your role in my becoming the writer and thinker I am today. There is a direct line between your mentorship and this book, and I feel so blessed to have landed in your classroom. It changed my life.

(Thank you also to Keith Sommers for telling me you'd fire me if I didn't go back to school. I promised you I'd have you in my acknowledgments one day.)

Thank you to Melissa Lewis, for waking me up; to Andrew Brischler, for catching me again and again; and to Emily Roberts, for making me brave. To Katie Heaney, Caitlin Sempowich, and Jackie DeStefano, thank you for keeping me alive, whether you knew you were doing so or not. To Rose Lewis, Natasha Barnes, Annelyse Gelman, and Juliet Shafto, thank you for over a decade of hehsh braowns, for being my home, for getting it. To Billy Kermode, thank you for talking me down.

I owe an immense debt of gratitude to Mike Alsup, for giving me not only permission to share Alice's work but also the blessing to describe a small portion of her life. Thank you for your openness, and for allowing me—and now, readers—to better see her. Thank you, also, to Gary Granger for expanding a story I thought I already knew.

Thank you, Alice.

Thank you, Elizabeth, for your deep well of compassion and insight, and for holding my sadness. In more ways than I can count, this book couldn't exist without you.

Acknowledgments

To my parents, Carlo and Linda: Thank you for raising me right, for teaching me about the world, for reading to me, for never letting me doubt that I am loved, and for being okay with me writing this book. To UG and Aunt Denise, thank you for your constant support. To Nena, Jordan, and Dylan: Any time I've ever doubted my ability to love wholly, I've remembered you and come to my senses. Jordan, thank you for staying. I love the three of you so much it's stupid.

Brendan, thank you isn't enough, but I'll keep saying it forever. You made this possible, and it's just one of a googolplex of reasons I love you. Theo, when you're old enough to read this, if you do choose to read this: Thank you for making everything brighter. I hope you don't mind that I wrote about Butt World. You are the two loves of my life.

And to you, reader: Thank you for reading.

Selected Bibliography

The following is an incomplete list of books and other media that I consumed, consulted, and found useful throughout writing *Better*, the majority of which didn't make it into the text. Most are about suicide; others are suicide- or survival-adjacent, even if the connection is clear only to my mind. Each I recommend.

BOOKS

Alsup, Alice. *The Poet Walks Away: Poems*. Pemberley Press, 2014.

Alvarez, A. *The Savage God: A Study of Suicide*. W. W. Norton & Company, 1990.

Antrim, Donald. *One Friday in April: A Story of Suicide and Survival*. W. W. Norton & Company, 2021.

baer, hannah. *trans girl suicide museum*. Hesse Press, 2019.

Bamford, Maria. *Sure, I'll Join Your Cult: A Memoir of Mental Illness and the Quest to Belong Anywhere*. Simon and Schuster, 2023.

Carrington, Leonora. *Down Below*. New York Review of Books, 2017.

Case, Anne, and Angus Deaton. *Deaths of Despair and the Future of Capitalism*. Princeton University Press, 2021.

Critchley, Simon. *Suicide*. Thought Catalog Books, 2016.

Cunningham, Michael. *The Hours*. Farrar, Straus and Giroux, 1998.

Danquah, Nana-Ama. *Willow Weep for Me: A Black Woman's Journey Through Depression*. W. W. Norton & Company, 1998.

Dazai, Osamu. *No Longer Human*. New Directions Publishing, 1958.

Selected Bibliography

Dillard, Annie. *Holy the Firm*. Harper & Row, 1977.

Goethe, Johann Wolfgang von. *The Sorrows of Young Werther*. Penguin Classics, 1989.

Gray, Spalding. *The Journals of Spalding Gray*. Vintage, 2012.

Hecht, Jennifer Michael. *Stay: A History of Suicide and the Philosophies Against It*. Yale University Press, 2013.

Jamison, Kay Redfield. *An Unquiet Mind: A Memoir of Moods and Madness*. Vintage, 1997.

Jamison, Kay Redfield. *Night Falls Fast: Understanding Suicide*. Vintage, 2000.

Joiner, Thomas. *Why People Die by Suicide*. Harvard University Press, 2009.

Levé, Edouard. *Suicide*. Deep Vellum Publishing, 2014.

Li, Yiyun. *Dear Friend, from My Life I Write to You in Your Life*. Random House, 2017.

Li, Yiyun. *Where Reasons End: A Novel*. Random House, 2019.

Mailhot, Terese Marie. *Heart Berries: A Memoir*. Counterpoint Press, 2018.

Nguyen, Diana Khoi. *Ghost Of*. Omnidawn Open, 2018.

Ozawa-de Silva, Chikako. *The Anatomy of Loneliness: Suicide, Social Connection, and the Search for Relational Meaning in Contemporary Japan*. University of California Press, 2021.

Paperny, Anna Mehler. *Hello I Want to Die Please Fix Me*. The Experiment, 2020.

Plath, Sylvia. *The Journals of Sylvia Plath*. Anchor, 1998.

Radtke, Kristen. *Seek You: A Journey Through American Loneliness*. Pantheon, 2021.

Rankine, Claudia. *Don't Let Me Be Lonely: An American Lyric*. Graywolf Press, 2004.

Sexton, Anne. *The Complete Poems*. Ecco, 1999.

Shneidman, Edwin. *Voices of Death*. Harper & Row, 1980.

Toews, Miriam. *All My Puny Sorrows*. Bloomsbury Publishing, 2019.

Wang, Esmé Weijun. *The Collected Schizophrenias: Essays*. Graywolf Press, 2019.

Williams, Mark. *Cry of Pain: Understanding Suicide and Self-Harm*. Penguin Group, 1997.

Williams, Terry. *Teenage Suicide Notes: An Ethnography of Self-Harm*. Columbia University Press, 2017.

Woolf, Virginia. *Moments of Being: A Collection of Autobiographical Writing*. Mariner Books, 1985.

Woolf, Virginia. *A Writer's Diary: Being Extracts from the Diary of Virginia Woolf*. Mariner Books, 1973.

MULTIMEDIA

Cole, Sean, host. *This American Life*, episode 622, "Who You Gonna Call?" Chicago Public Media, August 4, 2017. https://www.thisamericanlife.org/622/who-you-gonna-call.

Daldry, Stephen, dir. *The Hours*. Paramount Pictures, 2002.

Goldstein, Jonathan, host. *Heavyweight*, episode 49, "Another Roadside Attraction," Gimlet Media, November 17, 2022. https://gimletmedia.com/shows/heavyweight/wbhx37x.

Harjo, Sterlin, and Taika Waititi, creators. *Reservation Dogs*. Television series. FX Productions, 2021–2023.

Joffe-Walt, Chana, host. *This American Life,* episode 557, "Birds & Bees," Chicago Public Media, May 15, 2015. https://www.thisamericanlife.org/557/birds-bees.

Lovelace, Paul, and Jessica Wolfson, dirs. *Radio Unnameable*. Kino Lorber, 2012.

Mars, Roman, host. *99% Invisible*, episode 259, "This Is Chance: Anchorwoman of the Great Alaska Earthquake," May 16, 2017. https://99percentinvisible.org/episode/chance-anchorwoman-great-alaska-earthquake/.

Moe, John, host. *The Hilarious World of Depression*. Podcast series. American Public Media, 2016–2020. https://www.hilariousworld.org/.

Rosin, Hanna, host. *Invisibilia*, season 4, episode 1, "I, I, I. Him," National Public Radio, March 13, 2018. https://www.npr.org/2017/06/30/593135007/podcast-i-i-i-him.

Steel, Eric, dir. *The Bridge*. IFC Films, 2006.

Wells, Charlotte. *Aftersun*. A24, 2022.

Notes

AUTHOR'S NOTE

xii   *"how it felt to me"*: Joan Didion, "On Keeping a Notebook," in *Slouching Towards Bethlehem* (New York: Farrar, Straus and Giroux, 1968), 134.

PROLOGUE

1   does not take insurance: Joshua Breslau et al., "Availability and Accessibility of Mental Health Services in New York City," *Rand Health Quarterly* 10, no. 1 (2022): 6, https://www.ncbi.nlm.nih.gov/pmc/articles/PMC9718065/.

CHAPTER 1: DO IT

10   "We must be together": Roman Mars, host, and Jon Mooallem, writer, *99% Invisible*, episode 259, "This Is Chance: Anchorwoman of the Great Alaska Earthquake," May 16, 2017, https://99percentinvisible.org/episode/chance-anchorwoman-great-alaska-earthquake/.

12n   the most prescribed category: NIH MedlinePlus Magazine, "Commonly Prescribed Antidepressants and How They Work," National Library of Medicine, September 21, 2023, https://magazine.medlineplus.gov/article/commonly-prescribed-antidepressants-and-how-they-work.

CHAPTER 2: BETTER

39n   "before and after": Yiyun Li, *Dear Friend, from My Life I Write to You in Your Life* (New York: Random House, 2017), 3–4.

Notes

47 On our second day there: "El Santuario de Chimayo," National Park Service, updated March 23, 2024, https://www.nps.gov/places/el-santuario-de-chimayo.htm.

53 one- and two-year-olds: Stephen Bates, "Son of Poets Sylvia Plath and Ted Hughes Kills Himself," *The Guardian*, March 23, 2009, https://www.theguardian.com/books/2009/mar/23/sylvia-plath-son-kills-himself.

53 hours before she died: Jane Feinmann, "Rhyme, reason and depression," *The Guardian*, February 16, 1993, https://www.theguardian.com/books/1993/feb/16/biography.sylviaplath.

54 public skepticism: Janet Malcolm, "The Silent Woman," *The New Yorker*, August 23, 1993, https://www.newyorker.com/magazine/1993/08/23/the-silent-woman-i-ii-iii.

54 "clearly defined immediate": Sylvia Plath, *The Journals of Sylvia Plath* (New York: Anchor, 1998), 251.

55 "part of nothing": Plath, *The Journals of Sylvia Plath*, 252.

55 "conquer childbirth": Plath, *The Journals of Sylvia Plath*, 241.

56 "I am nothing": Plath, *The Journals of Sylvia Plath*, 204.

58 But then there's a photo: Harry Ogden, *Ted Hughes; Sylvia Plath*, 1956, gelatin silver print, 9 7/8 in. x 8 1/8 in., National Portrait Gallery, ref. no. NPG P2012, https://www.npg.org.uk/collections/search/portrait/mw270579/Ted-Hughes-Sylvia-Plath.

58 "How clear and cleansed": Plath, *The Journals of Sylvia Plath*, 193.

58 "Much happier today": Plath, *The Journals of Sylvia Plath*, 261.

58 "Is it dangerous": Plath, *The Journals of Sylvia Plath*, 276.

58 "if ever I have come close": Plath, *The Journals of Sylvia Plath*, 59.

58 "free, spoiled, pampered country": Plath, *The Journals of Sylvia Plath*, 62.

59 "life [is] so tragic": Virginia Woolf, *A Writer's Diary: Being Extracts from the Diary of Virginia Woolf* (New York: Mariner Books, 1973), 27–28.

CHAPTER 3: THE AIRLOCK

64 "as if I had to": Sylvia Plath, *The Journals of Sylvia Plath* (New York: Anchor, 1998), 252.

64n "it's so over for everyone": u/coleisw4ck, "SAME," r/CPTSDmemes, Reddit, August 14, 2024, https://www.reddit.com/r/CPTSDmemes/comments/1eschvc/same/.

64 "lose their taste for life": Georges Minois, *History of Suicide: Voluntary Death in Western Culture* (Baltimore: The Johns Hopkins University Press, 1999), 51.

65n   "no other trans girls": hannah baer, *trans girl suicide museum* (New York: Hesse Press, 2019), 41.

65n   disproportionately represented: Norik Kirakosian, et. al., "Suicidal Ideation Disparities Among Transgender and Gender Diverse Compared to Cisgender Community Health Patients," *Journal of General Internal Medicine* 38, no. 6 (May 2023): 1357–1365, https://link.springer.com /article/10.1007/s11606-022-07996-2.

65n   trans youth: Myeshia Price-Feeney, Amy E. Green, and Samuel Dorison, "Understanding the Mental Health of Transgender and Nonbinary Youth," *Journal of Adolescent Health* 66, no. 6 (June 2020): 684–690, https://www.jahonline.org/article/S1054-139X(19)30922-X/fulltext.

65n   external factors: "6 Risk Factors for Transgender & Gender Diverse Suicide," CAMS-care, accessed November 22, 2024, https://cams-care .com/resources/educational-content/6-risk-factors-for-suicide-in -transgender-and-gender-diverse-adults/.

65n   increase suicidality universally: "Risk and Protective Factors for Suicide," CDC Suicide Prevention, April 25, 2024, https://www.cdc.gov/suicide /risk-factors/index.html.

65n   abuse: Andrew R. Flores, Ilan H. Meyer, Lynn Langton, and Jody L. Herman, "Gender Identity Disparities in Criminal Victimization: National Crime Victimization Survey, 2017–2018," *American Journal of Public Health* 111, no. 4 (April 2021): 726–729, https://ajph .aphapublications.org/doi/abs/10.2105/AJPH.2020.306099.

65n   poverty: "The Complexity of LGBT Poverty in the United States," The University of Wisconsin-Madison Institute for Research on Poverty, June 2021, https://www.irp.wisc.edu/resource/the-complexity-of-lgbt -poverty-in-the-united-states/.

65n   estrangement: "New research shows almost half of LGBT+ adults are estranged from family and a third 'not confident' their parents will accept them," Just Like Us, April 2023, https://www.justlikeus.org /blog/2023/04/19/new-research-shows-almost-half-of-lgbt-adults -are-estranged-from-family-and-a-third-not-confident-their-parents-will -accept-them/.

65n   incarceration: "Unjust: How the Broken Criminal Justice System Fails Transgender People," Movement Advancement Project and Center for American Progress, May 2016, https://www.lgbtmap.org/policy-and -issue-analysis/criminal-justice-trans.

66   "[a]s much spending": baer, *trans girl suicide museum*, 42.

66   "the most normal": baer, *trans girl suicide museum*, 42.

Notes

66 "I imagined us": baer, *trans girl suicide museum*, 41.

67 "Part of the museum": baer, *trans girl suicide museum*, 59.

67 "your body is the problem": baer, *trans girl suicide museum*, 60.

68 "I feel this pain": baer, *trans girl suicide museum*, 113.

68 "readiness": baer, *trans girl suicide museum*, 58.

68 "the question I'm asking": baer, *trans girl suicide museum*, 59.

69 "lost and desperate": Spalding Gray, *The Journals of Spalding Gray* (New York: Vintage, 2012), 47.

69n "I hope I can get down to some writing": Gray, *The Journals of Spalding Gray*, 75.

69n "out of it and ragged": Gray, *The Journals of Spalding Gray*, 77.

71 "We talked death": Anne Sexton, "The Barfly Ought to Sing," *TriQuarterly* 7 (Fall 1966): 89.

77 "[W]e pick up the pistol": Donald Antrim, *One Friday in April: A Story of Suicide and Survival* (New York: W. W. Norton, 2021), 92.

77 "beat back [the] pressing urge": Thomas Joiner, *Why People Die by Suicide* (Cambridge, MA: Harvard University Press, 2009), 22–24.

78n women's mental health: Amanda Koire and Reid Mergler, "Women's History Month: The Rise of Reproductive Psychiatry," American Psychiatric Association, March 3, 2023, https://www.psychiatry.org/news-room/apa-blogs/womens-history-month-reproductive-psychiatry.

78n "emerging field": "Reproductive Psychiatry Gives Birth to a New Era in Women's Mental Health," Psychiatrist.com, January 24, 2023, https://www.psychiatrist.com/news/reproductive-psychiatry-gives-birth-to-a-new-era-in-womens-mental-health/.

81 "There are these two": David Foster Wallace, "This Is Water," commencement speech, Kenyon College, Gambier, Ohio, May 21, 2005, transcript and audio, https://fs.blog/david-foster-wallace-this-is-water/.

82 power, force: Definitions and etymology of "vitality" come from Oxford English Dictionary, s.v. "vitality (n.), sense 3," https://www.oed.com/dictionary/vitality_n.

82 "a sense that one's actions": Ben Dean, "Vitality," Authentic Happiness, accessed August 24, 2024, https://www.authentichappiness.sas.upenn.edu/zh-hans/content/vitality.

82 communicate: Definitions and etymology of "inspire" come from Oxford English Dictionary, s.v. "inspire (v.), II.5.a," https://www.oed.com/dictionary/inspire_v.

82 motion: Definitions and etymology of "animate" come from Oxford

English Dictionary, s.v. "animate (v.), sense I.2," https://www.oed.com/dictionary/animate_v.

83   "life without having lived": Plath, *The Journals of Sylvia Plath*, 261.

83   claims of his misogyny: Mary K. Holland, "The Last Essay I Need to Write about David Foster Wallace," *Literary Hub*, November 29, 2021, https://lithub.com/the-last-essay-i-need-to-write-about-david-foster-wallace/.

CHAPTER 4: THE ARCHIVE

89   "[S]ometimes, in a panic": Sylvia Plath, *The Journals of Sylvia Plath* (New York: Anchor, 1998), 104.

89   "twinge of glory": Plath, *The Journals of Sylvia Plath*, 192.

90   "capture moments like this": Plath, *The Journals of Sylvia Plath*, 65.

90   "note more symptoms": Virginia Woolf, *A Writer's Diary: Being Extracts from the Diary of Virginia Woolf* (New York: Mariner Books, 1973), 32.

90   "This was perhaps": Edouard Levé, *Suicide* (Dallas, TX: Dalkey Archive Press, 2014), 62.

91   "Where had they gone?": Levé, *Suicide*, 26.

91   "looked for explanations": Levé, *Suicide*, 46.

91   "my bank account": Edouard Levé, *Autoportrait* (Dallas, TX: Dalkey Archive Press, 2012), 7.

91   "the big toe": Levé, *Autoportrait*, 10.

91   "a female hamster": Levé, *Autoportrait*, 13.

91   "I archive": Levé, *Autoportrait*, 5.

92   "so only-once": Plath, *The Journals of Sylvia Plath*, 72.

92   "How I envy her the task": Woolf, *A Writer's Diary*, 7.

92   "I fancy old Virginia": Woolf, *A Writer's Diary*, 23.

93   "This second is life": Plath, *The Journals of Sylvia Plath*, 4.

93   "Life piles up": Woolf, *A Writer's Diary*, 9.

95   "that most fearsome": Plath, *The Journals of Sylvia Plath*, 241.

96   "our memories tell more": Yiyun Li, *Dear Friend, from My Life I Write to You in Your Life* (New York: Random House, 2017), 5.

97   "Nothing is real": Plath, *The Journals of Sylvia Plath*, 5.

97   "past or future": Plath, *The Journals of Sylvia Plath*, 18.

98   "To forget frees me": Levé, *Suicide*, 94.

CHAPTER 5: THE UGLY MASK

108   Chemical imbalance?: Joanna Moncrieff and Mark Horowitz, "Depression Is Probably Not Caused by a Chemical Imbalance in

the Brain—New Study," The Conversation, July 21, 2022, https:// theconversation.com/depression-is-probably-not-caused-by-a-chemical -imbalance-in-the-brain-new-study-186672.

108　Genetic inheritance?: Maria Shadrina, Elena A. Bondarenko, and Petr A. Slominsky, "Genetics Factors in Major Depression Disease," *Frontiers in Psychiatry* 9 (July 23, 2018): 334, https://www.frontiersin.org/journals /psychiatry/articles/10.3389/fpsyt.2018.00334/full.

108　"a distillation both": Kay Redfield Jamison, *An Unquiet Mind: A Memoir of Moods and Madness* (New York: Vintage, 2011), 5.

109　"generalised emotion-numbing effect": Moncrieff and Horowitz, "Depression Is Probably Not Caused by a Chemical Imbalance in the Brain—New Study."

109　"be[ing] . . . disproven": u/papitopapito, "If the chemical imbalance theory has been disproven, why do SSRI work for so many people?," r/antidepressants, Reddit, June 29, 2022, https://www.reddit.com /r/antidepressants/comments/vnbzcg/if_the_chemical_imbalance _theory_has_been/.

109n　hasn't been categorically debunked: Laura Sanders, "A Chemical Imbalance Doesn't Explain Depression. So What Does?," ScienceNews, February 12, 2023, https://www.sciencenews.org/article/chemical -imbalance-explain-depression.

111　"great muscular owl": Sylvia Plath, *The Journals of Sylvia Plath* (New York: Anchor, 1998), 240.

111　"demon": Plath, *The Journals of Sylvia Plath*, 177.

113　"beyond help": Plath, *The Journals of Sylvia Plath*, 62.

113　"ugly dead mask": Plath, *The Journals of Sylvia Plath*, 67.

113　"gay, friendly person": Plath, *The Journals of Sylvia Plath*, 69.

114　"You have forgotten": Plath, *The Journals of Sylvia Plath*, 67.

114　"Scared, Spoiled Baby": Plath, *The Journals of Sylvia Plath*, 82.

114　"You just better learn to know yourself": Plath, *The Journals of Sylvia Plath*, 86.

115　Reporting on Suicide: "Best Practices and Recommendations for Reporting on Suicide," Reporting on Suicide, accessed August 25, 2024, https://reportingonsuicide.org/recommendations/.

115　National Institute of Mental Health: "Frequently Asked Questions About Suicide," National Institute of Mental Health (NIMH), revised 2023, https://www.nimh.nih.gov/health/publications/suicide-faq.

115　World Health Organization: "Preventing Suicide: A Resource for Media

Professionals, Update 2023," World Health Organization, September 12, 2023, https://www.who.int/publications/i/item/9789240076846.

115 "international suicide prevention": "About," Reporting on Suicide, accessed November 22, 2024, https://reportingonsuicide.org/about/.

116 "person-first language": "Person-First and Destigmatizing Language," National Institutes of Health, August 11, 2022, https://www.nih.gov /nih-style-guide/person-first-destigmatizing-language.

116 discourse dominated by censure: Brian Barraclough and Daphne Shepherd, "A Necessary Neologism: The Origin and Uses of Suicide," *Suicide and Life-Threatening Behavior* 24, no. 2 (Summer 1994): 113–26, https://pubmed.ncbi.nlm.nih.gov/8053006/.

116 gruesomely punishable crime: Gerry Holt, "When Suicide Was Illegal," *BBC News*, August 3, 2011, https://www.bbc.com/news/magazine-14374296.

117 "Eight Ways to Actively Fight Depression": This headline and "Recognize and Conquer Your Critical Self Attacks" come from Lisa Firestone, "Eight Ways to Actively Fight Depression," *Psychology Today*, October 6, 2011, https://www.psychologytoday.com/us/blog /compassion-matters/201110/eight-ways-actively-fight-depression.

117 "To combat depression": Lisa Firestone, "6 Truths About Depression and How to Overcome It," HuffPost, October 2, 2013, https://www.huffpost .com/entry/depression-help_b_4018957.

117 "defeat" it: The Sun, "Just One Hour of Exercise per Week Can Help Defeat Depression," *New York Post*, October 3, 2017, https://nypost .com/2017/10/03/just-one-hour-of-exercise-per-week-can-help-defeat -depression/.

122 "I can't even guess": Osamu Dazai, *No Longer Human* (New York: New Directions Publishing, 1958), 21.

123 "People talk of 'social outcasts'": Dazai, *No Longer Human*, 67.

123 "[H]e was a good boy": Dazai, *No Longer Human*, 177.

123 "be argued into silence": Dazai, *No Longer Human*, 35.

123 "Nothing was so hard": Dazai, *No Longer Human*, 24.

123 "Practical troubles": Dazai, *No Longer Human*, 25.

CHAPTER 6: WAIT

132 "For me, the question": Simon Critchley, *Suicide* (Brooklyn: Thought Catalog Books, 2016), 16.

136 "We were enemies": Miriam Toews, *All My Puny Sorrows* (New York: Bloomsbury Publishing, 2019), 38.

Notes

136   "never adjusted to the light": Toews, *All My Puny Sorrows*, 24.

137   "Just stop lying to me": Toews, *All My Puny Sorrows*, 31.

137   "Elf was up in arms": Toews, *All My Puny Sorrows*, 50.

139   "I am so, so sorry": yayatizz, "What I Wish Someone Said to Me When I Wanted to Kill Myself," TikTok, April 16, 2023. https://www.tiktok.com/@yayatizz/video/7222730970712067371.

140   "cursed genetically": Toews, *All My Puny Sorrows*, 90–91.

140   "a sustained argument": Alice O'Keeffe, "Miriam Toews: 'I Worried People Would Think, What Is Wrong with This Family?,'" *The Guardian*, May 2, 2015, https://www.theguardian.com/books/2015/may/02/miriam-toews-interview-all-my-puny-sorrows-mennonite.

140   "guilt for not having": Spalding Gray, *The Journals of Spalding Gray* (New York: Vintage, 2012), 56.

141   gaining legal and public approval: Roger Collier, "Assisted death gaining acceptance in US," *Canadian Medical Association Journal* 189, no. 3 (January 23, 2017): E123.

141   A large swath of the country: Rachel Yi, "Most Americans Favor Legal Euthanasia," Gallup, August 8, 2024, https://news.gallup.com/poll/648215/americans-favor-legal-euthanasia.aspx.

142   data suggest that: "Facts About Suicide," CDC Suicide Prevention, July 23, 2024, https://www.cdc.gov/suicide/facts/index.html.

142   "built to self-destruct": O'Keeffe, "Miriam Toews: 'I Worried People Would Think, What Is Wrong with This Family?'"

142   "the part that makes sense": Stacey Freedenthal, *Helping the Suicidal Person: Tips and Techniques for Professionals* (New York: Routledge, 2018), 8.

143   "understand the essence": Israel Orbach, "How Would You Listen to the Person on the Roof?: A Response to H. Omer and A. Elitzur," *Suicide and Life-Threatening Behavior* 31, no. 2 (Summer 2001): 129–39.

143   "actually 'convince' [him]: Israel Orbach, "Therapeutic Empathy with the Suicidal Wish: Principles of Therapy with Suicidal Individuals," *American Journal of Psychotherapy* 55, no. 2 (February 2001): 166–84.

143   "I never wanted to die": Donald Antrim, *One Friday in April: A Story of Suicide and Survival* (New York: W. W. Norton, 2021), 95.

144   "my reasons, my certainties": Antrim, *One Friday in April*, 21.

144   "Are you a gentleman?": *Radio Unnameable*, directed by Paul Lovelace and Jessica Wolfson (Kino Lorber, 2012), YouTube, https://www.youtube.com/watch?v=DNmFebpg3DU.

145   Years later, Valenti called: Sean Cole, host, *This American Life*, episode

622, "Who You Gonna Call?," August 4, 2017, https://www
.thisamericanlife.org/622/who-you-gonna-call.

146   this has happened often enough: Kathryn McDonald, "The Radio Phone-in and the Suicidal Caller," in *The Bloomsbury Handbook of Radio*, ed. Kathryn McDonald and Hugh Chignell (London: Bloomsbury Academic, 2023), 190–207.

147   "scrambl[ed] from fire escape": Antrim, *One Friday in April*, 16–17.

147   "white, middle- and upper-class kids": Terry Williams, *Teenage Suicide Notes: An Ethnography of Self-Harm* (Ithaca, NY: Columbia University Press, 2017), 17.

147n   "I was much further": Stevie Smith, *All the Poems: Stevie Smith* (New York: New Directions Publishing, 2016), 347.

CHAPTER 7: ARTIFACTS

155   a designation she hated: Nathan Rabin, "I'm Sorry for Coining the Phrase 'Manic Pixie Dream Girl,'" Salon, July 16, 2014, https://www
.salon.com/2014/07/15/im_sorry_for_coining_the_phrase_manic
_pixie_dream_girl/.

155n   "In real life": Alice Alsup, *The Poet Walks Away: Poems* (Austin, TX: Pemberley Press, 2014), 68.

159   "Favorite quotes from suicide notes?": Alice Alsup, "Favorite quotes from suicide notes?" Facebook, private post, May 30, 2014.

160   "narcissistic and poorly worded": Alice Alsup, "That post was narcissistic and poorly worded," Facebook, private post, June 6, 2014.

161   "lover of words": Harbeer Sandhu, "There Is Nothing Left Now That Goes Unsaid: Thanks and RIP Alice Alsup," *Free Press Houston*, June 11, 2014, https://freepresshouston.com/there-is-nothing-left-now-that
-goes-unsaid-thanks-and-rip-alice-alsup/.

163   "We came": Alsup, *The Poet Walks Away: Poems*, 44.

164   "a peculiar inversion": Simon Critchley, *Suicide* (Brooklyn: Thought Catalog Books, 2016), 61.

166   Oliver had cut himself out: Diana Khoi Nguyen, "Po(i)sed for Action: At the Intersection of Poetry and Drama, Part I," Poetry Foundation, October 7, 2019, https://www.poetryfoundation.org/featured
-blogger/82825/poised-for-action-at-the-intersection-of-poetry-and
-drama-part-i.

166   "what has a form": Diana Khoi Nguyen, *Ghost Of* (California: Omnidawn Publishing, 2018), 166.

166   "radical eulogy": Peter Mishler, "Poet Diana Khoi Nguyen on Family and

Writing a Radical Eulogy for Her Brother," *Literary Hub*, October 23, 2019, https://lithub.com/poet-diana-khoi-nguyen-on-family-and -writing-a-radical-eulogy-for-her-brother/.

167   "a picky eater": Nguyen, "Po(i)sed for Action: At the Intersection of Poetry and Drama, Part I."

167   "cathartic [and] therapeutic": Mishler, "Poet Diana Khoi Nguyen on Family and Writing a Radical Eulogy for Her Brother."

168   "I did not have": Nguyen, "Po(i)sed for Action: At the Intersection of Poetry and Drama, Part I."

168   "at once both deeply unpleasant": Critchley, *Suicide*, 12.

169   "How many words": Miriam Toews, *All My Puny Sorrows* (New York: Bloomsbury Publishing, 2019), 217.

169   "icy flood": Sylvia Plath, *The Journals of Sylvia Plath* (New York: Anchor, 1998), 175.

170   "dumb and dumber on Lamictal": u/RedElfRN, "Dumb and Dumber on Lamictal, Does It Ever Get Better?," r/BipolarReddit, Reddit, August 24, 2015, https://www.reddit.com/r/BipolarReddit/comments/3i6m0j /dumb_and_dumber_on_lamictal_does_it_ever_get/.

170   "a bad case of the stupids": Jshect, "Has Anyone Gotten a Bad Case of the Stupids on Lamictal?," My Support Forums, January 2, 2012, https:// mysupportforums.org/bipolar/211379-has-anyone-gotten-bad-case -stupids-lamictal.html.

171   "Am I losing my mind": Anonymous, "Am I Losing My Mind While Trying to Save It?," MetaFilter, July 25, 2006, https://ask.metafilter .com/42883/Am-I-losing-my-mind-while-trying-to-save-it.

CHAPTER 8: COMFORT

183   "looked at [him] with skepticism": Donald Antrim, *One Friday in April: A Story of Suicide and Survival* (New York: W. W. Norton, 2021), 92.

185   "The depressed person": David Foster Wallace, "The Depressed Person," *Harper's Magazine*, January 1998, https://harpers.org/wp -content/uploads/HarpersMagazine-1998-01-0059425.pdf.

187   "begging shamelessly": Wallace, "The Depressed Person."

189   "I have weapons": Sylvia Plath, *The Journals of Sylvia Plath* (New York: Anchor, 1998), 240.

189n   "I-related pronouns": James W. Pennebaker, *The Secret Life of Pronouns: What Our Words Say About Us* (New York: Bloomsbury Publishing, 2011), 109.

190   "You hang on to": *Six Feet Under*, season 4, episode 12, "Untitled,"

written and directed by Alan Ball, featuring Michael C. Hall and Richard Jenkins, HBO, aired September 12, 2004.

190   "make [her]self ": Plath, *The Journals of Sylvia Plath*, 246.

192   *Jessica Meets Vanessa*: dmchatster, *Jessica Meets Vanessa, and Assures Her She's Fine*, May 13, 2010, YouTube, https://youtu.be /7Ygcl_DQ-Q4.

193n   "critical underlying issue": Chikako Ozawa-de Silva, *The Anatomy of Loneliness: Suicide, Social Connection, and the Search for Relational Meaning in Contemporary Japan* (Berkeley: University of California Press, 2021), 3.

194   "one is and becomes": Ozawa-de Silva, *The Anatomy of Loneliness*, 21.

194   "Dependency is not": Simon Critchley, *Suicide* (New York: Thought Catalog Books, 2016), 33.

194   "a person's experience": Ozawa-de Silva, *The Anatomy of Loneliness*, 28.

195   "intimat[e] connect[ion]": Ozawa de-Silva, *The Anatomy of Loneliness*, 180.

195   "social bases of self-respect": Neely Anne Laurenzo Myers, "Recovery Stories: An Anthropological Exploration of Moral Agency in Stories of Mental Health Recovery," *Transcultural Psychiatry* 53, no. 4 (2016): 427–44.

196   "We *are* burdens": Antrim, *One Friday in April*, 92.

196   "reason to worry": Antrim, *One Friday in April*, 120.

197   "Peer support for anyone": r/SuicideWatch, Reddit, accessed August 24, 2024, https://www.reddit.com/r/SuicideWatch/.

198   "It gets better": u/SQLwitch, "What's Wrong with 'It Gets Better'? What if it Doesn't?," r/SuicideWatch, Reddit, May 14, 2014, https:// www.reddit.com/r/SuicideWatch/comments/25igd7/whats_wrong _with_it_gets_better_what_if_it_doesnt/.

199   "I want to be alone": Ozawa-de Silva, *The Anatomy of Loneliness*, 81.

199   "If you're standing on the edge": Amanda Hess, "Please Do Not Downvote Anyone Who's Asked For Help," Slate, March 3, 2015, https://slate.com /technology/2015/03/reddit-and-suicide-intervention-how-social-media -is-changing-the-cry-for-help-and-the-answer.html.

200   "We thought we knew how": Kay Redfield Jamison, *Night Falls Fast: Understanding Suicide* (New York: Alfred A. Knopf, 1999), 3.

203   "only lonely rooms are safe": Antrim, *One Friday in April*, 29.

CHAPTER 9: REAL LIFE

210   his favorite video: Fuseguy is Cool, *MTA NYC Bus: World of Buses at*

Sutphin Blvd/Archer Ave, YouTube, October 22, 2016, https://youtu.be/gPv0VdAepPU.

210 becoming complacent: William Cummings, "More than 176,000 in US have died of COVID-19; 57% of Republicans polled say that is 'acceptable,'" *USA Today*, August 23, 2020, https://www.usatoday.com/story/news/politics/2020/08/23/republicans-coronavirus-deaths-poll/3424673001/.

211 simply deciding: Michael Wilson, "The Pandemic Isn't Over. New Yorkers Are Acting as if It Were.," *New York Times*, June 18, 2020, https://www.nytimes.com/2020/06/18/nyregion/coronavirus-ny-social-distancing.html.

215 "so basically everyone I know": @AriannaRebolini, "so basically everyone I know is depressed . . . ," Twitter (now X), January 28, 2021, https://x.com/AriannaRebolini/status/1354973263290621952.

215 "Everyone just acts like": Michelle (@amigadehelado), "I work in a restaurant. . . . ," January 28, 2021, Twitter (now X), https://x.com/amigadehelado/status/1354984175015702532.

215 "And your employer wants": Dani (@alwayscriticism), "Somehow apparently yes . . . ," January 30, 2021, Twitter (now X), https://x.com/alwayscriticism/status/1355485328463831040.

215 "Not to mention": Amanda M. (@mandaleigh1687), "Not to mention . . . ," January 29, 2021, Twitter (now X), https://x.com/mandaleigh1687/status/1355197491826855936.

215 "Really tired of living": Spencer LaBelle (@spencelabelle), "Really tired of living in this dystopian apocalypse . . .", January 29, 2021, Twitter (now X), https://x.com/SpenceLaBelle/status/1355368041463353345.

215 "I work at Amazon": @RagefulAries, "I work at Amazon . . .", January 29, 2021, Twitter (now X), https://x.com/RagefulAries/status/1355147575255568387.

216 "It's getting increasingly difficult": Ethan (@crazyquantum), "It's getting increasingly difficult . . . ," January 29, 2021, Twitter (now X), https://x.com/crazyquantum/status/1355219775903948800.

217 "I haven't seen most of my friends": Aria Velz (@ariavelz), "Good thing I have all of these screens to remind me of everything," TikTok, February 17, 2021, https://www.tiktok.com/t/ZP8RVxeat/.

217 dehumanizing systems: Anna Flagg, Jamiles Lartey, and Shannon Heffernan, "How the US failed people in prisons during Covid: 'Really important to learn from what happened,'" *The Guardian*, April 18, 2024,

https://www.theguardian.com/us-news/2024/apr/18/incarcerated
-people-covid-death-rates.

219   violations of workers' rights: Caroline O'Donovan, "The US Labor
       Board Isn't Strong Enough to Protect Workers from Amazon. Some
       Union Organizers Want to Go Around It.," *BuzzFeed News*, March 30,
       2021, https://www.buzzfeednews.com/article/carolineodonovan
       /amazon-union-labor-violations-nlrb.

219   the years preceding: Mark Di Stefano, "Amazon Workers Are Planning
       Black Friday Protests at Its UK Sites," *BuzzFeed News*, November 21,
       2018, https://www.buzzfeed.com/markdistefano/amazon-workers
       -planning-black-friday-protests.

219   collective bargaining: Caroline O'Donovan, "Amazon Fired an Employee
       Involved in Workplace Organizing in Minnesota, Sources Say," *BuzzFeed
       News*, April 14, 2020, https://www.buzzfeednews.com
       /article/carolineodonovan/amazon-fired-employee-involved-in
       -workplace-organizing-in.

219n   "directly attributable transactions": Jonah Peretti, "BuzzFeed in 2020,"
       BuzzFeed, January 3, 2020, https://www.buzzfeed.com/jonah
       /buzzfeed-in-2020.

220   customer service: Olivia Solon and April Glaser, "Amazon Ring call
       center workers in Philippines 'scared' to go to work during pandemic,"
       NBC News, October 15, 2020, https://www.nbcnews.com
       /tech/security/we-don-t-have-choice-amazon-ring-call-center
       -workers-n1243439.

220   the wealthiest man in the world: Giacomo Tognini, "After Two Weeks at
       No. 2, Jeff Bezos Is Once Again the Richest Person in the World," *Forbes*,
       June 10, 2021, https://www.forbes.com/sites/giacomotognini
       /2021/06/10/after-two-weeks-at-no-2-jeff-bezos-is-once-again-the
       -richest-person-in-the-world/.

220   by more than half: Aimee Pichi, "Billionaires Got 54% Richer During
       Pandemic, Sparking Calls for Wealth Tax," *CBS News*, March 31, 2021,
       https://www.cbsnews.com/news/billionaire-wealth-covid-pandemic
       -12-trillion-jeff-bezos-wealth-tax/.

220   "death grip": Sandeep Vaheesan and Tara Pincock, "Throwing the Books
       at Amazon's Monopoly Hold on Publishing," *The Nation*, January 8,
       2024, https://www.thenation.com/article/economy/throwing-the
       -book-at-amazons-monopoly-hold-on-publishing/.

220   "a Rube Goldberg [machine]": Peter Shamshiri (@The_Law_Boy),
       "same day delivery is the most American shit of all time, you run out of

deodorant or something and with a single click start a Rube Goldberg of human suffering in an Amazon warehouse twenty miles away," Twitter (now X), September 4, 2019, https://x.com/The_Law_Boy /status/1169263666912534528.

220n   decrease in household income: Emily A. Shrider, Melissa Kollar, Frances Chen, and Jessica Semega, "Income and Poverty in the United States: 2020," U.S. Census Bureau, September 14, 2021, https://www.census .gov/library/publications/2021/demo/p60-273.html.

220n   up to 13 percent: Roxanna Edwards, Lawrence S. Essien, and Michael Daniel Levinstein, "U.S. labor market shows improvement in 2021, but the COVID-19 pandemic continues to weigh on the economy," U.S. Bureau of Labor Statistics Monthly Labor Review, June 2022, https:// www.bls.gov/opub/mlr/2022/article/us-labor-market-shows -improvement-in-2021-but-the-covid-19-pandemic-continues-to-weigh -on-the-economy.htm.

222   "unhappy places": Anne Case and Angus Deaton, *Deaths of Despair and the Future of Capitalism* (New Jersey: Princeton University Press, 2020; reprinted with new preface by the authors, 2021), 1. Citations refer to the 2021 edition.

223   As of 2022: "Suicide Statistics," American Foundation for Suicide Prevention, accessed September 22, 2024, https://afsp.org/suicide-statistics/.

223   Native Americans: Joseph Friedman, Helena Hansen, and Joseph P. Gone, "Deaths of Despair and Indigenous Data Genocide," *Lancet*, 401, no. 10379 (March 11, 2023): 874–76.

223n   "interpreted with caution": "Suicide Data and Statistics," U.S. Centers for Disease Control and Prevention, July 18, 2024, https://www.cdc.gov /suicide/facts/data.html.

224   "nowhere to be seen": Nicholas Bloom, "Corporations in the Age of Inequality," *Harvard Business Review*, March 21, 2017, https://hbr .org/2017/03/corporations-in-the-age-of-inequality.

225   rapid decline in membership: Diane Katz, "The Decline of the American Labor Union," Geopolitical Intelligence Services Reports, April 28, 2023, https://www.gisreportsonline.com/r/decline -american-union/.

225   "higher wages": Case and Deaton, *Deaths of Despair and the Future of Capitalism*, 238–239.

225   workers' satisfaction in life: Bernice Lott, "Social Class Myopia: The Case of Psychology and Labor Unions," *Analyses of Social Issues and Public Policy* 14, no. 1 (December 2014): 261–80.

225   psychological well-being: Kyoung-Ok Park, Mark G. Wilson, and

Myung Sun Lee, "Effects of Social Support at Work on Depression and Organizational Productivity," *American Journal of Health Behavior* 28, no. 5 (September–October 2004): 444–55.

226 and so did the suicide rate: F. T. Green, "Money Can Make or Break Your Mental Health," Slate, November 19, 2021, https://slate.com /technology/2021/11/suicide-risk-money-research-mental-health.html.

226 studies in the United States: Gaby Galvin, "Study: Higher Poverty Tied to Increased Youth Suicide Risk," *U.S. News & World Report*, January 27, 2020, https://www.usnews.com/news/healthiest-communities /articles/2020-01-27/higher-poverty-tied-to-increased-youth-suicide -risk-study-shows.

226 in Sweden: Charlotte Björkenstam, Kyriaki Kosidou, and Emma Björkenstam, "Childhood Adversity and Risk of Suicide: Cohort Study of 548 721 Adolescents and Young Adults in Sweden," *BMJ* 357 (April 19, 2017): j1334.

226 Even just the forecasting: "Increases in Suicide Rate Linked to 'Shocks' in the Economy," M2 Presswire, March 11, 2024, https://link-gale -com.i.ezproxy.nypl.org/apps/doc/A786033684/GBIB?u=nypl&sid =ebsco&xid=52346c9.

226 "People are likely": Sylwia J. Piatkowska, "Poverty, Inequality, and Suicide Rates: A Cross-National Assessment of the Durkheim Theory and the Stream Analogy of Lethal Violence," *Sociological Quarterly* 61, no. 4 (January 2020): 787–812.

227 "America does this": Case and Deaton, *Deaths of Despair and the Future of Capitalism*, 191.

227 higher rates of suicide: "New CDC Report Shows Suicide Risk Tied to Local Economic and Social Conditions," CDC Newsroom, September 10, 2024. https://www.cdc.gov/media/releases/2024/s0910-vs-suicide-risk.html.

227 half can't access: Annie Waldman et al., "Why I Left the Network," ProPublica, August 25, 2024, https://projects.propublica.org/why-i-left -the-network/.

227 "I am never going to make": Waldman et al., "Why I Left the Network."

228 "interfered with [their] patient's care": Waldman et al., "Why I Left the Network."

229n employer-sponsored coverage: Kat Tretina and Heidi Gollub, "How Much Does Health Insurance Cost in 2024?," *USA Today*, November 23, 2023, https://www.usatoday.com/money/blueprint/health-insurance /how-much-is-health-insurance/.

234 See Arizona mother Denise: Denise Schatt-Denslow, "Our Insurance

Halted Our Son's Mental Health Care, and He Paid with His Lfe," AZ Central, June 20, 2022, https://www.azcentral.com/story/opinion /op-ed/2022/06/20/mental-health-services-should-up-doctors-not -insurers/7629980001/.

234 See Rochelle and Michael of Ohio: Rhitu Chatterjee, "Teen with Life-Threatening Depression Finally Found Hope. Then Insurance Cut Her Off," NPR, April 17, 2023, https://www.npr.org/sections/health -shots/2023/04/17/1164782264/teen-suicide-health-insurance-denial -mental-health-parity.

234 most therapists are white: "Demographics of U.S. Psychological Workforce [interactive data tool]," American Psychological Association, retrieved November 22, 2024, https://www.apa.org/workforce/data -tools/demographics.

235 depression in Black youths: Arielle H. Sheftall, "The Tragedy of Black Youth Suicide," Association of American Medical Colleges, April 11, 2023, https://www.aamc.org/news/tragedy-black-youth-suicide.

235 "like an outsider": Christina Caron, "Why Are More Black Kids Suicidal? A Search for Answers," *New York Times*, November 18, 2021, updated June 22, 2023, https://www.nytimes.com/2021/11/18/well /mind/suicide-black-kids.html.

235 is underfunded: Melissa Rohman, "Funding Disparities Research and Underrepresented Minority Scientists," Feinberg School of Medicine, Northwestern University, January 22, 2020, https://news.feinberg .northwestern.edu/2020/01/22/funding-disparities-research-and -underrepresented-minority-scientists/.

235 "very accepting communities": "2024 U.S. National Survey on the Mental Health of LGBTQ+ Young People," The Trevor Project, https://www .thetrevorproject.org/survey-2024.

235 Native American LGBTQ youths: Claire Urbanski, "As Rates of Suicide for Native American Youth Increase, Culture Is Key to Prevention," The Claymon Institute for Gender Research, Stanford University, May 24, 2023, https://gender.stanford.edu/news/rates-suicide-native-american -youth-increase-culture-key-prevention.

236 Native Americans receive those degrees: "Educational Attainment of Young Adults," National Center for Education Statistics, May 2023, https://nces.ed.gov/programs/coe/indicator/caa/young-adult -attainment.

236 twice as likely to kill themselves: Julie A. Phillips and Katherine

Hempstead, "Differences in U.S. Suicide Rates by Educational Attainment, 2000–2014," *American Journal of Preventive Medicine* 53, no. 4 (October 2017).

236 · lowest tier of tuition: Sarah Wood, "See the Average College Tuition in 2024–2025," *U.S. News & World Report*, September 26, 2024, https://www.usnews.com/education/best-colleges/paying-for-college/articles/paying-for-college-infographic.

236 Racial discrimination increases: Bruno Messina Coimbra et al., "Meta-analysis of the Effect of Racial Discrimination on Suicidality," *SSM Population Health*, 2022.

236 75 percent of Black adults: Kiana Cox, "Racial Discrimination Shapes How Black Americans View Their Progress and U.S. Institutions," Pew Research Center, June 15, 2024, https://www.pewresearch.org/race-and-ethnicity/2024/06/15/racial-discrimination-shapes-how-black-americans-view-their-progress-and-u-s-institutions-2/.

241 "social disease": Donald Antrim, *One Friday in April* (New York: W. W. Norton, 2021), 15.

241 "a global sickness": Antrim, *One Friday in April*, 126.

CHAPTER 10: TOUCHING DEATH

250 "does no harm": David Hume, *The Philosophical Works of David Hume*, Volume 4 (Boston: Little, Brown and Company, 1854), 544.

251n fatal police shootings: "Fatal Force Database," *Washington Post*, accessed January 2, 2025, https://www.washingtonpost.com/graphics/investigations/police-shootings-database/.

252 assuming that *I* was: Philippe Rochat, "Five Levels of Self-Awareness as They Unfold Early in Life," *Consciousness and Cognition* 12, no. 4 (December 2003): 717–31, https://www.sciencedirect.com/science/article/abs/pii/S1053810003000813?via%3Dihub.

253 "It isn't the pain": Maggie Nelson, *The Argonauts* (New York: Graywolf Press, 2016), 134.

About the Author

ARIANNA REBOLINI is a writer from New York. She is the coauthor, with Katie Heaney, of the novel *Public Relations*. She lives in Queens with her husband, son, and two cats.